"An important book, *Devil's Den to Lickingwater* is a fine environmental and industrial history of the Mill River in Williamsburg and Northampton. Its lively text, accompanied by beautiful maps and illustrations, tells a dramatic story of the river's many transformations through community enterprise and development, ecological challenges, disaster, decline, and rejuvenation. Both as an account of how the Mill River came to be as it is, and as an inspiration for ensuring its healthy future in the life of the region, this book will have lasting influence."

— Christopher Clark, author of *Rural Roots of Capitalism* and *The Communitarian Moment*, Chair, Department of History, University of Connecticut, Storrs

"Sinton's engaging history of the land and people along the Mill River is essential reading for anyone in Western Massachusetts seeking a better understanding of where they live. It combines the attention to detail of the best local histories with a sophisticated analysis placing those details in a broader social, economic, and ecological context."

— David Glassberg, Professor of History, UMass, Amherst author of *American Historical Pageantry and Sense of History: The Place of Past in American Life*

"With rich knowledge and clear, evocative language, John Sinton interweaves the natural and engineered history of the Mill River in Western Massachusetts with the complex stories of settlements along its course. Sinton deftly traces the interactions of the river and its flooding waters with the forces that built farms, villages, towns, and cities alongside its banks—forest clearing, agriculture, industrialization, dams, transportation, and politics. Abundant maps and images enhance understanding and help bring this past world to life. Today, inspired by environmental awareness, interest in recreation, and tourism, a growing number of river walks allow new appreciation of the Mill River's beauty. Sinton offers a compelling story and an important contribution to the growing literature of the interplay between nature and human action."

— Helen Horowitz, Parsons Professor Emerita of History and American Studies, Smith College, author of *Traces of J.B. Jackson* coming in 2019

"This gem of a book offers an elegant yes to the question 'Does nature have a history along with us humans?' The Mill River had a heroic past as a sacred place to the early Native Americans and an invaluable resource to the first Anglo American settlers and to later generations that harnessed its power to the region's first mills and factories. John Sinton captures the history of the Mill in loving detail, exposing the changing shape of its flora, fauna, and aquatic life and larger impact on our landscape. It is beautifully written, richly detailed with maps and other illustrations, and informative throughout—a must and compelling read for everyone from environmentalists to local historians and general readers wishing to learn why we reside in such a special place."

— Bruce Laurie, Professor Emeritus of History, Universityof Massachusetts, Amherst, author of *Rebels in Paradise: Sketches of Northampton Abolitionists*

"John Sinton has given us a masterpiece that is at once environmental history, local history, and a microcosm of New England, American, and global history. It interweaves the latest findings on all manner of scholarly topics with countless anecdotes of human beings, both inventive and foolish. Especially notable for incorporating Native Americans' presence and perspectives. Beautifully written and illustrated."

— Neal Salisbury, Professor Emeritus in History, Smith College, author of *Manitou and Providence: Indians, Europeans, and the Making of New England*

"This is a must read for anyone interested in New England cultural and environmental history. John Sinton is a companionable and knowledgeable guide as he brings to life the cultural and landscape history of Northampton and Williamsburg through the story of the region's lifeblood, the Mill River. Aided by one hundred newly crafted maps and illustrations, Sinton describes in great clarity the river's geologic history, its use and meaning to indigenous people, its industrial phase, and its revived place in the landscape today. A cogent discussion of the environmental impacts of deforestation, pollution, and invasive species places the Mill River in a national context. This highly readable volume should be on every New Englander's bookshelf."

— Elizabeth M. Sharpe, co-director of Historic Northampton, author of *In the Shadow of the Dam: The Aftermath of the Mill River Flood of 1874*

"John Sinton takes us on a full-immersion journey in environmental history with his book *Devil's Den to Linkingwater: The Mill River through Landscape and History*. He utilizes intensive historical research, a la Paul Krugman and William Cronon, to give 'voice to the river' in what he terms an *awikhigan* – the Abenaki word for representing the world in different ways. He covers the Mill River's history from early geologic times, through Native American eras and the period of early European settlers all the way up to the present. Major hydrologic events like floods and river diversions are covered, as well as their interactions with riverine communities. This book will be of interest to those whose appetites include; natural and cultural landscape history, environmental interpretation, cultural ecology, and river-related planning and management."

— Richard Smardon, SUNY (Syracuse) College of Environmental Science and Forestry, Distinguished Service Professor, author of *Sustaining the World's Wetlands*

"A beautifully written microhistory that will make you care deeply for this winding little New England tributary in ways you never dreamed. A remarkable book and lavishly illustrated to boot."

— Ted Steinberg, Distinguished Professor of History and Professor of Law at Case Western Reserve University, author of *Gotham Unbound*, *Down to Earth*, and *Acts of God*

Devil's Den to Lickingwater

The Mill River Through Landscape & History

John Sinton

Levellers Press

AMHERST, MASSACHUSETTS

Cover photograph by Janine Norton used with permission

Levellers Press, Amherst, Massachusetts
Printed in the United States of America
ISBN 978-1-945473-65-4

DEDICATION

To Wendy, the love of my life; and to
Toby, Josh, Alex, Chris, and Jonathan,
with thanks for their love, their teachings,
and fruitless attempts to keep me within boundaries.

IN MEMORIAM

Elizabeth J. Farnsworth

and

Ralmon Jon Black

Table of Contents

CHAPTER FOUR
1840–1880

Great Floods and Political Turbulence at the Height of the First Industrial Revolution

CHAPTER FIVE
1880–1940

Flood, Contamination, and Diversion

Maps and Images

Front Cover

Hulbert's Pond (Janine Norton photo)

Fold-out from back cover

Map of Mill River Villages, Devil's Den to Lickingwater.
(Transit Authority Figures)

CHAPTER ONE

CHAPTER TWO

CHAPTER THREE

CHAPTER FOUR

CHAPTER FIVE

PREFACE

> *No group sets out to create a landscape, of course. What it*
> *sets out to do is to create a community, and the landscape*
> *as its visible manifestation is simply the by-product of*
> *people working and living, sometimes coming together,*
> *sometimes staying apart, but always recognizing their*
> *interdependence.*
>
> — J. B. Jackson

How This Book Came About

One of my first sensual memories comes from the age of four: I am on my father's back, arms loosely around his neck as he frog legs out into the main current of the Truckee River, two miles south of Tahoe City, California. Our bodies glide and bump down the rapids, slowing as the pool shallows out into the gravel bar at the end of the run. I stand up and walk toward the right bank, where the back eddy will return me to the head of the fast water, and wait for my father to do it again.

I am a river rat. I grew up near rivers in the San Francisco Bay Area in the 1940s and '50s, with all my summers on the Truckee or some other western river. I fished and floated and swam and listened to rivers. I still read the water, looking for a paddler's line or the eddy at the end of a run where a trout waits for its buggy dinner to arrive. But I never imagined writing about rivers until middle age. I had taken side roads in my life that eventually circled back to rivers. I earned a doctorate in Russian and Early Modern European History but wrote my dissertation on a Turkish minority group on the Volga. I steeped myself in Fernand Braudel's *Annales* school of history while taking daily walks along the Seine.

I moved to Western Massachusetts in the late '60s and was married in a backyard of bluets and a side yard of marsh marigolds. While living along the banks of the Connecticut River, I cast aside the strict study of history to become an environmental planner, and later conducted environmental impact assessments of the Red River in Kentucky and the Cheat in West Virginia. I worked my way through the postdoctoral world by researching the Charles River. After moving to southern New Jersey in 1972, I worked on the New Jersey Pine Barrens for several years and paddled the little rivers of that place.[1]

In the 1980s, I returned to my roots as a river rat and went full bore into the study of rivers, beginning with the Delaware.[2] After that, it was a year in Cologne working on the Rhine.[3] In 1999, after twenty-five years, my wife Wendy and I returned to the Connecticut River where we had married and settled in the village of Florence in the city of Northampton. I immediately started pondering how to write about the Connecticut, and, as had been my custom, I went onto the river to experience it. For two years Wendy and I, along with my friend and colleague Elizabeth Farnsworth, paddled all the paddleable reaches of the Connecticut, from its source on the Canada/New Hampshire border to its mouth at Old Lyme and Old Saybrook on Long Island Sound. Out of these experiences sprang a boating guide for the river's steadfast guardian, the Connecticut River Conservancy.[4]

The sheer size and complexity of the Connecticut River's 11,000-square mile watershed has made it such a daunting project that no author has successfully tackled it. I turned instead to the Mill River, which I can see and hear from my back porch. This book is the result of living near the banks of a river that has witnessed thousands of years of human history. It derives whatever authority it has from friends and colleagues who know far more than I; and particularly from Ralmon Black, who is a product of the hilltown soils of Williamsburg. Ralmon, whose knowledge of the Mill River is as intimate as mine is acquired, was born in 1939, a day after me.

Why the Mill River?

This story takes place in Western Massachusetts, a region of New England bordered on three sides by Vermont, Connecticut and New York State; and extending east to within some thirty miles of the city of Worcester, and south to the city of Springfield. It is a "betwixt" place, sandwiched east to west by Worcester and Albany, New York; and north to south by two states with strong identities (Vermont and Connecticut). The Native American peoples of Western Massachusetts were also betwixt and between, consisting of mixed populations from more distinct tribes such as the Pequot, Nipmuck, Mohican, and Abenaki.

This is a place that tends to partake of everything around it rather than trying to take on a particular character. It clearly feels like New England, but with an openness that invites argument and tolerance. It's an accepting place whose inhabitants would rather look away, if they must, than confront those they might object to.

I chose to write about this place for a number of reasons, not least of which is its long habit of participating in the affairs of the world. This little watershed is a microcosm of American history, a perch from which I can pick up my historical binoculars and witness events stretching back to the ice ages. It allows me to see history and geology made palpable, from dinosaur footprints to the remnants of Indian corn-hills, from peaceful Arcadian valleys to spectacular floods to landscapes so dramatically changed that they're almost impossible to recognize. This is a gloriously substantial place, where you hike on rocks and roots and await winters that could be twenty degrees below zero with six-foot snow drifts or forty degrees above with three cords of wood still waiting for you to burn them.

I have other reasons to use this watershed to tell a global tale. With a length of about twenty miles and an area of about fifty-two square miles, the Mill River and its watershed are big enough to be diverse and small enough to get one's head around. Telling the stories of large rivers is made extremely difficult by the diversity of their landscapes and their huge geographic extent.[5] Other waterways in the region, such as the Deerfield or the neighboring Mill Rivers of Hampshire County, are either too small or lacking in historical complexity to be satisfying subjects. The Mill River, like Goldilocks' favorite chair, is just right.

This part of the world has a riveting story to tell, beginning with one of America's wondrous geological events—the appearance and disappearance of a huge lake left by the last glaciers, the remnants of which the first Americans may well have seen. This was followed by millennia of Native habitation, and then their disastrous contact with and removal by Europeans.

The history of Colonial America unfolds after the mid-seventeenth century, and I can watch it from my seat overlooking a 410-mile-long river that the Abenaki called the Long Everflowing River, or Connecticut (Kwinitekw). We are about ninety miles upriver from the Connecticut's mile-wide mouth on Long Island Sound. An astonishing 70 percent of the Sound's fresh water comes out of the Connecticut River. Our Mill River enters on the right bank of the Connecticut at the border of the cities of Northampton and Easthampton.[6]

I say "ours" because there are scores of Mill Rivers throughout eastern North America. Our Mill has the advantage of being well documented in all kinds of source materials, starting with first-settlement town records and lasting through 230 years of newspaper and other accounts. This trove of materials has received the attention of a host of local historians and genealogists, who have relentlessly pursued clues from gravestones, property titles, court records, diaries, and oral histories. Of all these local folks, one in particular rises to heroic status: Sylvester Judd, whose short biography is beautifully told in Bruce Laurie's *Rebels in Paradise.*[7] From the 1830s to the 1850s, Judd took not just voluminous notes, but actual *volumes* of notes on all matters of interest to him— endless lists of property transfers and the contents of wills, church and political affairs, the weather, and the dates of the blossoming of flowers and ripening of fruit, to name a very few.

The Maps and Images

This book began as a series of river walks and paddles along the twenty miles of the Mill, and became a series of brochures for self-guided historic tours. Although I didn't know it at the time, the brochures were a natural starting point for the book. The landscape, after all, was my first history teacher. I feel history more as a physical experience than an intellectual exercise, but, naturally, these two modes of human activity reinforce each other. If we adopt the eyes of a stranger in an alien landscape, our younger selves begin to ask pertinent questions: How come this path is so winding? What kinds of trees are those? That odd building, what's happening inside it? After a time, mental maps emerge and, with sufficient effort, we are able to memorize the key features of a place. History begins with the recovery of that memory of the place and how much it has changed since you were last there.

You will find a lot of maps and images in this book. The story of the Mill River would be incomplete without them because *Devil's Den to Lickingwater* is a palpable history. I urge readers to search out these two titular locations if they are able to walk a trail or follow a street pattern. Between the source and mouth of the Mill River lies a wealth of worlds, and my work is an attempt to bring them to life.

I believe there are many valid ways to describe a place by word, map, or image. What you hold in your hands happens to be a book, but it contains much more than words and images—it contains visions and worlds and ideas to explore.

Through the work of Abenaki historian Lisa Brooks, I discovered that there is a single Abenaki word for representing the world in different ways. An *awikhigan*, she explains in a section entitled "The Map and the Book are the Same Thing," is "a tool for image making, for writing, for transmitting an image or idea from one mind to another, over waterways, over time."[8] This same concept holds true for many Native people in the New World. *Devil's Den to Lickingwater* is my contribution to the Mill River *awikhigan*.

You will find here a series of maps intended to simplify and clarify ideas in the book. Rob Stewart of Transit Authority Figures in Northampton created the maps with all the skill and vision that I lack. I have looked at several of his maps only to discover new information and ideas that my cluttered mind had hidden. Chief among his contributions is the clarity of the physical space occupied by the Nonotuck and English villages, something words do not describe.

I have purposely included a few maps that are difficult to interpret with the intention of engaging readers in a game of envisioning a fully fleshed-out landscape from some two-dimensional scratches on a sheet of paper. Prime examples are the nineteenth-century Williamsburg maps. Twenty-first-century Americans are notoriously lacking in map-reading savvy, so I do not expect every reader to inspect all the maps with the same strange intensity that occupies map lovers. Still, I wanted to provide an opportunity to see the world from our ancestors' perspectives.

Finally, I have kept beautiful photographs of Mill River landscapes to a minimum because I would like readers to experience this watershed on their own time and in their own season. Treat this *awikhigan* as an invitation to steep yourselves in this place.

Giving Voice to the River

In this work, I have wanted to give voice to the Mill—to tell stories of how it shaped the land and the environmental transformations it has experienced. People have lived near its banks for millennia, and I have tried to describe some of what the river saw as one group of people after another turned to the river to serve them as a fishery, a source of drinking water, a sewer, a bathing place, a power source, and a landscape of leisure and pleasure. As human populations and technical innovation exploded, the river had to change, sometimes dramatically. It has seen plants and animals disappear and reappear and its water quality deteriorate and recover. Even its bed has been moved as people tried to control and tame its waters—with problematic results. For the past 370 years, people have been importing hundreds of non-native plants, animals, insects, and diseases that affect the Mill. As mentioned above, this little river has played a major part in New England's first two hundred years of European settlement, and its waters have reflected much of America's social, cultural, political and economic experience.

I tell the Mill River's story as a series of connected themes, sustained and revisited in each chapter. We begin with an introduction to the life and times of the river and its people, starting with a physical description of the river's reach. We move on to what the river saw along its banks: the dams, bridges, and mills that people built, the floods that swept downstream and backed up into town. We end each chapter with the ecological transformations that form the heart of the Mill River's story.

I have written a love letter to a place deep in my heart. I am a river rat returning to his home stream for a final journey and asking the reader to accompany him on this voyage. May the Mill River's path, gentle reader, open up for you a world hidden in plain sight.

CHAPTER ONE

From Lake Hitchcock to 1720: The First 20,000 Years

> *"Rivers aren't constrained by human desires and stories;*
> *they sing the beauty of their own randomness and drift."*
>
> — Jeremy Denk, "Flight of the Concord,"
> *The New Yorker*, February 6, 2012.[1]

Introduction

> *Start with an incline, which has no intent; add rain,*
> *whose only option is to fall; and time, which can do*
> *nothing but pass. This is how rivers begin.*
>
> — Barbara Hurd[2]

Like all rivers, the Mill has a simple purpose to fulfill—to move water and sediment. It picks up water from precipitation and underground springs and erodes rock and fine sediment from its valley, all of which it deposits downstream. The physics of the transport of its water and materials are also pretty simple: the more water the river carries and the steeper the gradient down which it flows, the more turbulent the river becomes as it carries material downstream. It appears counterintuitive, but in many rivers the current's velocity can be greater in downstream areas where the land is flatter and the river appears to run slower when in fact it runs faster.[3] In dry periods and on flat land, it erodes less and deposits less, while in wet periods and in steep terrain, the opposite applies. During catastrophic weather events the river's power becomes fierce, as it carries millions of tons of materials downstream, including trees and houses. Wherever the river finds a way to spread its water, the force becomes spent and whatever it carries is deposited on the flatland.

An array of plants and animals finds that different parts of the Mill River Valley suit their specific purposes. The upper reaches of the stream and tributaries support populations of algae and other submerged plants, a few flowering plants, some small brook trout and minnows, several species of aquatic insects (mayflies, stoneflies, and blackflies among them), and frogs, clams, crayfish, and worms—the sorts of creatures that children love to play with. Because the upper Mill runs through rocks with few nutrients to nourish the microscopic life on which insects feed, it supports a modest biota relative to downstream habitats. The upper part of the watershed, however, supplies people with drinking and bathing water.

As the water of the Mill River reaches the flatter sections of Williamsburg, it deposits its hilltown sediments—higher upstream in periods of low water, farther downstream in times of high water. Aquatic plants find anchorage in the slower waters, and those plants provide food and hiding places for more insects and minnows, so the diversity and abundance of fish begin to increase. Since the water here is cold even in summer, trout and minnows (dace, chubs, and shiners) remain the most common fish.

The number of birds also increases. The thriving insect, plant, invertebrate, and fish populations provide food for kingfishers and herons. Flycatchers, warblers, and waxwings feast on insects emerging from the stream. Mergansers, wood ducks and mallards feed on whatever is available, from grasses to crayfish, minnows to trout.

As the river winds through its steep-sided valley from Williamsburg through Haydenville, Leeds, and Florence to Paradise Pond in Northampton, it provides habitat for otter, mink, muskrat, and beaver. Although the water remains cold much of the year, it warms considerably during the low flows of the summer months when plenty of insects, minnows, and crayfish can be found. Trout find refuge in the deeper pools or near springs where they can escape the heat. It is only below Paradise Pond where sunfish, bass, perch and other warmwater fish show up in good numbers. As more nutrients get flushed downstream toward the Mill River's confluence with the Connecticut, the waters from different streams merge and become a nutrient soup for creatures large and small. By the time the Mill enters Hulbert's Pond (an ancient oxbow) in Easthampton, fish such as pike and enormous carp join the aquatic community. The broad floodplain where the Mill River meets its confluence with the Connecticut is very rich in common and rare wetland plants. Birders delight in the wealth of migrating and resident birds, from waders to raptors, sparrows, and waterfowl.

How did this unprepossessing stream shape the landscape and create the perfect valleys and flatlands for mill villages while laying down the rich agricultural soils that continue to support major cash crops to this day? For answers we turn to a series of tales that geologists have spun and to Native people whose stories tell of ancient shapers of the earth.

The First 20,000 Years

Twenty thousand years ago, there was no Mill River to be seen. This is not to say that no Mill River existed; there were river valleys prior to the most recent glaciers, perhaps even where the Mill River now runs. These last glaciers, which began to melt about 20,000 years ago, eroded and modified that preglacial landscape. Over the course of the next 7000 years and through a complex series of geological processes, the current landscape through which the Mill River now runs emerged.

Fig. 1.1 Visualization of the creation of Lake Hitchcock looking north ca. 20,000 years B.P. as the glaciers retreat (Courtesy Julie Brigham-Grette, Universtity of Massachusetts).

When the glaciers began to melt, the single most significant post-glacial feature in the Connecticut River Valley was a 250-mile-long series of interconnected post-glacial lakes called Lake Hitchcock, named after the nineteenth-century Amherst College geologist and president, Edward Hitchcock. Stretching from a huge dam of glacial material deposited at Rocky Hill, Connecticut, the lake reached all the way north to Burke, Vermont. Lake Hitchcock lasted several thousand years, long enough to begin the process of laying down the great agricultural soils of the Connecticut Valley. About 18,000 years ago, the lake began draining in fits and starts, first from the south where streams and rivers eroded away the front (south) side of the dam at Rocky Hill. It was only about 15,500 years ago that the ice margin around the Mill River watershed retreated from the higher-elevation areas that would one day become known as the hilltowns. Nonetheless, when Lake Hitchcock drained south of the Holyoke Range, a stable lake existed north of that point for some time. Geologists named it Lake Hadley. The lake completely drained from the local area about 14,000 years ago, but remnants of Lake Hitchcock persisted for several hundred years northward into Vermont and New Hampshire.[5]

Lake Hitchcock reached an elevation of about three hundred feet above sea level and remained in the Northampton region for about 3000–4000 years. As it began to retreat from Northampton about 16,000 years ago, it left behind the sediments from its lake bottom, the fine-grained silt, sand, and clay that comprise the meadows of Hadley and Northampton. Downtown Northampton would have been about one hundred fifty feet underwater at this

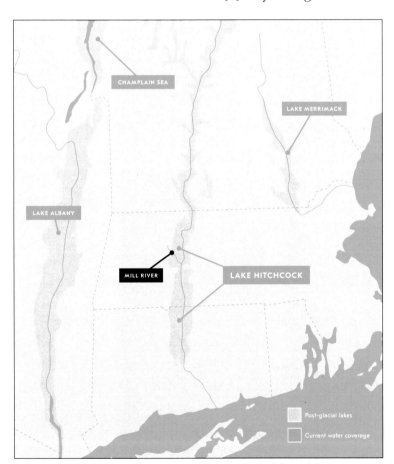

Fig. 1.2 *Map of Lake Hitchcock and other Post-Glacial Lakes in the Northeast. (Transit Authority Figures map based on map by Jack Ridge, Tufts University.)*

time, and Look Park and the land adjacent to Florence Meadows would have been beachfront property.[6]

For our purposes, it is useful to separate the Mill River watershed's landscape features into those that formed directly under the moving ice and those formed by the meltwater stream deposits that came later. As the ice thinned, sediment was deposited directly beneath it in the form of unsorted material of every size, from boulders to clay, all mixed together in a substance called glacial till. Soil formed from this material would one day become the bane of upland farmers, who had to contend with a terrain so rocky it appeared to grow boulders.[7] In some areas till was deposited in the form of rounded and spoon-shaped hills called drumlins, which to this day are oriented in the direction the ice flowed, from northwest to southeast. Examples include Baker's Hill in Florence, Yankee Hill in Bay State, and probably Round Hill in the center of Northampton.

The glacier released its enormous stash of ice water into meltwater rivers and streams that were powerful enough to carve valleys, such as Day Brook Valley in Haydenville. These rivers deposited vast amounts of sand and gravel in an array of landscape features, some snake-like and sinuous (eskers), others irregularly shaped terraces along valley walls (kames), and still others in braided fan shapes (outwash deltas). It was these meltwater streams which gave birth to the present day channel of the Mill River.[8]

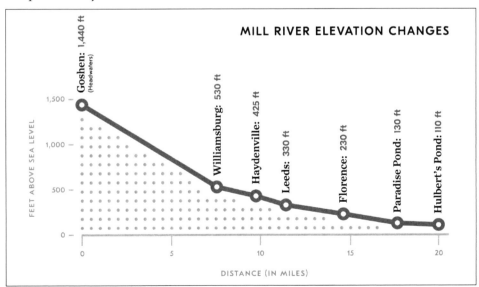

Fig. 1.3 *Height Above Sea Level of Village and Mill Locations on the Mill River (Transit Authority Figures)*

Every stream has a topographic profile that describes its voyage from source to mouth. The Nonotuck People were keenly aware of river profiles since they marked pathways through the landscape. European settlers relied on rivers for consistent power for mills and paid close attention to cascades and falls. Too small a drop in the river meant too little power to turn a waterwheel, and too great a drop challenged eighteenth-century dam-building technology.

Tumbling out of its headwaters at Upper Highland Lake in Goshen at 1440 feet above sea level, the Mill River's West Branch drops 910 feet to Williamsburg (at 530 feet), where it meets the East Branch flowing out of Conway State Forest, then down another 105 feet to Haydenville at an elevation of 425 feet. Picking up tributaries from Beaver Brook and Roberts Meadow Brook, it drops 95 feet to Leeds at 330 feet, another 100 foot drop to Florence at 230 feet, down to Paradise Pond at 130 feet, and slowly drops a final twenty feet to the meadows of the Connecticut River at 110 feet above sea level. That is a total drop of 1330 feet from Goshen to Hulbert's Pond, a distance of about twenty river miles. The Mill River fit early settlers' needs almost perfectly. Very few tributaries to the Connecticut provide a comparable size and length that also combine steep slopes in the upper reaches with falls and cascades along its middle course and plentiful water in its lower reaches. Few New England streams, therefore, have such long histories of factory villages.

Along the first steep drop of almost 1000 feet from the hilltowns of Goshen, Ashfield, and Conway down to Williamsburg, the meltwater stream which was to become the Mill River eroded away thousands of years of glacial till, depositing it ever farther downstream. Wherever the stream encountered underlying bedrock, such as in Devil's Den, it cascaded over cataracts. The valley broadened when the river reached the former area of Lake Hitchcock in Florence. There it meandered back and forth across its flood plain (the new Florence community gardens and Florence Recreation Fields) where it picked up the sediments of the former lake. From Florence downstream, the Mill was constrained by the drumlins and outwash deposits that dictated its course, especially those of Baker Hill and Yankee Hill. Where it eroded away the surface materials and hit bedrock (at today's Nonotuck Falls in Florence and Paradise Pond at Smith College), it cascaded again, forming the structures at which the English colonists placed their first mill dams. It then carved its way between Fort Hill and Meetinghouse Hill (Main Street in Northampton), which are likely outwash terraces from the Mill River into Lake Hadley.[9] The Mill River finally deposited all its eroded materials at Hulbert's Pond, an ancient oxbow of the Connecticut River, there to be carried by the Connecticut itself and ultimately deposited in Long Island Sound, another ninety miles downstream.

The Pre-Columbian People from Their Arrival in the Connecticut Valley to European Contact

The moment one imagines the peopling of this valley, two questions come to mind. Did the first humans arrive in time to see Lake Hitchcock before it disappeared? And who were they?

To begin with the second question, we are unlikely ever to have definitive answers about the exact origins of the first humans to see the valley. Archaeological evidence is sketchy because dramatic geomorphological change has occurred, leaving little chance for discovery of artifacts. Furthermore, the date and origins of humans in North America has turned out to be extremely complex, with some estimates going back to 30,000 years before the present.[10] New discoveries in genetics and renewed efforts from archaeologists will increase our knowledge, but the question of origins will remain a fertile ground for dispute for some time to come.

Judging by some of the origin stories from more recent Indian groups, it is well within reason to imagine that the first people arrived 15,000 years ago—in time to see the final remains of Lake Hitchcock. They would have arrived in a strikingly different landscape, with vegetation similar to the northern tundra, dominated by sedges with scattered birch, mountain-avens, and alder growing on the permafrost.[11] Over the next 8000 years, as the earth warmed, the Valley's vegetation changed dramatically. From 14,000 to 11,500 years ago spruce and jack pine prevailed, followed by white pine and then hemlock, which appeared about 10,500 years ago. From 10,200 to 8000 years ago, there occurred a spike in ragweed and other non-woody plants, suggesting forest decline as the region became significantly drier and the incidence of fire increased. From 9500 to 8000 years ago, oak predominated in the valley sections of our region, while hemlock was found in the highlands.

From 8000 to 5500 years ago, North America experienced a significant rise in temperatures, which allowed beech to move in. Simultaneously, megafauna, such as mammoths, disappeared and Native Americans shifted their focus on hunting to deer, bear, and other game similar to what exists today.[12] Then, 5500 years ago, hemlock declined significantly, and drought-tolerant hickory replaced many oaks, probably as a result of extended drought. Hemlock did not recover for nearly 3000 years. The next major shift occurred more recently, between 1500 and 1850 AD, when earth's climate cooled. This Little Ice Age gave New England a reprise of cold summers and often deadly winters.[13] And during most if not all of this post-glacial period, people lived in the Connecticut Valley.

There is plenty of archeological evidence of human settlement throughout the Connecticut River Valley, but in the Mill River watershed itself, few records of Native sites exist. Archeologists have found artifacts from different periods and places, suggesting that certain locations have been continuously occupied over the past 10,000 years. Unfortunately, records of artifacts are relatively scarce because so many sites were near riverbanks, which regularly eroded during periods of flood, burying some and eradicating others. Until the last century, little thought had been given to preserving and recording Indian sites and materials, so the historical record contains little to enlighten us. Many local residents have collected Indian artifacts over the last 350 years, but these remain simply collectors' items with no provenance. There has simply been too much disturbance, erosion, and sedimentation to hope that a major archeological site still exists. Still, the geographic setting of Northampton—the floodplain, river confluences, highlands, and adjacent wetlands—suggest that Native Americans used the site for a variety of purposes, from small encampments, to horticultural fields to permanent multi-family settlements.[14]

In their own stories of the origin of places on the landscape,[15] Native Americans replace the scientific forces of glaciers and climate with the powers of giant animals and humans—earthshapers and transformers—who mark the land with their limbs and bodies, creating rivers, battling superhuman forces and re-working megafauna into animals now recognizable to us.[16]

In the traditional Haudenosaunee (Iroquois) story, at first only a mass of water (and water animals) existed. Then Sky Woman falls through a hole in the sky, and the water animals gather in council to decide how to provide for Sky Woman to land. One after another of them fails until it comes to muskrat's turn. He dives to the bottom and finally rises to the surface with some mud. Gasping his dying breath, he lays the mud on turtle's back. As he does so, geese fly up to catch Sky Woman in their wings "and, as they lay her on turtle's back, the woman releases a seed she has carried from the Sky World, and the earth was born."[17]

From the Western Abenaki comes the voice of an elder from the Missisquoi or Mazipskoik (place of the flint), near Lake Champlain, who explained the origin of his people to Marge Bruchac:

> Our life began with the creation and transformation of this land, passed down to countless generations in the oral tradition. For those of us from Missisquoi and other Western Abenaki places, we were made near Bitawbagok, Lake Champlain, by Tabaldak: the Creator on aki, the earth. We were created out of the wood of a tree that still thrives here. We have always been here, kin to the ancient forests.[18]

All the elements of a landscape, argues Marge Bruchac, "serve as the tangible evidence of the Native past, and these echoes of the Paleolithic, in re-animated form, also stand as guideposts for Native people living in the modern world."[19] We know from the stories of Native people and the recovery of archeological evidence that the Pioneer Valley was hospitable to Native Americans for millennia.[20]

An Understanding of New England's Prehistoric Environmental History[21]

Native people throughout North America have manipulated their landscapes for millennia to encourage the growth of useful garden plants and forest trees. Indians fired over agricultural fields to plant corn-hills that were kept in cultivation for centuries. They used fire to clear the understory of many forest areas, encouraging nut trees both for themselves and game animals. But there has been a decades-old argument about both the intensity and origins of fires prior to the arrival of Europeans.[22] How many were caused by lightning, and how many purposefully set? How much land did Native Americans clear, and with what intent?

Those who support the theory that fire was used purposefully by Native Americans in the Northeast, such as the journalist and author Charles Mann, cite the example of bison that roamed eastern North America from Maine to Georgia. How, he asks, could bison have roamed if the forests were thick with trees and the grasslands few? Bison are grazers that require thousands of acres of grassland to sustain them, yet, argues Mann, Indians managed to clear sufficient land to keep these western animals in the eastern U.S. What early colonials thought was a separate species of bison, which they called the woodland buffalo, was simply the plains buffalo drawn eastward by Indians, who kept the grasslands free of woody vegetation.[23] As the historian William Cronon noted, "[The Europeans] accustomed to keeping domesticated animals lacked the conceptual tools to recognize that the Indians were practicing a more distant kind of husbandry on their own."[24] The local historian and journalist Sylvester Judd also argues the likelihood of extensive burning, citing seventeenth-century sources that suggest the English simply carried on the tradition of firing over landscapes they inherited from the Natives.[25]

On the other hand, a number of scientists insist that only the southern sections of New England witnessed high fire frequencies, and we really don't know whether most fires were caused by humans or by lightning. In short, small fires appear to have transformed landscapes at local scales. We must make do with speculation on the extent and cause of pre-colonial burning and its effects on New England's ecology. So much dramatic change has occurred these last four hundred years that we can only look through obscure lenses and enjoy the academic arguments.[26]

We do, however, have sufficient scientific clues to hazard guesses at the ecological composition of the Mill River watershed.[27] The area would have consisted of both young and very old forests, the former on flat and fertile alluvial floodplains, and the latter probably on steeper slopes that were not amenable to settlement and farming, but rather to hunting for game. Some old-growth forests might well have been three hundred years old when the settlers found them.[28] Early records of witness trees[29] from town surveys indicate that oaks and pines were the most prevalent species, followed by maples, hemlock, beech, chestnut, hickory, and several species of birch. Less frequent tree species included ash, cherry, poplar, basswood, elm, and spruce.[30]

A third of the land in New England was not forested but chiefly consisted of seven types of habitat:

> 1. Beaver meadows primarily dominated by grasses and plants rooted in water (scientifically called emergents) such as Canadian mannagrass, Canada blue-joint grass, and sweet wood-reed;

2. Floodplains and wet meadow, which would have contained native grasses and rushes, as well as silver maple, sycamore, black maple, and other trees;

3. Shrub wetlands with roses, buttonbush, and blueberries;

4. Bogs with wild cranberries, pitcher plants, and Labrador tea;

5. Fens with shrubby cinquefoil, many (now rare) sedges and orchids;

6. A few glacier-scoured summits of the Metacomet mountains;

7. Agricultural and early-successional fields opened by the Indians' use of fire.

Animals such as turtles, amphibians, reptiles, and insects would have been much more common than they were following colonization. According to the reports of astonished settlers, birds, fish, even ants swarmed in the millions during the height of summer.[31] A full array of mammals provided clothing and meat. For clothing and sinew there were otter, fisher, muskrat, beaver, fox, and wolf. Much of the meat came from the big three: deer, bear, and moose, plus rabbit, squirrel, raccoon, beaver, muskrat, otter, porcupine, and woodchuck, along with birds such as turkey, passenger pigeon, and waterfowl. For fish they had brook trout, perch, suckers, catfish, pickerel, sturgeon, lamprey, shad, herring, and salmon.

In fields by the Mill River, the Nonotucks grew white, yellow, and multicolored eight-row flint corn, kidney beans, gourds, pumpkin, summer squash, Jerusalem artichoke, and tobacco. From the woods they gathered such fruit as Solomon's seal, blueberries, raspberries, blackberries, strawberries, elderberries, and probably serviceberries. Other edibles from the woods included sumac, acorns, ground nuts, chestnuts, hickory nuts, and butternuts.[32]

How Native Groups Managed Space Before 1600

The Algonquian-speaking people, whom the Europeans first contacted, had migrated into the region in the distant past and probably numbered between 90,000 and 125,000 in New England when the Europeans arrived, although these estimates only provide a basis for further research and discussion.[33] All Native groups in New England spoke one of the Algonquian languages, most of which were closely related. The major language groups and their territories are located in Fig. 1.4. Note the central location of Nonotuck (Northampton) near the mouth of the Mill River, and its sister villages of Pocumtuck (Deerfield), Agawam (Springfield), and Woronoco (Westfield).

Tribes in eastern New Hampshire and Maine spoke Eastern Abenaki, while those in the Connecticut River Valley from Agawam and Nonotuck north to the St. Lawrence River spoke Western Abenaki. The Mohican, Nipmuc, Massachusett, Wampanoag, Narragansett, Mohegan, Pequot, and others in southern New England spoke their own related Algonquian languages or dialects. Individuals of every group were as deeply attached to the place in which they lived as they were to their family and language. In Abenaki (the People of the Dawn Light) *ndakinna* means "our land."

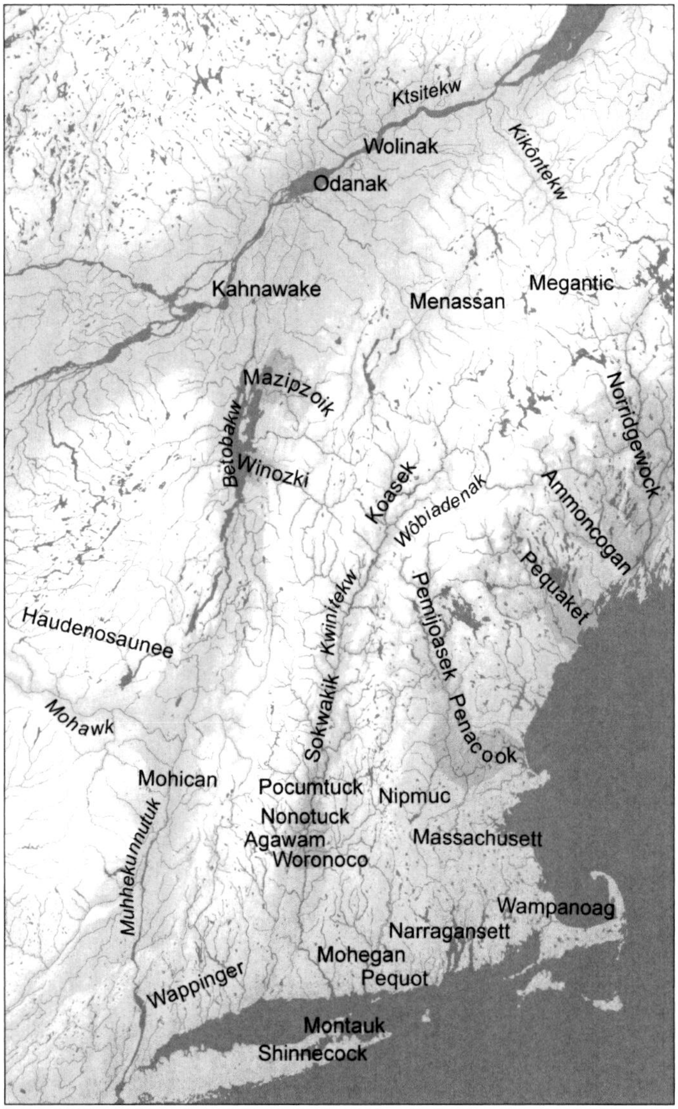

While Native Americans identified themselves chiefly as a member of a family and a group that spoke a single dialect, this was not their whole identity. The Abenaki historian Lisa Brooks has described the landscapes and people of the Mill River watershed as part of a "common pot," *wlôgan* in Abenaki.

The common pot is that which feeds and nourishes. It is the wigwam that feeds the family, the village that feeds the community, the networks that sustain the village. Women are the creators of these vessels; all people come from them, and with their hands and minds they transform the bodies of their animal and plant relatives into nourishment for their families. The pot is made from the flesh of birch trees or the clay of the earth. It can carry or hold; it can be carried or reconstructed; it can withstand fire and water, and, in fact it uses these elements to transform that which it contains. The pot is Sky Woman's body, the network of relations that must nourish and reproduce itself.[34]

Fig. 1.4 *Environs of Kwinitekw showing Wabanaki wôlhanak, mission, villages, and neighboring Native territories from Sobakw, the sea, to Ktsitekw, the St. Lawrence River. Courtesy University of Minnesota Press. The maps were created by Jenny Davis and Lisa Brooks, using ArcGIS 9.2, courtesy of Harvard University.)*

The concept of the common pot will recur in this book as an undercurrent. It emphasizes the idea that the landscape remains a whole entity regardless of whether individuals and governments try to divide it into parts. *Ndakinna* was part of the common pot just as were the family networks that held communities together. Permanent settlements in the Connecticut River Valley were located in the intervals of the Connecticut River (*Kwinitekw*), that is, the rich alluvial lands along the river and its tributaries. The planting sites were called *wôlhanak*, a word related to a pot or a dish. "These *wôlhanak* were fertile bowls between mountain ranges that were capable of sustaining the many families who gathered there, forming permanent communities and hosting trading parties who came through with news and goods from far away."[35]

Well traveled trails and canoe routes between scores of *wôlhanak* linked together all the Indians of the Northeast as part of the common pot, including tribes far to the west and east. The *wôlhanak* of Pocumtuck (Deerfield) and Nonotuck (Northampton), in what is now called the Pioneer Valley, were located at the nexus of New England's most important network of paths. To the northwest lay *Betobakw* (Lake Champlain), the origin site where Western Abenaki first emerged. From there one could travel north to the Abenaki *wôlhanak* of Odanak and Wolinak on the *Ktsitekw* (St. Lawrence River). Northeast trails led to the Eastern Abenaki territories of the Penacook tribe and the *wôlhanak* of Pemijoasek in the White Mountains, the place where all Abenaki first emerged according to their origin stories. Paths and canoe trails led past Mount Katahdin, the emergence place of Eastern Abenaki, and ultimately down the rivers of Maine to the Atlantic Ocean or east to the land of the Passamaquoddy and Mi'kmaq, the place of first morning light.

From Pocumtuck, Nonotuck, and Agawam, trails extended up the Millers and Chicopee Rivers east to Nipmuc country and the ocean. The Deerfield and Westfield Rivers led west to the *Muhhekunnutuk* (Hudson) river in Mohican territory and from there to the Mohawk and the rest of the *Haudenosaunee* (Iroquois) nations—Oneida, Onondaga, Cayuga, and Seneca. From western New York State it was not far to other tribes in the northern Great Lakes region, such as the Wyandot (Huron), who had allied themselves with the Abenaki, Mohawks, and French in the famous 1704 Deerfield Raid. Finally, trails also led south down the *Kwinitekw* to "the wampum-making nations of the Niantic, Mohegan, and Pequot gathered by (the river's) mouth."[36]

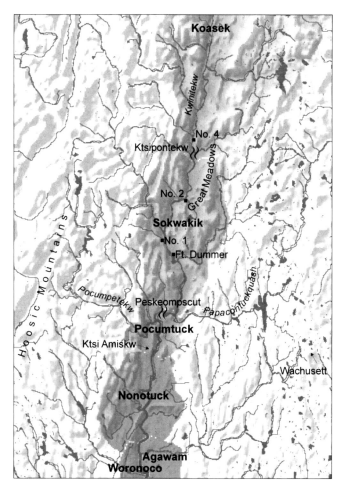

Fig. 1.5 *The river Kwinitekw from Ktsipôntekw to Peskeomp-scut, with Native wôlhanak highlighted. (Courtesy University of Minnesota Press. The maps were created by Jenny Davis and Lisa Brooks, using ArcGIS 9.2, courtesy of Harvard University.)*

The Abenaki name for the ancient crossroads on the Connecticut River at Pocumtuck (Deerfield) is *Ktsi Amiskw*, the Great Beaver, which contained the *wôlhanak* of Pocumtuck, Capawonk, and Nonotuck as well as the great falls at *Peskeompscut* (Turners Falls). The origin of *Ktsi Amiskw* is famous in Native literature, and is a clue that Indigenous people had arrived early enough to see Lake Hadley as it was draining. Note especially the reference to the huge pond at Mt. Tom, which would have been Lake Hadley.

The Great Beaver, whose pond flowed over the whole basin of Mt. Tom, made havoc among the fish and when these failed he would come ashore and devour Indians. A pow-wow was held and Hobomock [a benevolent spirit giant] was raised, who came to their relief. With a great stake in hand, he waded the river until he found the beaver, and so hotly chased him that he sought to escape by digging into the ground. Hobomock saw his plan and his whereabouts, and with his great stake jammed the beaver's head off. The earth over the beaver's head we call Sugarloaf, his body lies just to the north of it.[37]

Travelling a few miles north of Northampton, looking east (to the right) one can easily view *Ktsi Amiskw* from Interstate 91 as a double humped hill across the Connecticut River. What you see is *Ktsi Amiskw's* head, and the beaver is so great that its tail lies ten miles north in Deerfield. It still watches over the valley and its children. The beavers who currently live all around us have returned after a 200-year absence to create ponds for native trout and habitat for native plants and wildlife.

Several major *wôlhanak* were located in and around these crossroads: Agawam (the "landing place"), Woronoco (the "winding land"), Nonotuck or

Norwottuck ("in the midst of the river"), Capawonk ("protected place or place in the bend of the river"), and Pocumtuck (the "shallow, sandy river").[38] Natives also left a number of ceremonial stone landscapes in this area. Notable among them are those in Turners Falls near the tail of *Ktsi Amiskw*. One such group of stones are believed to relate to the Perseid meteor showers; another, a human effigy, may represent the spirit of the humans who used the site.[39]

The inhabitants of these settlements were autonomous groups, living in villages composed of family units, not members of more centralized "tribes," such as Mohawks or Pequots. They had no political "center," but rather sachems, or group heads. These were men and women of high status, although ultimate power was held principally by councils of elders of both sexes. They traveled extensively throughout New England and southern Canada, participating in a shifting pattern of alliances and war with Abenakis in the north, Mohegan/Pequots to the south, and Nipmuks to the east, as well as Mahicans of the Hudson Valley and Iroquoian Mohawks to the west.

The historian Peter Thomas pointed out that the idea of "tribe" as a centralized unit of people in a particular geographic place did not fit the Nonotucks or any of the Middle Connecticut River settlements: "The 'tribe,' as such, was a fleeting reality. It was episodic." At any one time there would have been Native Americans from other locales —Pequots, Abenakis, Nipmucs, and Mahicans—living as part of the Nonotuck settlement, and other inhabitants of the settlement moved in and out of the Mill River watershed seasonally or in times of war. Presumably, Nonotuck Indians could be found in other regions of the Northeast as well, since Indian alliances and groups were highly fluid.[40]

The Nonotuck and the Mill River

We can now look in detail at the most local landscape level: the watershed of the Mill River itself with its Native American village. Geology dictates settlement patterns, and so it was at Nonotuck Village, located at the point where the Mill River looped around Fort Hill on the north side, then along the base of the south side, and ultimately emptied into Hulbert's Pond. We can see this feature clearly on a map that the French scholar G.R.J. Cestre drew when he was studying the growth of Northampton while at Smith College on an exchange program. (see Fig. 1.7)

Bordered on three sides by the Mill River and extensive wet meadows, Fort Hill was a perfect spot for a Nonotuck village. It was defensible, and had both arable land and extensive fishing and hunting areas close by. There were, of course, other villages in the neighborhood, such as in the spots where modern-day Hatfield and Hadley are located, and even possibly in Bark Wigwam Meadow east of downtown Northampton, but we lack material or written evidence to determine the precise location of most of them.

In Fig. 1.7. note how the Mill River loops around the north, east, and south limits of Fort Hill. It would be convenient to ascribe the idea of Nonotuck as "People In The Midst of the River," to this looping feature, but the concept was perhaps more general. That is, it could well mean something akin to "the river people" or possibly "the people upriver."[41]

The Nonotucks, who spoke an Algonquian dialect[42] had managed their landscape carefully and had so efficiently cleared their fields and nearby forests that, according to town records "many large tracts were almost destitute of timber, and in some places covered with high coarse grass. This grass and other wild herbage furnished pasture for the cattle of the inhabitants of Northampton, Hadley, Hatfield, etc. for many years."[43]

The village's most important agricultural fields lay at the southwest corner of Fort Hill. A startling 1920 photo shows corn-hills, which were likely quite extensive, established in a swale between Fort Hill and Hospital Hill. There doubtless were other fields,[44] but these are the only ones whose location we know with some certainty, and their location makes sense in relation to the major settlement on Fort Hill. How extraordinary that these Nonotuck fields remained essentially as they appear in the photos for almost three hundred years.[45]

Cestre supposed that there were also horticultural fields where the current Smith College athletic fields are situated, although he provides no citation.[47] Cestre's interpretation of pre-contact Nonotuck (Northampton) seems quite plausible. Note the great extent of the meadows, the central place of Fort Hill, the proximity of the two areas of corn-hills, and the forested hill north of Fort Hill, directly across the Mill River, which was to become the colonists' Meetinghouse Hill.

Nonotuck occupied one of the most fortunate spots in all of New England. For millennia, Ktsi Amiskw, the Great Beaver, had watched over this *wôlhanak*.

Fig. 1.6 Corn-Hills: *This is a series of 1920 photographs of Nonotuck corn-hills in a meadow at the base of Fort Hill. Numbers 1-3 are taken from the east, number 4 from the middle of the field, number 5 is a detail showing the growth of hardhack (Spirea), and 6 is from the northwest showing the leveled hills near the railroad embankment, now part of the rail trail. The 1940 diversion destroyed any trace of the former landscape. (Courtesy American Anthropological Association – AnthroSource)*

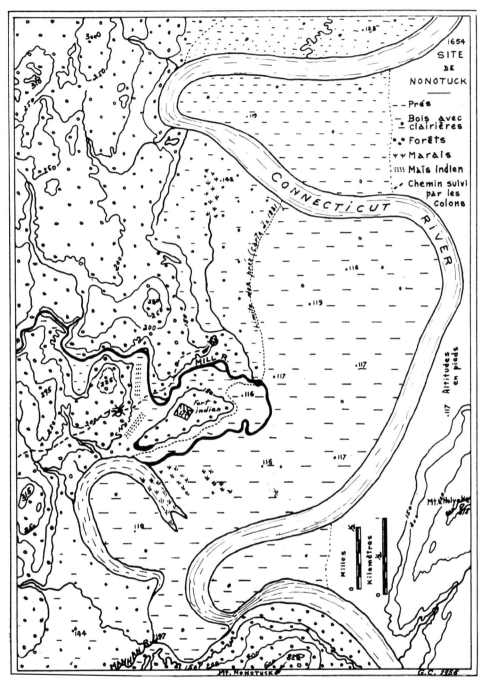

Fig. 1.7 Pre-colonial map of Northampton G. Cestre, 1963. (Courtesy Northampton DPW) Legend: Près = meadow; Bois avec clairières = open woodland; Forêts = forest; Marais = swamp; Maïs indien = Indian corn; Chemin suivi par les colons = road taken by the colonists

Nonotuck was integral to trade networks, blessed with rich lands for corn-hills, and was a major contributor to the common pot. Its blessings were just what the English had in mind when they began to arrive—first in trickles, then in droves. Whether or not the colonists were aware of it, they also became part of the common pot. Their contributions, from metal implements to smallpox, would begin a dramatic transformation of its contents.

Native American-English Contact 1654–1675

Pre-Settlement Disease Decimates the People of the Common Pot: "This Widowed Country"

Well before the actual colonial settlement of New England, smallpox, yellow fever, typhus, measles, and diphtheria made their way along trading trails and warpaths, leaving only one in ten alive among many coastal groups by the middle of the seventeenth century.[48] The historian Colin Calloway notes that

> these lethal pathogens were truly the shock troops of the European invasion of America, and the result was one of the world's greatest biological cataclysms. Long before the first invaders arrived, trade goods and diseases traveled along the trails and waterways that linked *Ndakinna* [Our Land] to Iroquoia, Canada, southern New England, and the Atlantic Coast. Disease produced famine and worked alongside increasing intertribal warfare to shatter the Indian potential for resistance [to colonial depredation].[49]

Disease decimated whole villages, leaving rotting corpses for dogs to eat, abandoned fields, dispirited and dislocated people. In one seventeenth-century Massachusetts contemporary account, the Indians "died in heapes as they lay in their houses ...[while the dying] were left for crows, kites, and vermin to prey upon."[50]

It was a human tragedy, and an ecological turning point as well. Until Columbus, Indigenous people occupied a vital role in the natural world, a role so important that their removal changed the character of the ecosystem and the contents of the common pot.[51] Indians had managed and modified the landscape for thousands of years. After Columbus, American landscapes were "widowed," to use the historian Francis Jenning's turn of phrase.[52]

Not only did invading [plants] and rats beset them, but native species, too, burst and blasted, freed from constraints by the disappearance of Native Americans. The forest that the first New England colonists thought was primeval and enduring was actually in the midst of violent change and demographic collapse.[53]

As disease decimated Indian populations, so the trade patterns of the French and Dutch dislocated social relationships. Starting in the mid-sixteenth century, the longstanding principles of trade reciprocity and equality among Indian groups gave way to the ethics and imperatives of commercial traders.[54] The impacts of trade and disease, however, were geographically scattered, depending on where the French or Dutch established trading posts—the Micmac homeland and Iroquoian Saint Lawrence for the French, the Hudson for the Dutch.

The first four decades of trading and disease changed intertribal relationships in New England so dramatically that early descriptions of the location of Indian groups must bear little relation to what the English settlers encountered in the mid-seventeenth century. The English in the 1640s, for example, described a unified, expansionist Pequot tribe that dominated southern New England, whereas Adriaen Block's Dutch foray in 1614 described the Pequot as a tribe composed of autonomous, stable groups near the coast. Something dramatic had occurred in the ensuing generation of trade relations and social disruption to transform southern Connecticut beyond recognition.[55]

As to the Pioneer Valley specifically, we know nothing in detail about the impact of trade and disease on the Native Americans in the middle Connecticut River Valley prior to English settlement.[56] We can surmise from Calloway's and historian Salisbury's work, however, that the tribes of southern New England were particularly hard hit by disease and social disruption. We also know from the account of William Bradford, governor of Plymouth, that a smallpox epidemic enveloped the southern Connecticut Valley in 1634.[57] The Nonotuck homeland occupied the space between the southern Mahican/Pequot and the northern Abenaki, whose homeland began near today's Vermont/Massachusetts border and whose loss of numbers by disease was significantly offset by refugees fleeing north. We can infer that the agricultural Nonotuck would probably have suffered a fate similar to their southern neighbors.[58]

Contact: *The Self-Governing Town vs. the Common Pot —War and Displacement*

English settlers began arriving in droves during the 1630s. They were products of a great upheaval that ran through English society from the mid-sixteenth to the mid-seventeenth century. Although commercialization of agriculture doubled the population during that period, the process also threw large numbers of families off their land. These changes swelled urban populations and created havoc that expressed itself in the breakdown of religious and political institutions, ultimately resulting in the English Civil Wars of 1641–52. The colonists were bringing with them not only new plants and animals, but also many of the forces that had been transforming English society.[59]

The newcomers streaming into the Connecticut Valley reflected the general pattern of English settlers. Some were rural folk escaping the vagaries of agricultural markets and uncertain land tenure, others were urban tradesmen and artisans hoping to return to the land.[60] Puritanism enjoyed its greatest reception with these latter two groups.[61]

English Puritans arrived in New England with a pre-conceived idea of how to settle upon the Algonquian landscape by establishing a series of discrete communities of worshippers linked by faith. The idea was to have the governor and legislature mark out the boundaries of independently governed towns with a church at the center of public life—Governor John Winthrop's "city upon a hill." The strain of Puritanism practiced in New England came to be called Congregationalism, in which every believer is a priest and every congregation has its own covenant. The English were replacing the common pot with a communal religious belief and scores of independent, self-governing towns geographically centered on a meetinghouse. The common pot was both a concept and an array of landscape and human features that had developed over centuries in which the people and the place had become a unity, sometimes in balance, sometimes not. The English idea had little to do with accommodation to nature and everything to do with the manipulation of nature, as well as unity through faith, work, and righteousness.

I pose this question for the reader to ponder: would the Europeans be able to obliterate the common pot? Or would the common pot survive? We will let history play out to find an answer.

The arrival of the English colonists to Nonotuck is an often-told tale, generally taken from J.R. Trumbull's nineteenth-century history of Northampton, which he based on town records.[62] The English first settled the lowest section of the Mill River watershed in the 1650s, and in a quite separate arrangement, took over the hilly, upper section a hundred years later. In 1654, a group of twenty-three Connecticut men, plus one man from Dorchester, petitioned the General Court (the legislature) for permission to plant a town at Nonotuck. John Pynchon, the wealthy son of William, founder of Springfield, used his good offices and large land holdings at Nonotuck to help the Connecticut Yankees succeed.

The colonists' first job was to evict the Nonotuck Indians by way of treaty, which they did in short order: From Trumbull, writing in the 1890s, we get a

Fig. 1.8 Original deed by which John Pynchon acquired rights to the Nonotucks' lands. "On September 24, 1653, title to the land known to the Native Americans as Norwottuck or Nonotuck and subsequently became the English town of Northampton, was conveyed to John Pynchon of Springfield by "Chickwallop, alias Wawhillowa, Neessahalant, Nassicohee, Riants, Paquahalant, Assellaquompas and Awonusk ye wife of Wulluther all of Nanotuck" in "consideration of One Hundred fathom of wampam by Tale, & and ten Coates besides some small gifts..." (Source: J. Trumbull History of Northampton)

description of the treaty process that encapsulates the idea of "Indian" held by nineteenth-century Northamptonites:

> [The Nonotuck's] land, of which they made scant use, and which was really of little value to them, was honorably purchased. In fact the establishment of the new settlement at Northampton did not dispossess the Indian owners of any thing held sacred by them... No Indian village then existed within the limits of the town. There were here no burial places...[and] on the meadow, at suitable intervals they raised a little corn.[63]

Shades of a widowed landscape!

At first, colonists tended to treat Native groups as sovereign nations, savvy trading partners, and formidable enemies.[64] Certainly from the Nonotuck perspective, the treaties they signed were usufruct agreements, rather than title transfers, that is, a mutual willingness to use different parts of the shared territory for their own purposes.

Citing Northampton town records, Marge Bruchac noted that the Nonotucks and John Pynchon got along well for at least a short time, and the Indians allowed the English to create a village on the condition that "Pynchon shall plow up or cause to be plowed up for the Indians sixteen acres of land on ye east side of the Quinnoticott River...[where] the Indians have liberty to plant their present corn fields."[65] Although there is no indication that the English ever did plow those sixteen acres in Hadley, the actions of the Nonotuck, in planting corn on both sides of the Connecticut, indicated they never intended to leave the area permanently.

The upper half of the Mill River watershed, now the hilltown of Williamsburg, was founded very differently than was Northampton. Indeed, Williamsburg was never even part of Northampton; rather, it was broken off from Hatfield, the town directly north of Northampton. Three years after the Indians' agreement to sell Nonotuck lands, the sachem Umpanchala sold to Northampton men the area called Capawonk "in the bend of the river," north of Northampton, a section that became the town of Hatfield in 1670. Hatfield extended six miles west into the woods, and the Hatfield proprietors divided the town into four sections, the third and fourth of which included what is currently called Williamsburg on the Mill River.[66] The Nipmuck name is Unquomonk, "the ending place at the boundary." The Unquomonk moniker was later bestowed on many entities, including Unquomonk Hill, Unquomonk Brook and Road, and in the nineteenth century, Unquomonk Woolen Manufacturers and the Unquomonk Silk Mill.[67]

During the seventeenth century, Hatfield's third section remained without a permanent settler. Local stories were told about the dangerous third and fourth sections, where one might well run into Mohawk warriors, who were enemies of both the Connecticut River tribes and the English at that time.

Despite their initial trade relations, the Nonotuck and English soon became uneasy neighbors, and significant numbers of Indians in Northampton continued only about twenty years. By the middle of the seventeenth century,

20,000 Englishmen and women had settled in New England, exacerbating conflicts not only among Native Americans but among Europeans, namely Dutch, French, and English populations themselves, as well as struggles between Europeans and Natives. Indian survival was challenged both from within by inter- and intra-tribal friction and from without by Europeans.[68]

That first fateful decade after contact dramatically altered the whole of Nonotuck life. Having come under the suzerainty of the English, "the Natives at Fort Hill were compelled to comply with a list of conditions imposed by the town that forbade… working on the Sabbath, drinking, hosting visitors, and holding the religious observances known as powows."[69] When the beaver became scarce and the Natives were forced from their cornfields, the Nonotuck lost their two most important trade items. Death from disease and the loss of intertribal trade ensured that poverty overwhelmed the remaining Nonotuck. In 1660 the English forced the Nonotuck sachem Umpanchala to give up much of his land along the river as payment for his debts, which included a fine of two fathoms of wampum for being drunk.[70] Debt and credit, in fact, were the most powerful tools the Pynchons used to control commercial and land transactions in the Connecticut Valley.

William and his son John Pynchon were the lynchpin in the quick success of Springfield and Northampton. William, one of the original settlers of Roxbury (now part of Boston) in 1630, purchased land in Springfield shortly thereafter. In 1636 he created an extraordinarily productive commercial, social, and political network in the Connecticut Valley. Pynchon founded Springfield as a commercial enterprise and it has remained so to the present. I would add that the same goes for Northampton.[71] Springfield was, in Stephen Innes' words, a company town run much like an English manor, in which William and John were the largest landowners, the largest employers and principal merchants, and held critical judicial and political offices. With their control over both Indian and English indebtedness, they essentially controlled banking and real estate.

How did the Pynchons achieve so much so quickly? Salisbury suggests a fortunate confluence of personal traits, timing, and geography. William Pynchon arrived in 1630 "an ambitious, well-heeled merchant gentleman," qualities not unique in England, but requisite for success. Second, he arrived in the Valley at the very start of the Pequot War, which eliminated the Dutch and

Pequots, the Pynchons' strongest trading competitors. Third, the geography of the Connecticut Valley was favorable for both the fur trade and English-style farming, and allowed the Pynchons to control trade from the St. Lawrence to the Hudson, and from Long Island Sound to Boston. English settlers poured in, requiring land and cash. The Pynchons could provide both, along with the capacity to export the new commodities of beef and wheat, now supplements to the beaver trade.[72] Salisbury summed up the situation as follows:

> In the face of these and other developments the Indians of the region were squeezed in a veritable vice-grip. It was in this setting that John Pynchon stepped up his acquisition of Indian land. By the mid 1670s, [John] Pynchon no longer needed the Indians, nor did anyone else. It is hardly surprising, then, that they joined the uprising led by Metacom [King Philip].[73]

Salisbury is referring here to the famously bloody series of episodes called King Philip's or Metacom's War, the origins of which lay in a tangle of tribal relationships.

The immediate antecedent of King Philip's War occurred less than a decade after the English occupied Nonotuck land. Bitter inter-tribal warfare broke out in a series of raids in *Ktsi Amiskw* known as the Beaver Wars. The supply of beaver pelts had been exhausted in New York State in the mid-seventeenth century, and the Mohicans of the Hudson, who had acted as the major middlemen for trade with the Mohawks, began to acquire fur from the people in the Connecticut Valley through alliances and marriages. When trade no longer sufficed to acquire pelts, the Mohawks began to raid the Mohicans, resulting in full-scale war between the two nations. Realizing that the common pot was out of balance, the Mohicans, Penacooks, and inhabitants of *Ktsi Amiskw* gathered a large crowd of people for a three-month-long conference in the early 1660s, and in 1663 built a fortification at Pocumtuck. In short order, Haudenosaunee warriors mounted an attack, and several years of war ensued. After a particularly savage Haudenosaunee raid on the whole of *Ktsi Amiskw*, the Pocumtuck scattered to the far winds, abandoning their fields and fishing and hunting grounds. "A year later, Englishmen from Massachusetts Bay targeted the seemingly 'empty' site for a new settlement. [In 1673] they would come to call it Deerfield."[74] Many Nonotuck likely participated in the warfare at *Ktsi Amiskw* and, like the Pocumtuck, scattered north to friends and relatives outside the region.

On the heels of inter-tribal strife came King Philip's War in 1675. Sometimes called America's bloodiest war, this series of battles capped off the earliest round of warfare between Native Americans and English settlers in New England. *Ktsi Amiskw* was near the northwestern front of the battles, which stretched southeast to the Wampanoag country of Metacom in southeastern Massachusetts. Because so many authors have scrutinized this subject, we have no intention of diving into the extraordinary complexities of King Philip's War, certainly one of the most perplexing and cruel in the long history of American violence.[75] It would be satisfying to have a single narrative of events, tracing the origin of the war to one or two incidents, and the end of it to the death of Metacomet in 1676. English accounts conclude that a rebellion of Native people had been squashed, the Indians subjugated, and land titles cleared.

The realities, however, are otherwise. In her remarkable study of King Philip's War through the lens of Native people, Lisa Brooks insists that, "Naming the conflict "King Philip's War" created an impression of finality."[76] What occurred, however, was a series of battles that continue to this day, fought by a network of Native American resisters from Vermont and Maine to Massachusetts and Connecticut. They have never given up their quest to regain their lands. We cannot, on the other hand, underestimate the heavy losses that Native Americans suffered during the 1670s. King Phillip's War created a diaspora of Indians from southern New England and spelled the end of their way of life.

When King Philip's War came to *Ktsi Amiskw*, John Pynchon tried to neutralize the local valley Natives through treaties and trade, but many in 1675 joined Metacom's attacks on Northfield, Deerfield, Hatfield, Hadley, and Northampton. The English retaliated in 1676, massacring nearly four hundred Native refugees, including elderly men, women, and children who had gathered at Peskeompskut (Turners Falls). Marge Bruchac has labeled King Philip's War a milestone in the historical memory of the northern colonies, "a marker for the *supposed* [my italics] end of Native occupation of New England, and a justification for later Indian removals."[77]

Few Native Americans were left in Northampton after King Philip's War. Many retreated north to their Abenaki relatives, who had long ago established a number of villages, such as St. Francis and Odanak, along the St. Lawrence. Hundreds from *Ktsi Amiskw* made their way north in the 1670s and 80s, finding sanctuary outside French forts. Over the next century, they maintained contact with their relatives in northern New England. As Haefeli and Sweeney note in their book on the 1704 Deerfield raid, whenever peace was restored, "they would return to their homelands [to find that] the English had claimed more of their lands."[78]

Those who remained would travel about, following kinship and intertribal networks. They marketed baskets and brooms, hiring out as day labor and dispensing traditional medicine.[79] James Trumbull tells of early eighteenth-century visits from Nonotucks who "always came when Clapp's corn was green, and would devour it in large quantities," whenever they visited Mrs. Clapp, the former Mary Sheldon, who was captured by Abenaki in the 1704 Deerfield raid and ransomed back to the Valley in 1706.[80]

By the time this historical period ended in 1677, the English and French had set the stage for their eighteenth-century wars and the Iroquois had taken "a step toward their ideal of peace and cooperation among peoples. To the southern New England Algonquians, it marked the end of political autonomy and reciprocity."[81]

Warfare in New England broke out sporadically over the next hundred years, and the English residents of Northampton found themselves the northernmost safe haven for colonists at the end of the seventeenth century.[82] Attacks on both sides occurred with some frequency just north of Northampton at Deerfield, Turners Falls, and Northfield. During the series of eighteenth century wars between England and France, Connecticut Valley Indians of *Ktsi Amiskw* allied with their neighbors against the English and captured hundreds of colonists, many of whom were incorporated into Native kin networks.[83] During the largest of the Anglo-French conflicts, the War of the Spanish Succession (1701–13), the greatest French victory occurred with the 1704 Deerfield Raid, when the French and their Native allies killed forty-seven and captured 112 English settlers. More than half the colonists whom the Indians captured remained with their captors and became members of Native American families. Those same "captives" often returned to visit their former friends and relatives in the Middle Connecticut Valley.[84]

Despite myths of their disappearance from their homeland, the Western Abenaki remain in small clusters of families. Vermont stories of brave pioneers pitted against roving savages, however, only added to the myths and to "prolonged white racism against Indigenous people in New England," as Bruchac has observed.[85] The Western Abenaki continue to this day their legal struggle for recognition in Vermont and for title to at least some of their homeland.

The English Settlers in the Seventeenth Century

The English Subsistence Strategy and Its Impact on the Woodlands

The English came from a world radically different from that of the Nonotuck. Their intention was to re-create the world from which they came. And what kind of world was that? Some, like William Pynchon, came from well-watered rural areas where people were accustomed to raising livestock on meadowland and growing small grain, mainly wheat. Those who were born in Northampton, England, came from a city famed for its leather trade and the manufacture of shoes and boots. There were a large number of non-conformist believers (separatists from the Anglican church) in Northamptonshire, who had sided with Cromwell during the English Civil Wars of the 1640s and supported his short-lived government. In revenge, when King Charles II returned to power in 1660, he destroyed the walls and castle of Northampton. Nonotuck's first English settlers had grown up in England during troubled times. They were deeply invested in their faith and well aware of the ravages of war. At the same time, they were chiefly men and women with at least modest wealth, possessing artisan skills in several crafts, as well as expertise in farming and warfare.

In comparing English and Native American subsistence strategies, Peter Thomas estimated that a colonial town of 250–300 persons utilized very similar amounts of farm land (1700–2400 acres) as did an Indian village of 400 (990–2320 acres).[86] The English used plants from wet meadows for grazing, while Indians used reeds, rushes, and sweetgrass (*Hierochloe sp.*) for basketry and mats, and plants such as blue flag (*Iris versicolor*), cattail (*Typha latifolia*), and pickerel weed (*Pontederia cordata*) for food. Colonists cleared and logged uplands, which altered them dramatically for hunting, and the open grazing of cattle and pigs in marginal areas around the town produced competition between domestic and wild animals for the same resource, further reducing hunting opportunities.

Colonists and Indians interacted continually, using one another to whatever advantage they could. Maize allowed the English to survive, while trade in wild game, furs, beads, and wampum (strung beads of whelk and clam shells), which was regarded as legal tender in the mid-seventeenth century, provided income for the Natives.[87] Wampum served many purposes, from trade to ceremonial events, storytelling, and record keeping. Nonotucks also served as messengers, guides, and haulers, while settlers granted Indians credit and a judicial framework to redress grievances, such as corn lost due to the depredations of cattle.

The English quickly set about to establish gardens and fields for food and woodlots for heat and housing. We have a general idea of what forests might have looked like prior to English settlement, but imagining the forests of the Mill River watershed in detail is problematic. Sylvester Judd wrote that "no early writer has given a description of this part of Massachusetts, nor indeed of any portion of the country on the borders of this river."[88] Two factors, both elusive to historians, affect our interpretation of the settlers' impact on the woodlands.

First, we must try to figure out the extent to which the Nonotuck fired over these particular woods. It could well have been on a regular basis if Judd is correct in asserting that Northampton home lots did not require much clearing, since horses and carts could pass through the forest already with little trouble. Colonists, Judd stated, were simply following the precepts of the Nonotuck. "According to tradition," he wrote, "there were some splendid burnings in the woods on the hills and mountains, around this valley, especially at night."[89]

Second, we might wonder whether the Nonotucks, so decimated by disease, would have been able to deploy the manpower to manage the woodlands. It seems likely, from the healthy state of the corn-hills in 1654 as described by the original settlers, that the Nonotucks still formed a viable community. If they had enough people to tend their fields, they would have had sufficient numbers to fire over the woodland and/or wet meadows for hunting and gathering.

During the first half-century of settlement, the English expanded the Natives' use of fire, suppressing the growth of shrubs and understory trees. One account from seventeenth-century Hadley described the forest as so open "that a deer could be seen [at] 40 rods [660 ft.] on the wooded hills."[90] The clearing of the woodlands began immediately after settlement, even though a large number of towns throughout the Pioneer Valley enforced regulations to constrain the cutting and export of wood. This suggests that wood and saw-timber would have been somewhat scarce immediately adjacent to town centers by 1700. Whether the lack of timber was due to the open nature of the forests or to the regimen of swift cutting and felling in those years we do not know.

The English depended on a variety of trees for multiple uses:

- Firewood: settlers favored oak, walnut, maple, and elm for firewood and cut many thousands of cords annually to cook and heat their homes, keeping fires burning right through the summer months. We know that in the early eighteenth century, towns provided fifty to eighty cords of wood a year for each of their clergymen, who, granted, were men of some standing. Judd estimated that the one hundred families in Hadley required about 3000 cords of heating wood per year by the mid-eighteenth century.[91]

- Construction timber: the English favored oak for all parts of their homes, but soon came to use pine as well. They used oak not only for framing, but for clapboards and shingles.

- Rift timber: this is any timber that could be riven, meaning split or cleaved apart for rails, clapboards or shingles. Again, oak and pine were the preferred woods.

- Clapboards: these pieces of house siding were originally cloven, and so called clove-boards or clapboards, generally using oak and pine. Only later were they sawn.

- Saw logs: pine was most often used for saw logs for construction because sawn oak was prohibitively expensive.

- Woodland Pasture: cattle, oxen, swine, and horses were primarily pastured in the open woodlands at the beginning of settlement, while the meadows were generally reserved for hay.[92] Townspeople kept a few sheep and goats on their home lots. Towns in the Valley generally hired herdsmen to put animals out to pasture and keep them from intruding onto cropland and hayfields, thus ensuring that the woodlands remained quite free of brush.[93]

Although not extensive in area, the impact of settlers on local woodlands was significant. By 1700, most of the forests adjacent to Northampton had been heavily timbered, while much of the rest of the woodlands to the west had open understories. The English penchant for oak and white pine began to clear the way for an increase in red and sugar maple, which, over the next two centuries, would become a much greater part of the region's woodland.[94] The following two centuries would witness enormous change in the forests, which were cleared by the mid-nineteenth century only to return to woodland in the twentieth. The changing wooded landscape would dramatically affect the Mill River.

How the Mill River Dictated the Layout of Northampton

Before we describe the original bed of the Mill River in the mid-seventeenth century, we need to be clear that a river has two kinds of beds. The first is the channel between two banks in which it runs most of the year. The other, which we generally refer to as a floodplain, is directly adjacent to the banks. For our purposes, however, it is more useful to think of the floodplain as the extra bed during times of high water—just like the extra beds we borrow when we have an overflow of aunts, uncles, and cousins coming into town. The river claims both beds on occasion, often to our consternation, but both serve the river's purpose of carrying and depositing sediments and water.

Almost the whole of the Mill River we see today runs down its original course from Goshen to Florence, despite the twelve dams and barriers which impede its flow.[95] Only four extensive secondary beds, or flood plains, exist: the first (Sweetfern Plain) in the former Williamsburg village of Skinnerville, the second in Florence at the Northampton Community Farm, the third at the fields adjacent to Paradise Pond, and the fourth along the meadows surrounding downtown Northampton. As we shall see over the course of this story, the Mill did indeed shift its bed quite dramatically in Florence, but the greatest changes occurred in downtown Northampton, where, in partnership with the Connecticut River, the two rivers ran almost annually into their flood plain, called "the Meadows." The Mill, in particular, became such a nuisance to the town, that the people of Northampton diverted its channel three times between 1710 and 1940.

Fig. 1.9 shows how the Mill River ran down from Paradise Pond to the north face of Fort Hill, then eastward until it cut through the post-Lake Hitchcock outwash plain, separating Meetinghouse Hill on the north from Fort Hill on the South. Following the path of least resistance, the Mill ran along the northeast face of Fort Hill and then along its south face toward Hulbert's Pond two miles to the west in Easthampton.[96] During major flood events, the river would

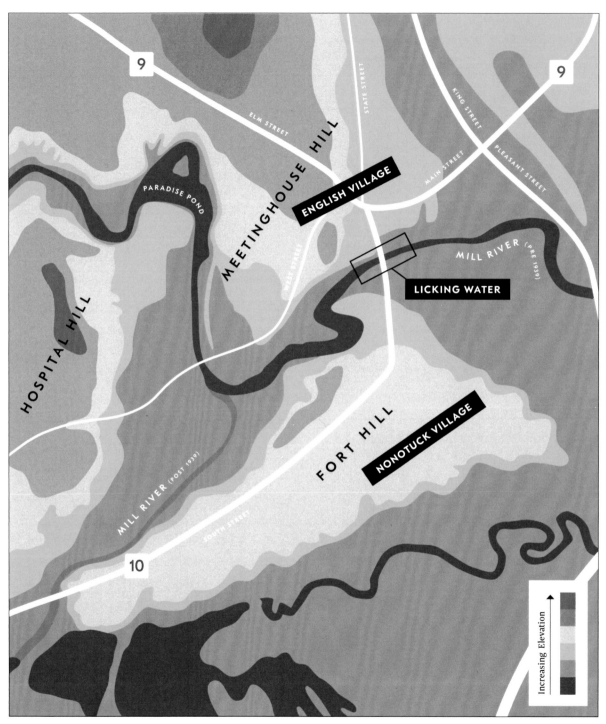

Fig. 1.9 *Relief Map showing the locations of the Nonotuck village on Fort Hill and the English village on Meetinghouse Hill in 1654. (Transit Authority Figures map based on LiDAR image supplied by Robert Newton, Smith College)*

overflow into its flood plain, namely, the Meadows, which were more extensive 350 years ago. Both the Nonotuck and English knew that any permanent buildings on the Meadows would risk destruction on a regular basis, since the Mill River claimed it as its second bed whenever necessary.

The Mill River had created an obvious choice for the English: Meetinghouse Hill was located high enough to avoid floods and was adjacent to the valuable meadowlands. Furthermore, the natural overland route to Springfield was the Indian path now known as West Street or Route 66 that leads west and south either into the hilltowns or toward Springfield. The Nonotuck already occupied Fort Hill. During the first few years of settlement, the colonists had a village on the north section of the severed outwash plain while the Nonotuck lived on the south section.

Having chosen a location, the English then had to lay out their new town, a problem already faced by the previous generation of colonists. Consider just a few of the many variables that New England settlers faced: topography, geography, village of origin, economic status, climate, availability of food and water. The challenge is almost as great for the researcher. Given the large number of studies that have been done on New England towns, one can easily find oneself going down Alice's rabbit hole. Richard Judd (not to be confused with Sylvester), in his environmental history of New England, nicely summarizes the town-founding process as one of practical application to the landscape mixed with a set of principles based on which families should be given which lands according to their need, status, number of their children and other criteria. Looking at maps of some original town lots, the historian Brian Donahue finds "a baffling jigsaw puzzle of irregular pieces."[97]

At first glance, the layout of Northampton appears to be just such a puzzle, but the key is not difficult to find. The settlers of Northampton built their first houses on the first six streets they laid out: Main, King, Pleasant, Market, Hawley, and Bridge streets. Shortly thereafter, lots were laid out on South, Fruit, and Maple streets, and the Meeting House was built on the site of what is currently the Old Courthouse. The proprietors developed rules to divide up their town into three categories — homesteads, fields, and meadows. The rules, however, are not quite clear to us in the twenty-first century. For example, in Sheffield's history of the village of Florence, he quotes the town records as stating that "every singell [unmarried?] man [will receive] foare acres and every head of a phamily six acres of meadow." He then states that each proprietor was granted a homestead and "fifteen acres to the head of a family, three acres to a son, twenty acres to a one hundred pound estate."[98] One consistent rule, however, was that every household lot should back onto one of the several small brooks that ran through downtown Northampton.[99]

While this is hardly the place to detail the inner workings of the complex system of private and common property rights, it is worth noting that the resource economist Barry Field has untangled the threads of this cat's cradle. Suffice to say that the sharing of common land made economic and social sense over the course of the first three or four generations of settlers, and that sharing took several forms, from the free use of outlying lands to sharp limitations on the number of animals allowed on common grazing lands. In Northampton, the shift from common property to private enclosed lands took almost one hundred years, with the town of Northampton granting its communally used land to settlers several times until it was all given out by 1742. Even so, there existed "continuing commonage rights to a large portion of the land for ten more years."[100]

Any current visitor to Northampton immediately notices the peculiar arrangement of streets, with a winding Main Street that splits in two on the west end and, at its east end, a set of parallel north/south streets (Market-Hawley and King-Pleasant). Finally, the principle street leading south (Old South Street) dips oddly downhill off Main Street, then curves immediately uphill, taking a sharp left toward Easthampton. Knowing what we know about the site's geomorphology, we can see that the proprietors had to configure streets that would navigate across the Mill River and between the severed outwash terrace that formed Meetinghouse Hill and Fort Hill. Then they had to take advantage of a pair of parallel tributaries (King Street Brook and Market Street Brook) that joined together as they passed under Bridge Street, which is the eastern continuation of Main Street. Thus, as many households as possible would have had access to water on their land. Bridge Street is named for the bridge over the confluence of King Street and Market Street Brooks, which is clearly delineated on maps drawn in 1831 and 1860.[101] Those brooks are now underground, but the remnants of the old riverbed can be seen as a ditch alongside the railroad tracks between King and Market Streets. The only roads south toward Springfield were South Street and West Street. Bridge Street and Pleasant Street led out into the Meadows to the Hadley and Hockanum ferries.

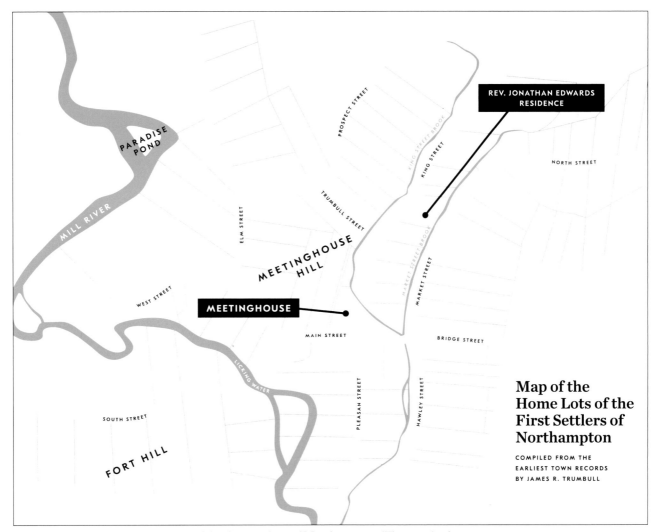

Fig. 1.10 Map of the Home Lots of the first settlers of Northampton (Transit Authority Figures. Source: J. R. Trumbull)

We have unscrambled the puzzle of the strange configuration of streets in the town of Northampton, and all we had to do was to follow the Mill River and its tributaries along King and Market Streets. The curves in the streets reflect the curvature of the river and its tributaries on the east that flanked King Street. The next problem for new settlers was how to cross the river without having to wade across a ford that could flood on a whim.

The First Bridge Over the Mill River at Lickingwater

In 1660, six years after their arrival, settlers crossed the Mill River at Licking-water where they were planning their first bridge. They then laid out house lots on Maple (now called Conz) and Fruit Streets on uplands bordering the Man-han Meadows to the east and just downstream from the original fording place across the river called Lickingwater. Here were the shallows that allowed both for fording and for the watering of livestock, hence "Lickingwater." Standing at the Round House below Pulaski Park in Northampton, one can easily imagine the shallows that would have existed in the parking lot at the point where the Mill River cut through the outwash delta separating Fort Hill from Meeting House Hill.

J. R. Trumbull, the Victorian historian of Northampton, was clearly troubled by the name of this place.

> 'Licking Water' was the absurd cognomen at one time applied to that portion of Mill River near the old South Street bridge. The appellation was occasionally used upon the town records, but is now obsolete... A school house was located in the vicinity of the river on the south side, in 1784, which was for many years known as the 'Lickingwater school.'[102]

Eighteenth-century citizens were not as fastidious as was James Trumbull, and named the street leading from Main Street to Lickingwater—logically enough—Lickingwater Street. We know it today as Old South Street.[103]

The first bridge over the Mill was not constructed until 1673, no doubt because the settlers were squabbling over who should pay for it. According to the town meeting notes of December 9, 1662, the town

> voted affirmatively that they will build a bridg ouer [sic] the Mill River: that is when the meeting house is finished so as is comfortable to meet in, likewise this vote satisfied the inhabitants on the other side for the present: also they haue liberty in the meane time to build a bridg [sic] if they see cause: So they are freed from working in the common highways til the town do build a bridg ther.[104]

Bridges, of course, need upkeep, and, as we shall soon see, tend to lead short lives. A major reason is floods, such as the one in 1691, which damaged the South Street Bridge. Apparently nothing was done for several years, so the town chose Joseph Parsons and Enos Kingsley to "make good foot Bridges ouer the Mill riuer so as to Sute the Inhabitants on that sied of the riuer vpon the

Towne charge in a way of proportion As we repair other high waies." The town never made good on its promise to repair the bridge after 1691, so in 1698 the inhabitants of Fruit and Maple Street apparently took the matter all the way to the Court of General Sessions (the colonial legislature), which required Mr. Parsons and Mr. Kingsley "to repair and make good the bridge at the town's charge and call out men to work," with a penalty of two shillings eight pence a day should no work be done.[105]

The South Street Bridge is but one disagreement of what will be many in this town of contentious citizens.

Environmental Transformation I:
Meadows and Wetlands

Environmental Transformations

The natural world is filled with transformations, with metamorphoses, with unpredictability. Such change grips the imagination of anyone who pays even slight attention to the outside world. Some people welcome the change, others become nostalgic, and some even try to stop it, but there it is. Landscapes, often despite our best efforts, are in constant flux, whether slowly or quickly.[106]

Early in life, I fell in love with metamorphosis when I collected caterpillars and stuck them in jars with their preferred leafy food, then watched them change into chrysalises and finally into butterflies. In high school biology I discovered that their magic shapeshifting lay deep in their evolutionary development, which allowed the immature and mature stages to dine on completely different foods. There, I also discovered the singularity of the Latin language when, in Mr. Hatch's Latin class, we struggled to make sense of Ovid's *Metamorphoses*. Ovid's origin tales are far closer to those of the Abenaki people than to the rationalist branch of my Western heritage, namely scientific explanations. Ovid describes scores of metamorphoses—bones become rocks, rocks become people, tears become streams, people become all manner of other living things—coral reefs, lions, lizards, snakes, seals, wolves, birds (woodpeckers, jackdaws, doves), plants (narcissus, hyacinth, reeds, mint), and myriad trees (myrrh, oak, laurel, willow, and the like).[107] It is the becoming that entices, not the stasis. In human life it is the shift into different stages of life. In tai chi, it is all about the transition, not the pose. The landscape's common pot is always in a state of balance and imbalance.

In non-industrial societies, before the anthropocene, the pace of transformation in the natural world seemed to proceed in more cyclical than linear fashion, marked by seasons, astral movements and migrations. With the advent of the seventeenth-century scientific revolutions, however, linear thought became ascendant. The idea of Progress dominated western philosophy—the belief that human society was forever advancing.[108] With the advent of the Industrial Revolutions, it became commonplace to predict that the world into which a person was born would metamorphose into something almost unrecognizable at death some seventy or eighty years later. It is within this context—the shock of the new—that I have framed the sections on environmental transformation.

With the arrival of Europeans, human disturbance patterns drove the pace and quality of environmental transformations here and throughout the New World. Chief among the tools for change were the triad of logging, fire, and the import of non-native animals, plants, and their accompanying diseases. Technological progress merely increased the pace and intensity of the disturbances, making it appear as though the contents of the common pot were so transformed as to become unrecognizable over the course of three hundred years.

The Importance of the Meadows and their Transformation

We begin with the transformation of the meadowlands, the introduction of European biota, and the extirpation of some native species. Of all the types of land available to the English, meadow was the most highly prized because it produced the most valuable commodity, namely provender and forage for cattle and sheep.[109] The Manhan Meadows, hard by the early dwellings and directly on the banks of the Mill River, must have been a fair sight indeed.

William Pynchon, father of John, was possibly reminded of home when he first spied the landscape of Northampton. The elder Pynchon was born in 1590 in Springfield, Essex. This region northeast of London is noted for its meadowland, which contains a rich mixture of some three dozen plant species high in nutrition—including red fescue, knapweed, and ox-eye daisy, all now common in America.[110] The eminent English geographer H. C. Darby explained that meadowland formed a crucial part of English agrarian economy, with an acre of meadow generally much more valuable than another of tillable land. It had long been recognized that riverside meadows benefitted greatly from inundation, which replenished the soil, and by the early seventeenth century the English had learned to manipulate flooding, increasing the fertility of the meadows and the output of manure while fattening their wallets.[111] Essex had "rich marshlands for fattening cattle and sheep and for dairying along the Thames-side."[112]

We can visualize the intimate relationship between meadow and town from the 1831 map (Fig. 1.11). Many of the seventeenth-century names still apply to the twenty-first century landscape, although the meadows' margins have been reduced as the town expanded eastward. Here are Old and Young Rainbow on the north with Venturer's Field and Bark Wigwam adjacent to them. Then, moving south are King's Bottom and Middle Meadow with Manhan Meadow to the southwest, bordered by Fish Place and Pynchon's Meadow. On the south end are Hockanum Meadows (a part of Hadley until 1840) and Hog's Bladder.[113]

It is both enticing and frustrating to imagine exactly what the meadows looked like in the mid-seventeenth century. Would that we could strip away all the invasive plants so that we could compare the 1650 "original" with the later landscape. But we cannot begin to grasp the full extent of the changes the settlers brought.[114]

We do, however, know something about the native vegetation of New England's wet meadows. Our intrepid diarist Sylvester Judd, who was also an amateur botanist, mentioned three species of *Andropogon* or thatch grass, and there are many other native plants that would have composed the meadows' flora: various sedges (*Carex*), mannagrass (*Glyceria*), bluestem grasses (*Schizachyrium*), and several well-loved New England flowering plants, such as Joe Pye weed, several asters, cardinal flowers, cattails, and bulrushes (*Scirpus*).[115] Early settlers in eastern Massachusetts had already discovered, however, that these native grasses and forbs were far inferior to English meadow grasses for forage and hay, which were necessary to feed the growing number of livestock that the English had been importing since 1620. In fact, the colonists had shipped so many cattle early on that by the mid-seventeenth century, farmers had enough cattle to breed, so no further imported stock were necessary.[116] Over the grueling New England winters, the earliest farmers were unable to keep their livestock in good condition solely on native grasses and resorted to slaughtering

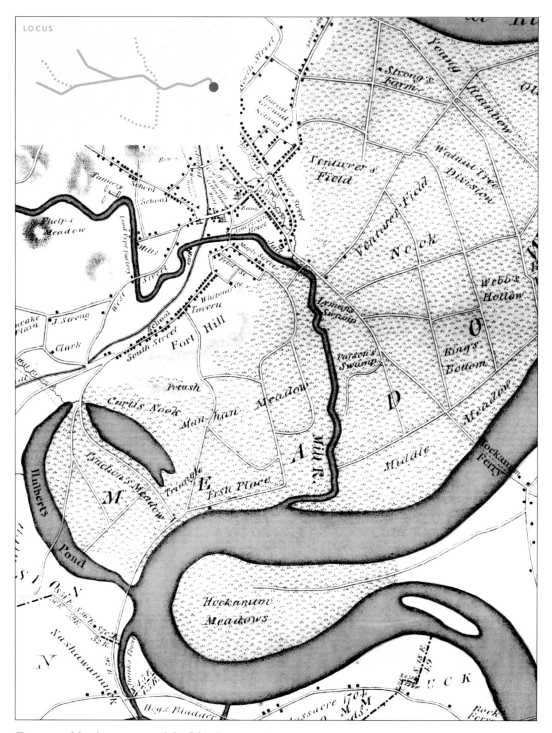

Fig. 1.11 *Northampton and the Meadows in 1831.*
(*Courtesy Forbes Library and Northampton DPW*)

some animals in the fall. Even in good years, livestock were sometimes on the verge of starvation.[117]

By the time the Connecticut Yankees settled Northampton, they probably knew they had to transform the meadows from mostly native to mostly English forage and hay crops such as timothy (herdsgrass) and fescue. Other more modern types of fodder, such as alfalfa, were introduced in the middle of the eighteenth century. To accomplish this transformation would require plowing the meadows to introduce new seed and, since they lacked oxen in the first few years of existence, it would have meant digging by hand or horse. No direct evidence exists of the exact methods or time it took to bring the meadows into full production.

Neither do we know the condition of the meadows in 1654. Were they free of shrubs and woody plants? If so, it is likely that the Nonotuck had conducted a regular regime of burning to grow rushes and grasses for basketry and clothing. In this scenario, the new proprietors would have been ready to make their six acres of meadow immediately productive without having to remove woody plants. Furthermore, we might suppose that the meadows were seasonally dry enough to plow and mow, for there is no evidence of the settlers draining the meadowlands.

English hayseed had become available by the middle of the seventeenth century, and John Pynchon was buying and selling it by the bushel as early as 1655.[118] Seed came in the form of chaff or "hay sweepings," which were broadcast over the fields in the late summer and fall. This practice continued well into the twentieth century; Ralmon Black of Williamsburg remembers broadcasting the sweepings of his family's hayloft over cornfields with his father, returning them to hayfields.[119]

The first heavy introduction of invasive plants to our region were the haying crops brought into the wet meadows and upland fields. Within the first two generations of settlement, certainly by 1700, the meadows were no longer recognizable as native wet meadows. In the eighteenth century, with the importation of newer crops such as clover and alfalfa, they began to resemble the meadows of Europe.

A most humble hitchhiker rode with the plants, seeds, and dirt along the route from Europe to North America—the earthworm. It radically changed the soil structure of both meadow and woodlands. The glacial period had killed off the species of earthworms formerly native to New England. Without worms, leaf litter in the forest built up and only slowly rotted into the soil, going deep to the roots of trees, nourishing them more richly than today. European earthworms, introduced in the roots of plants and ballast of ships, quickly digested the litter, preventing the nutrients from going deep into the soil, and impoverishing the forest soil. But what was bad for the forest was good for agriculture because earthworms keep nutrients close to the soil surface, aerate the soil, and increase soil fertility for agriculture.[120]

One more transformation occurred to the wetlands, but this one occurred throughout the watershed, indeed, throughout the whole Northeast. It had nothing to do with the introduction of new species. Instead, it was the extirpation of a native species, the beaver, which changed the landscape. Beavers significantly rearrange wetlands, removing many trees and shrubs, eating large amounts of alder, aspen, birch, cottonwood, red maple, poplar and willow. By controlling the growth of those species, it left other trees, such as hickory, pine, or spruce, to thrive. Beaver dams slow the velocity of streams, reducing the sediment load they carry. When beavers were active in pre-colonial times, streams throughout New England tended to run slower and clearer, especially in their upper reaches.[121]

By the early eighteenth century, Indians and Europeans had trapped out most beaver in the Connecticut Valley. With the beaver gone, their landscapes disappeared.[122] Beaver ponds turned into shrub wetlands filled with alders, buttonbush, blueberries, and native loosestrife while the emergent, aquatically rooted plants, such as Canadian mannagrass and water lilies, disappeared. It was only after the re-introduction of beaver to Massachusetts in 1932 that the species once again became common, re-creating the landscapes of their ponds and riverbanks.[123]

Climate, Floods, and Diversions

The English were not only moving into a region subject to flooding, but they had the ill luck of immigrating at one of the coldest periods during the "Little Ice Age," between 1300 and 1850 when temperatures in the Northern Hemisphere dropped quite dramatically, reaching their lowest point in the second half of the seventeenth century. This was not a true ice age, such as those prior to 20,000 years ago, but a period marked by anomalous weather events, such as storms and droughts that led to a general cooling of the climate, especially in the Northern Hemisphere. Early colonists were not vulnerable to flood and famine because of unrelenting cold, but because of the variable and unpredictable nature of the weather. Temperatures began rising again only in the nineteenth century, but well into the twentieth century, unusually cold winters could create conditions for deep icing of the Connecticut and Mill Rivers that could result in destructive freshets at times of ice out.[124]

Several major New England floods occurred prior to European settlement of the Mill River. Among these were the Category 5 hurricane of August 1635, which scored a direct hit on eastern Massachusetts; and two great spring floods in Connecticut, in March of 1639 and May or June of 1642. The first flood to be recorded by the English in Northampton occurred in 1667, a freshet that carried off one of Northampton's early grist mills near the old South Street Bridge. In 1680, the Governor of the Colony declared a Proclamation for a Fast Day in Massachusetts after another destructive flood. Such days of public fasting and prayer were often proclaimed by royal governors to repent for calamities, such as plagues, floods, crop failures and other disasters, which were thought to result from the sins and evil thoughts of the inhabitants.[125]

Trumbull and Judd briefly wrote of a great flood that occurred in February 1691, "the highest experienced in this section of the valley previous to 1801."[126] Medad Pomeroy's contemporary account describes the rain that fell

> for five days almost continuously, during which time the 'sun was not seen,' and 'the water rose to such a height as was scarce known in the country before.' Much damage was done throughout this entire region... [In] Northampton several horses were drowned and two corn mills and one saw mill much damnified.[127]

The Mill and Connecticut rivers also flooded almost annually, especially during spring freshets when river ice broke free, often backing up water behind an ice dam and sending their flow out onto the flood plain, the river's secondary bed. The first settlers had laid out Northampton high enough to escape major floods, but the annual floods irked them sorely because the water ran willy-nilly into the Meadows. In the late seventeenth-century, the settlers just were at the beginning of a long struggle with the river. The Nonotuck, on the other hand, had lived with an easy understanding of hydrodynamics—when the river carries a lot of water and material, simply move to the high ground, and when it runs quietly, return to its banks. The seasonal nature of Native American life fit quite well into the natural patterns of the river. It was only when the new settlers created more permanent land-use patterns on flood plains that trouble began, and we will tell the stories of how, year after year, mills, houses, and barns were destroyed by violent floods.

After laying out the town, the proprietors quickly discovered that the Mill River inconveniently overflowed its banks almost annually into what was then called the Great Swamp at the lower end of Pleasant Street, leading into the Manhan meadows, the town's prized grazing and mowing lands. As was its habit, the Mill claimed land adjacent to its channel where it could deposit the sediments and other materials it carried during periods of high flow. The medowlands closest to the town center abutted the lower parts of Maple (Conz) and Fruit Streets, which were adjacent to the Manhan Meadows. Maple and Fruit were the two anomalously low-lying streets in Northampton and were simply the result of a mistake, since they clearly lay in the Mill's second bed. These two-block-long streets ran off Lickingwater Street (now Old South Street), the connector across the Mill River between Meetinghouse Hill and Fort Hill. It was a case of people thinking they could outwit the river.

A major reason for settling in Northampton was the presence of valuable meadowland, as the English were long accustomed to working with similar landscapes. But New England was not England, and the damnably fickle weather did not allow for easy management of the meadows. In southeast England, the temperate, rather equable, damp climate accommodated the easy grazing of livestock. New England springtime, with its annual freshets, became impossible to manage. The term "freshet" seems a placid phrase for an annual river flood, but it is often fierce in the Connecticut Valley, and, as we shall see, freshets confounded the best attempts to control the water and sediments that the Mill River transported from the hilltowns down into the meadows.

Having chosen what they thought the most amenable site for Northampton, the settlers quickly found they could not manage the annual Mill River floods, which disrupted their spring schedule of grazing and mowing. Year after year, they tried to prevent the Mill from occupying its flood plain at inopportune times. Thus, in 1699, forty-five years after settlement, the town of Northampton voted to "stop the mouths of the gutters that carry the water out of the Mill river into the great swamp [Manhan Meadows]." They chose Joseph Hawley, John Clark, and Thomas Shelden to oversee the work of building dikes, employing "all persons [who] shall work eight hours in a day and those which come with teams shall work six hours."[128] Apparently the job was well done, but did no good. The river broke down the dikes and flooded the meadows as before. The townspeople had taken extraordinary time and trouble to build a dike along the southern edge of Fort Hill, where the Mill ran, but to no avail. The river's purpose, to carry its water and sediment, clearly conflicted with the settlers' need to prevent the water and sediment from flowing into the Meadows during planting, mowing, and stock-raising season.

Relying on methods well known in England, the settlers decided to divert the river. In 1710, proprietors who owned meadowlands, which included several of the town's leading families, appealed to the town for funds to dig a new channel for the Mill directly into the Connecticut River. Trumbull recorded that the town

> took into consideration a motion made concerning turning Mill river through the common field, in which motion was set forth the great inconvenience and damage done both to the publick and private by reason of the river's overflowing and so wronging men's land. The town rejected the motion...but voted liberty for those that had their land damnified to turn the river through the common field...provided the proprietors of the damnified land will be at the whole charge of it.

Fig. 1.12 illustrates the original bed of the Mill as it wandered along the southern base of the outwash terrace that is Fort Hill. One can see how easily the Mill would overflow its banks since it was already on a flood plain shared by the Connecticut River, and it was a fool's errand to attempt to retain the river within dikes at the base of Fort Hill. Whether the English were raising hay or simply grazing livestock, the meadows could flood at inopportune times, leading to heavy losses in hay or animals. Diversion was the only remaining choice, but we have no details about who surveyed and carried out the work, what difficulties they encountered, or how long it lasted. Neither do we know the exact point where the diversion began, although it must have been not far from what is now the junction of Pleasant and Conz (Maple) Street.[129]

So it was, that over the next ten years, from about 1710 to 1720, the landowners themselves paid to re-direct the Mill River away from the base of Fort Hill directly into what we now call the Oxbow of the Connecticut River. The Mill still flowed through town, however, where it remained for another 230 years, providing mill power, wash water, waste removal, recreation, and a constant source of anxiety over flooding.[130]

We are left wondering why Northamptonites continued to occupy residences on Fruit and Maple (Conz) Streets, which flooded so often. Indeed, it was only in the late 1880s that the marshlands at the foot of Fruit and Maple streets were finally drained.[131] Of course we long for the answer, but it is hard to put ourselves inside the heads of seventeenth-century colonists. Originally, Fruit and Maple Streets occupied the territory between Meetinghouse Hill and Fort Hill, just across the Old South Street Bridge, the primary means of overland transport and travel to and from Westfield and Springfield. The colonists' most important contacts were located downriver; for instruction and example, they turned first and foremost to their relatives and co-religionists to the south. North of neighboring Hatfield and west into the Berkshires was Native American territory. East was Hadley, a purely agricultural community, with strong connections to Northampton but without commercial appeal. So the natural space for expansion was Fort Hill, the former Nonotuck village, along which ran South Street. Still, it strikes us as a strange decision, given their early experience with Mill River floods.

Although there are only sparse descriptions of seventeenth-century floods, our survey of eighteenth- and nineteenth-century accounts in a later chapter will make clear that Northampton residents, especially in the Fruit and Maple neighborhood, were frequently uprooted when their houses and barns went underwater. Northampton's people, it appears, had a great willingness to acknowledge and accept their perilous fortunes. Let us move on, however, to Northampton's first dams and their impact on the river.

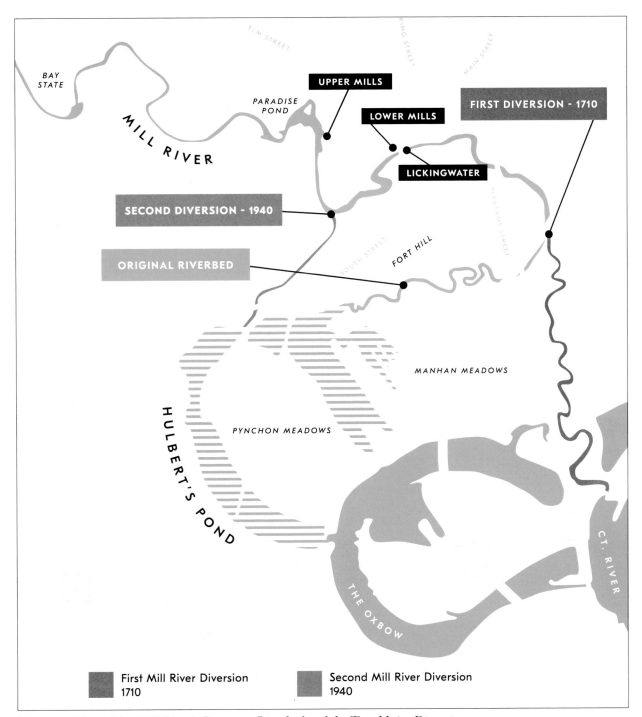

Fig. 1.12 *Map of the Mill River's Pre-1710 Riverbed and the Two Major Diversions in 1710 and 1940. (Transit Authority Figures)*

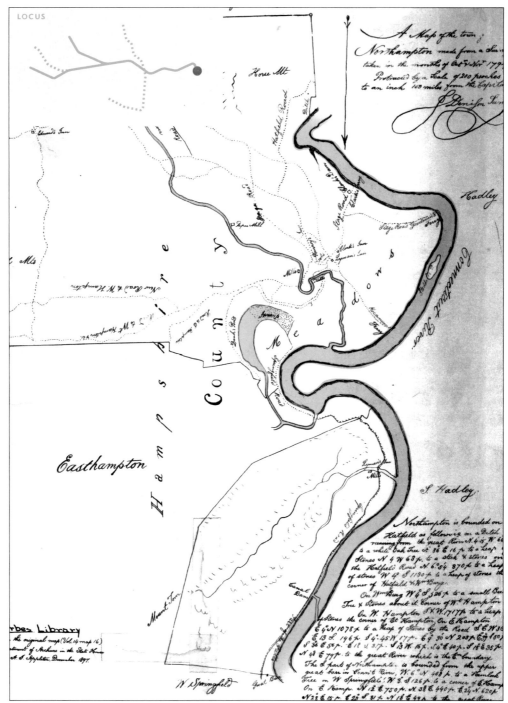

Fig. 1.13 *Oldest official map of Northampton surveyed in 1794. It focuses on waterways, roads, and meadows. The only buildings on the map are mills and inns plus a small drawing of the meetinghouse between Pomeroy's and Lyman's Inn. (Courtesy Forbes Library)*

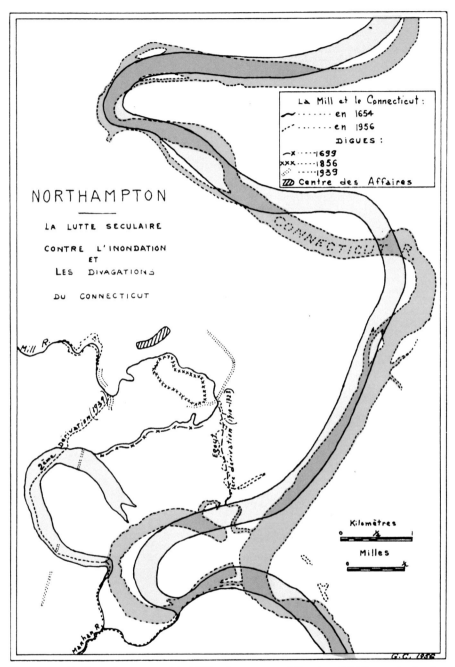

Fig. 1.14 G. Cestre's map entitled "Northampton – The Age-Old Struggle Against Flooding and the Meanders of the Mill and Connecticut Rivers." Note how widely the undiked Connecticut River (blue) meanders across its flood plain (yellow). (Courtesy Northampton DPW) Source: G. Cestre, 1963. Legend: Digues = Dikes; Centre des Affaires = City Center; Dérivation = Diversion; Egout = Drainage.

The First Mill Dams[132]

The English arrived at Nonotuck with a full range of needs that were foreign to the Natives, who had acclimated themselves over centuries to the vagaries of the local rivers. Just as New Jersey suburbanites, when they move into rural New England, expect to build McMansions and shopping malls to fulfill their idea of a proper lifestyle, so the English settled at Nonotuck with their own list of requirements, many of which had significant impacts on the Mill River.

First were food, clothing and shelter. We have already glimpsed the settlers' need to try to control the river for grazing and mowing on the meadows. Just as important in their minds were the needs for grinding grain, fulling (felting) woven wool for clothing, and sawing timber for houses. The proprietors made it clear that they would reward any capable millwright with free land and water rights if he would build a gristmill and sawmill. Fulling mills always took second place to grain: some clothing could be spun by women at home; other items were imported from England.

But where on the Mill could one find a significant drop? Not even a waterfall, but a drop of merely ten feet, to provide sufficient head to power a waterwheel?[133] Remember that the river drops almost 1400 feet from its headwaters to its discharge, but only twenty feet from Paradise Pond to the meadows, and most of the latter at the pond itself, about a mile from Northampton center.

Charles Dean, the late local historian and indexer of the *Hampshire Gazette*, found reference to a grist mill as early as 1659 that was probably built in 1657 or 1658 on the Mill's north bank upstream from Lickingwater.[134] This was a two-acre site, given to William Clark, Joseph Parsons, Alexander Edwards and Samuel Wright, Sr., who hired Robert Hayward to run it. We know the approximate location, which appears as unsuitable today as it apparently did to those first settlers. The first mill quickly went out of business in 1666, probably because there was insufficient head to run it. It was Northampton's first mill, later called the Lower Mills, but no more mills were built there for another seventy-five years.

The early mills were very basic structures, which nonetheless required a good deal of work to carve grooves in the millstones and shape the spindle, gears, and waterwheel. Millers also had to contend with a milling season that was only seven or eight months between ice-out and ice-up. Furthermore, the mills needed a controlled flow of water rather than the quirky free run of the

Mill's seasonal flow, and therefore the mill owners had to build dams to ensure enough head to power the waterwheel in times of low flow. A trench, called a raceway, would then be dug upstream, adjacent to the bank, into which a flow of water was diverted when the miller needed to run the waterwheel, and another trench, the tailrace, was dug to direct the water away downstream of the mill.

It was a risky business to invest in a building that was at the whim of flood and fire, so the community ensured that all citizens shared in that risk by providing incentives to mill owners, much as towns today court business opportunities. Residents struggled to maintain the infrastructure of their seventeenth-century town—its buildings and roads were so exposed to natural disaster. No wonder the colonists had little thought of preserving "wilderness," which to them was a dangerous state of nature just beyond their doorsteps.

A new mill site was needed, so in 1666

> Lt. William Clark & Thos. Meekins asked [the town] to be released from their promise to build a grist mill under the old conditions [of 1656] & made a new proposition contingent on town to help furnish the gravel for a foundation & other work. A bridge would be maintained & a road for access [built]. The highway was to be taken out of Lt. Wm. Clark's home lot.[135]

Thus began the construction of Green Street, built to gain access to what was to become the Upper Mills at Paradise Pond where the only logical dam site existed close to the center of Northampton. Clark and Meekins built Northampton's second gristmill "about midway between Paradise Pond and College Lane,"[136] but it was carried off by a flood in 1667, a year after its construction.[137]

These little mills led an ephemeral existence, which must have made for a harrowing livelihood for the mill owners and millers. Undaunted, Clark built another mill and a long raceway a bit upstream at the Upper Mills. Two conflicting stories are told about its fate. According to some, the Nonotucks burned the mill, but Rev. Solomon Williams wrote that in 1675 the Indians were thwarted in such an attempt as it was too well defended.[138] Whatever the case, Clark built yet another mill at that same site in 1678. That makes four Northampton gristmills built in the span of twenty years.

Looking out over bucolic Paradise Pond and the Smith College athletic fields, a scene of deep nostalgia for Smith alumnae, one is hard put to imagine the frantic activity at the Upper Mills during the last quarter of the seventeenth century, a time when Northampton's industry was focused at that site, and Green Street was a hubbub of carts carrying grain and lumber. Here's what happened after William Clark built that fourth gristmill in 1678:

1678   John Parsons builds a sawmill a few rods (1 rod = 16.5 feet) below Clark's mill; it operates until 1688.

1680   Samuel Clark and Joseph Parsons build a gristmill on the opposite (river right) bank of Clark's mill. Both mills use the same dam and are connected by Green Street.

1685   Joseph Parsons builds a sawmill as an addition to his grist mill.

1686   Clark and Parson's mills burn down.

1688   Samuel Clark and John Parsons build a new gristmill at the same site. A new road, Welsh End, is built, which became West St.

1692   A new bridge, and probably new mills, are built after the flood of 1691.

1697   The Upper Mills all burn down and are rebuilt that same year. The site remains in continuous use until the land is sold to William Edwards around 1800.[139]

While the Upper Mills hosted the largest number of industries in Northampton, two other sites were found for mills, both of which would become permanent industrial locations. Although there was likely a sawmill built in the 1660s, the first one recorded was in what we now call Bay State, and formerly Paper Mill Village. In 1670 the Reverend Solomon Stoddard and his partner Joseph Parsons constructed Northampton's first recorded sawmill at a small falls area near the current day Yankee Hill Machinery Co.[140] Shortly thereafter, in 1702, John Coombs established a fulling mill at the same site near the historic Bay State Cutlery.[141]

Another sawmill was built in 1681 at the best mill site yet discovered, this one in Florence at what became the Corticelli Silk Factory and later the Pro Brush or Nonotuck Mills building, on a piece of land that had been granted in 1657 to John Broughton, one of Northampton's original settlers. Town records note that Thomas Lyman, Samuel Wright, and Samuel Parsons were allowed to construct the mill "if [there would be] no damage to the corn mill," so we must assume a grist mill was already located there.[142] While these dam sites were superior to those of the Upper Mills, they were almost three miles from the center of town, an inconvenient distance to transport their products.

The thousand souls who resided in Northampton in 1720 managed to build enough dams, mills, and infrastructure to support themselves and their church. The Mill River had provided a good place for them to grow and begin to expand over the next century.

The Environmental Impact of Dams and Diversions

The manipulation of the Mill River began in the mid-seventeenth century and continued through the middle of the twentieth, with both beneficial and devastating consequences. The benefits of mill power and flood control were offset by a decline in the fishery and increased pollution. But the full impact of ecological damage would become unbearable only in the twentieth century.

Dams, necessary though they are, disrupt that signal purpose of a river we have discussed before—to move water and material downstream. Materials such as sand, mud, and brush build up, making the pond behind the dam more and more shallow and depriving the downstream river of its customary flow of sediments and nutrients. As well, dams block the free movement of fish and aquatic invertebrates, segmenting the stream and separating populations of fish.

The fishery of the Connecticut River and its tributaries provided a rich and vital resource to the people of the Valley, with migratory fish populations so abundant that seventeenth-century society considered the eating of shad disreputable to the point that one family in Hadley hid their dinner of shad under the table when a neighbor came knocking.[143] There were runs of 20,000 to 80,000 Atlantic salmon and shad, alewives, lamprey, and American eel in the millions. "The Connecticut was a fisheries highway for a multitude of species of which we now only see a tiny fragment."[144]

The Mill River did, of course, have a population of native fish, such as brook trout, shiners, dace, chub, perch and pickerel, but none of those would have provided much sport or victuals.[145] It is quite possible that salmon and

shad entered the Mill River from the Connecticut, although there is no historical mention of men catching them in the Mill River itself. Since the mouth of
the Mill originally flowed through sluggish water in Hulbert's pond, and thence
into the Manhan River in Easthampton, there may have been insufficient current to attract migratory fish, which make their way upstream going against the
current. The Mill's diversion directly into the Connecticut in 1710 would have
made the faster current more attractive to migrating fish, but by then, the people of Northampton had already dammed the Mill, and, in any case, the town's
sewage and pollution from such industries as tanneries might have prevented
fish from swimming upstream.

Over the course of the next two chapters, we will follow the demise of
the fishery as the people of Northampton celebrated the rise of their social,
political, and economic status in New England history. Through the heart of
the story runs the Mill River.

CHAPTER TWO

1720—1780: *The Mid-Eighteenth Century—A Gathering Turbulence*

Introduction

During the seventeenth century, the English had focused their attention on the lowest reach of the Mill River that bordered the Meadows, which they had transformed from native grasses and reeds to European fodder for livestock. In the eighteenth century, Northamptonites turned their attention to the stretch of river between the Meadows and Paradise Pond.

Paradise Pond is the iconic feature of the Mill River in the minds of most local citizens and visitors, and we begin this chapter with a walking tour from Paradise Pond to Lickingwater and the South Street Bridge, which linked Meetinghouse Hill to Fort Hill. Our walk starts at the upstream end of Paradise Pond by the beautiful white house and hillside garden of the Smith College president. Walking down College Lane we glance to the right to see whether the pond may have a flock of geese on it or a few canoes. On the left will be the botanical garden, and across the Pond lie the athletic fields where some Nonotuck corn-hills were located. Bordering the fields are the slopes of Hospital Hill, a drumlin that serves as Northhampton's sledding hill in winter.

The pond's bucolic character belies its historic importance as the mill center of Northampton from 1666—1820. The Paradise Pond dam marks the first major drop of water that the English encountered upstream of the Meadows. Prior to the dam, it was a series of steep cascades starting near the President's House and falling some fifty feet to the level of the river at the bottom of the current dam. It was called "the red rocks" in the early colonial days because it is an outcropping of the red sandstone, called arkose, that serves as an extensive band of bedrock all the way south to New Haven, Connecticut.

Continuing our walk, we follow the right bank of the Mill about a quarter mile to a bridge on what is now called West Street, originally named Welsh

End. This was the fording place for the first settlers as they came up from the south. Just downstream from the bridge, we encounter a fifteen-foot riprap wall of stone and cement lining the 1940 ditch that the Army Corps of Engineers constructed to divert the Mill to the southwest. Instead of following that sterile ditch, we turn northeast to follow the old riverbed. On our right will be a twenty-foot drop to a wetlands, which is all that remains of the Mill River's channel. Bordering the wetlands, we detect the obscure outlines of Fort Hill, hidden by vegetation in summer and barely visible in winter through the thick woodland. After another four hundred yards, we pass a small three-acre floodplain on the right, at the base of Fort Hill. A few hundred yards beyond that, after passing under a bridge, we reach the short stretch of the river called Lickingwater, at the foot of Pulaski Park on Main Street where the Roundhouse stands, a reminder of the kind of mid-nineteenth-century coal-gasification plant once common in New England. We now stand at the location where the Mill River severed the post-glacial outwash plain leaving Meetinghouse Hill on the left and Fort Hill on the right. We end our walk a few hundred yards farther downstream at the site where the South Street Bridge was dismantled in the 1940s (now a parking lot). Nothing exists to memorialize the route that had served for two hundred years as the high road to Springfield.

The people of eighteenth-century Northampton focused many of their activities on this very spot. Downstream, the Mill River picked up its tributaries flowing along King and Market Street and entered the Connecticut, carrying all Northampton's effluent. Upstream led to two mill sites where the town's flour was ground and timber sawn or riven. Follow the river farther upstream and townspeople could ponder the quiet of the woodlands and rush of the water. The pond, the river, and Old South Street Bridge formed the southern and western flank of Northampton in the eighteenth century, and its Congregationalist community of about a thousand souls created the outlines of the landscape that still exist.[1]

The temper of the times and its people in the eighteenth century are now foreign to us. Yes, we can read and understand their writings, but it takes a leap of empathy to put ourselves in their homemade boots and listen to their Bible readings at fireside on nights unimaginably cold, in winters so long that ice built up two and three feet thick on the Big River. War and economic expansion marked their lives from 1720 to 1780, a time when Northampton became the most important town in Western Massachusetts. The Hampshire County Courthouse symbolized its primacy when both Franklin County to the north and Hampden County (Springfield) to the south were part of Hampshire County. The congregational church, led by America's most famous preacher, Jonathan Edwards, placed Northampton at the center of American cultural life, and the rich agricultural fields and concentration of commercial enterprises made it an important economic center.[2]

This was a tightly bound Congregationalist community, limited to its location on the Mill River with no settlement upriver from the town. The Nonotuck had been thrown out, and there were not yet any Methodists or Catholics to upset the primacy of the Congregationalists, who showed plenty of energy to argue vigorously among themselves. People lived in a strictly stratified society based on "natural" distinctions among those with dignity and those without. The high born were addressed as "Mister," for example or "Goodman," or "Goodwoman/Goodwife," while those in the military were addressed by their rank.[3] Rank in the military was a crucial mark of status during this period of almost constant warfare.[4]

Acknowledging the primacy of rivers in their lives, contemporary authors referred to those who presided over this society as River Gods: men of considerable wealth and status, such as those from the Williams, Stoddard, Stebbins, and Worthington families. The term "River God" carried forward into the nineteenth century when historians used it to refer to those who derived their power and wealth from a combination of military and commercial activities with administrative, political, and judicial appointments. River Gods often distinguished themselves in war, and men in the Pioneer Valley could make names for themselves by joining the militia, and participating in any number of British expeditions. In the eighteenth century, "the military system was so big and so important in colonial Massachusetts that it touched in some way every aspect of colonial life."[5]

Preeminent among the River Gods was the Reverend Jonathan Edwards, who undoubtedly knew the river well and looked to the natural world for inspiration. Indeed, he appears in some of his writings as the forerunner of the Transcendentalists, sometimes even sounding like Walt Whitman. God's world, he wrote, is saturated with beauty and can be seen in a flower, a rainbow, and throughout nature.[6]

God's excellency, his wisdom, his purity and love, seemed to appear in everything: in the sun, moon, and stars, in the clouds, and blue sky; in the grass, flowers, trees; in the water, and all nature. I often used to sit and view the moon, for a long time; and so in the daytime, spent much time in viewing the clouds and sky, to behold the sweet glory of God in these things: in the meantime, singing forth with a low voice, my contemplations of the Creator and Redeemer.[7]

Jonathan Edwards, born downriver from Northampton in East Windsor, Connecticut in 1703 and educated at Yale, became America's leading eighteenth-century intellectual. He spent his most productive years as minister of Northampton's Congregational Church from 1727 to 1749. An extraordinary scholar and theologian, he stood at the center of the maelstrom of the Great Awakening, an enormous religious revival throughout the American colonies in the 1730s and 1740s.[8] Edwards, however, was a most difficult character, strong-willed and stiff-necked. By 1745, Edwards' parishioners had had enough of him and threw him out. In 1750, he took a position in Stockbridge, Massachusetts where he would minister to the Stockbridge Indians, most of whom were Mahicans. In February 1758 he became president of Princeton University, replacing his late son-in-law Aaron Burr. Hoping to encourage the widespread use of smallpox vaccine, Edwards had a doctor inoculate him as an example to the people of Princeton. The inoculation proved too much for Edwards' body to handle. Already in declining health, he died thirty-seven days later at the age of fifty-four.[9]

Edwards symbolized the contentious spirit of the River Gods and their lesser contemporaries, who were often torn between the Court Party and the Country Party—between the wealthy establishment and those whom Edwards described as "jealous of them, apt to envy 'em, and afraid of their having too much power and influence in town and church."[10] Such concentration of wealth and power in the hands of a few families, however, created a rising level of conflict between the Hampshire County elite and the common people.[11]

The River Gods ruled in an era prior to the Industrial Revolution, when colonial technology resembled that of Renaissance Europe—blacksmiths, gristmills, sawmills, oil mills, tanneries, and fulling mills all operated in the same manner in 1780 as in 1600. The Gods became wealthy by accumulating their capital from the increasing demand for agricultural products and commerce rather than through increases in efficiency and technology. Meanwhile, the mercantile system, under which British colonies were prevented from developing their own manufactured goods, meant that no true manufacturing facility could be built in the region.

But New Englanders had no need for large factories to produce the necessities of life. In an extraordinarily thorough study of household manufactures in early America, the historian Rolla Tryon argued that there existed a system of household factories through which families produced plenty of goods—from shoes and underwear to breeches and cookware—to live healthy lives even if insufficient to accumulate capital.

The near economic independence of many homes and communities was a great asset to the people of the Revolutionary days in their struggle for political liberty. War and blockade only drove them back to more primitive conditions and established an industrial independence of both foreign and domestic markets. After seven years of costly warfare, England finally realized the difficulty of conquering colonists who could within their homes manufacture the necessities that her blockade aimed to keep out.[12]

Economic independence and technical expertise had prepared the citizens of the Mill River to rush eagerly into a post-Revolutionary world that would leave the River Gods behind. The socially stratified society of colonial America would unravel at the end of this period. The Industrial Revolution began even as the ferment of the American Revolution frayed old ties and loyalties. The River Gods had aligned themselves so closely with the British power structure that, after the American Revolution, their close ties with the crown turned into a deadly embrace.[13] From 1774 on, the River Gods lost much of their financial base as new entrepreneurs emerged. Even so, the Gods retained a good deal of their political power, while others were engaged in building factories and inventing technologies.[14]

The Mill and Connecticut Rivers provided the wherewithal to succeed throughout the Industrial Revolution. The Mill would provide the power to produce goods while the Connecticut became the lane by which the goods could get to the outside world and new ideas and commodities could enter. Power and connectivity meant that Northampton could prosper into the next century.

Industrial Development: Dams and Mills in Communities of Competence

Northampton turned its focus in the eighteenth century from the Meadows to two dam sites on the Mill River, which would ensure its future in commerce and industry. The work ethic, the inquisitive minds, and acquisitive tendencies of the people of Northampton led to a community of competence, a group of citizens who were simultaneously grasping for God and wealth. The mills on the river provided a place for Northamptonites to make things and innovate technologies. While this only became obvious during the Industrial Revolution, expertise of all sorts, from banking to felting, developed during this period.[15]

The Battle Between the Upper and Lower Mills

Surely the most intriguing Mill River dam story of the eighteenth century was the resuscitation of the Lower Mills, where Northampton's first gristmill was built at a spot on what is now Clark Avenue, just upstream from Lickingwater. Given the growth of the agricultural economy, it is no surprise that more grist-mills were needed, and in 1742 Samuel and Moses Kingsley received permission to build such a mill at the abandoned Lower Mills site. Since there is so little natural drop on that part of the river, they built a very high dam to gain sufficient head to run the waterwheel.

Dam and mill were completed in 1746, and in no time, the water backed so far upstream that it interfered with the operation of the grist- and sawmills at the Upper Mills on Paradise Pond. The Upper Mills' owners—Deacon Noah Cook, Capt. Jonas Hunt, and Ebenezer Edwards—were outraged when they discovered that their waterwheels no longer had sufficient drop for the water to power them. A forty-five-year legal battle ensued. In 1759 the Kingsleys persuaded the town to investigate the problem, charging that the Upper Mill owners were persecuting them. The town then voted to save the Kingsleys' mill and water rights "provided said Moses and Samuel Kingsley keep their mill in order and do not raise the dam over 7 feet, or do not raise the water to the Depth of over 7 feet."

Feeling themselves ill-used, the dissatisfied owners of the Upper Mills petitioned the town in 1765 to render a new decision, so the town established a committee of three people from three surrounding towns and without any member from Northampton itself. The Kingsleys, however, refused to recognize the new committee, demanding that the town indemnify them for damages, which the town awarded them in 1766.

Legal matters remained in limbo another twenty-five years. Finally, in 1791, forty-five years after the original legal suit, the controversy ended when Daniel Pomeroy and Moses and Enos Kingsley bought the Lower Mill property, built a new dam, waterwheel, and machinery, and agreed to keep the water at the same level as an iron bar that the selectmen set in a rock thirty-six feet above the dam.[16]

Such was the behavior of Jonathan Edwards' Northamptonites—a community of folks who were "not the most happy in their natural temper... famed for a high-spirited people, and close, and of a difficult, turbulent temper."[17]

Mills in Florence and Leeds

According to Charles Sheffeld's nineteenth-century history, the original Northampton proprietors had insufficient meadowlands close to the center of Northampton for every household, so they doled out meadowland in Florence to John Broughton as compensation.[18] Perhaps Broughton visited his land, but certainly never lived there, for he had sold it by 1675. The picture that emerges from Sheffeld's perusal of the Proprietors' Book is of landowners selling their Florence land for quick profit because every few years the town had to draw up new lists of owners and the metes and bounds of all the properties, Fig. 2.1, the 1754 map of landowners, beggars the imagination.[19] Can one conceive of the problems one would encounter trying to clear title to any of these lands?

There appears to have been no permanent household in Broughton's Meadow during the first century of Northampton's existence, and the land was used chiefly for grazing and orchards, as suggested by the many references to fence maintenance in the Proprietors' Book. Parts of Broughton's Meadow were almost certainly wet. We know, for example, that in 1673, Joshua Pomeroy was granted six acres of "swamp and upland" at that spot.[20] And one more hint we get of eighteenth-century Broughton's Meadow comes from the manuscript of the tireless Sylvester Judd, who described a change in the Mill River's bed that moved the property on the west side of the river to the east side.

Fig. 2.1 *1754 Map of landowners in Florence. This map in Sheffeld's History of Florence was drawn before the section of Northampton, originally named Broughton's Meadow, was settled. The Mill River is highlighted in green. The current site of Florence Fields/Northampton Community Farm is the tan-shaded area that the river runs through. The plethora of property owners of both orderly long lots and disorderly metes and bounds lots resulted from the rapid turnover of speculative land deals at that time.*

The falls at Florence, however, did attract millers, who established grist and sawmills by 1681, as noted by the Town Records:

> On a Motion of Richard and Thomas Lyman, Samuel Wright and Samuel Parsons to have a place and liberty to set up a Sawmill, the Town...granted their request on Consideration...The place they desired is [at] Broughton's Meadow on the Mill river.[21]

That mill is the first recorded enterprise on the river at Nonotuck Falls, where at least one industry has operated to the present day. In the eighteenth century the mill passed into the hands of the Hulbert family and was known as Hulbert's Mill into the early nineteenth century, operating as a saw- grist- and/or linseed oil mill.[22] The owners of the land and mills at Broughton's Meadow, however, did not establish households there. There are no references to mills farther upstream in Leeds prior to 1780.

Williamsburg's Settlement

When the Peace of Paris in 1763 ended the French and Indian War (Seven Years War) between England and France, young families increasingly moved into the upland region of the Mill River and other Connecticut River tributaries, establishing the hilltowns on the eastern slopes of the Berkshires.[23] Williamsburg was carved out of Hatfield in the mid-eighteenth century, and unlike Northampton, its terrain consists solely of glacially carved sediments in steep terrain with very little flat agricultural land and no extensive meadows. The Hatfield proprietors did not get around to surveying the lots of most of Williamsburg until 1752.[24] Hampshire County then ordered a road laid out from Hatfield to "the Great Bridge" in Chesterfield to link up with the Pontoosuc Road to Albany.[25]

Only in the 1760s did settlers move to the Upper Mill River watershed, most of which became Williamsburg, which was incorporated in 1771. No industrial and very little agricultural activity had taken place prior to 1760 despite the oft-repeated journalistic story of John Miller building a cabin and taking up permanent residence in 1735.[26] However, Williamsburg did attract settlers prior to the founding of the downstream villages of Leeds and Florence. In 1771, the district of Williamsburg had at least two sawmills in operation and about sixty households. This was a full decade before Joseph Warner built the first house in Florence, and twenty-five years before a house and mill existed in what is now Leeds.[27]

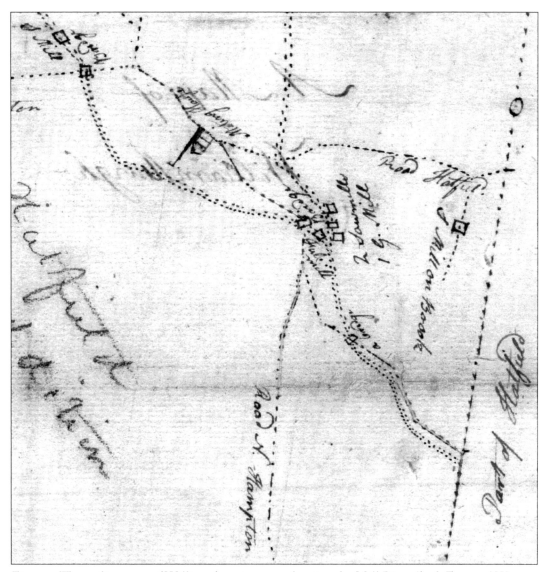

Fig. 2.2 *The earliest map of Williamsburg in 1795 showing the Mill River (both East and West Branch) as double-dotted lines and the roads in single dotted lines. There is a bridge and sawmill at the upper left corner, which is Searsville. The meetinghouse is on Village Hill Road between Searsville and what would become Williamsburg Center where several houses are located. Note that there is one gristmill for the town and three sawmills in this section of Williamsburg, attesting to the importance of timber. (Courtesy Eric Weber and Ralmon Black. Source: State Archives)*

Northampton and Williamsburg were settled a hundred years apart, and the Mill River never served to link the two towns. River Road, which now connects Leeds to Northampton along a narrow gorge to Haydenville, was only constructed by the county in 1838, and the railroad was built in 1867. One reached Williamsburg from Leeds along a trod path via Unquomonk well off the west bank of the river on what is now called Audubon Road and South Street. The earliest road to the Upper Watershed from Northampton or Hatfield was at Williamsburg's eastern border.[28]

Northampton and Williamsburg would always remain separate in terms of their social and economic relationships as well as their identities. Northampton was founded by interconnected families, who were chiefly born in England and moved upriver from Springfield and Connecticut. They settled what became the most important town in the most important region of Western Massachusetts. Their men had fought wars together and developed a contentious commercial spirit. Northampton had River Gods, artisans, yeoman farmers, and rich bottomlands to exploit.

In contrast, after most of the eighteenth-century wars had ended, Williamsburg was settled by a dissociated lot from Hatfield, Northampton, Connecticut and several eastern coastal towns around Boston, Braintree, Stoughton, Taunton, the Cape, and even from Martha's Vineyard. They ventured to exploit the commercial agricultural potential of the standing hardwood forest, turning much into an important cash crop—potash. Felling the forest opened up sufficient land for crops and a good deal of pasturage, along with a sufficient yield of capital from potash to construct mills that would add value to their agricultural products. Diverse as were their origins, they quickly became a tight-knit community, with many of the second generation marrying each other.

The first households distributed themselves in a scattered pattern with ten families on lots of forty acres and twelve on about two hundred.[29] Josiah Dwight owned one of the largest properties, 275 acres, with his the only house on it.[30] With some few exceptions, no houses were right across the road from each other, and next door was usually hundreds of yards away.

Gleaning court records, deeds, account books, newsprint, and family papers, Ralmon Black has bundled together his perceptions of the early settlement of Williamsburg. If one looks at the 1795 sketch map, it's clear that by the turn of the nineteenth century, the center of town was located on the hilltop between the West and East Branches of the Mill River where it reads "Meeting House" on Village Hill Road. On this map there is no road along the river; the road we now call Route 9 was built in 1829. At the upper left corner are a bridge and a sawmill at what would become Searsville. At the other end of Village Hill, in the center of the map, is Williamsburg Center with a fulling mill, two sawmills, and a gristmill. The surveyor who drew the map, Nehemiah Cleavland, failed to include what is now Haydenville because it wasn't considered an official part of Williamsburg until the mid-nineteenth century.[31] Had the cartographer sketched in that area, it would have shown a sawmill at the site of what is now called the Brass Works.

While the town center, symbolized by the meetinghouse, was located on top of Village Hill with a store, a tavern, and the home of the pastor, most of the population lived on scattered properties with enough land to support their families. A gravestone at the Mountain Street Cemetery on the east side of Williamsburg claims that William Warren, who died in 1768, was the "1st settler of the town and father of his family."[32] It is possible that Mr. Warren may have lived on Mountain Street from time to time in the 1740s, and Widow Warren and her sons are included in the Royal Charter. By 1760, Thomas Howe had built a house on Village Hill, known as the "Mansion House," and later "The Parsonage." Samuel Fairfield settled in the early 1760s, as did Downing Warner, and in 1763, Jesse Wild documented accounts of his activities. There were some who came to take potash from the most accessible places and sold the land they had cleared soon thereafter. Opportunities quickly opened up for other young families, and Wild, along with several others, established farmsteads on sites where they could develop water-powered mills on the West Branch in Searsville.[33] By 1780 there were sawmills, gristmills, and tanning yards on the West Branch, all powered by waterwheels.

Environmental Transformation II:

Potash, The Felling of the Forests, and Its Impact on the River and Its Fishery

The second great environmental transformation began with the first clearing of the woodlands. Williamsburg's original European settlers came from many parts of New England to a thick, unkempt forest that Natives had either avoided (because of the danger of Mohawks coming from the west) or used for hunting game. The newcomers, having been granted lots by the town of Hatfield, immediately began logging the timber and clearing the land for homesteads. They felled hemlock and oak, stripping them of bark for tanneries. Together with pine, the men bucked these trees into logs that could be dragged by oxen to the local mill for boards, shakes, or shingles. Decay-resistant chestnut furnished excellent timber for framing buildings and planking bridges, and the smaller stuff was worked into posts and rails for fencing. Sugar maple was left for the making of syrup.[34]

This great felling came at the very onset of the Industrial Revolution in the mid-eighteenth century, when textiles began to be mass-produced in the factories of Europe and the English Midlands. Whereas the land that was cleared for a garden, grain field, and livestock grazing could provide sustenance, the dense hardwood forest was the only standing cash crop worth silver specie—potash.[35] The insatiable demand for potash literally fired the first major industry in the Upper Watershed and America's first chemical industry.[36] The forest clearing traumatized the landscape, deeply harming the Mill River system, as we shall see.

Fig. 2.3 The Ashery, a nineteenth-century drawing by David Hamilton. (Courtesy Ralmon Black)

Potash, long an essential ingredient in ceramics, glass, glazes, gunpowder, leather tanning, paper manufacturing, and many other applications, became by 1750 an integral ingredient in the soap and bleach used in the rising mechanized textile industry. Potash was obtained from plant ash, chiefly hardwoods, but Europeans had long since depleted their forests. English textile millers bought potash from Russia with silver coin. Realizing that the great American forests could supply all the potash they desired, English manufacturers turned to New England for their supply, keeping silver in house.

To this end, British experts came to Boston and other port cities with manuals on the production of potash and disseminated the process widely. Potash became a ubiquitous American export. There is no better description of the potash-making process in Williamsburg than a mid-nineteenth-century account written when potash was still being made in the hills.

Fig. 2.4 The Merritt potash kettle with Floyd Merritt of Goshen and Ralmon Black on the left. The kettle measures 44" x 25" and weighs about 600 pounds. (Courtesy Eric Weber)

Timber was cut down in immense quantities and drawn, after being cut into logs, to the ash-pits, for making potash. Ash-pits were cellars dug ten to twenty feet wide, twenty to forty in length, and four to six in depth, and stoned up around the sides. In these a fire was built, the logs were drawn and kept piling on, many times for weeks together, until the whole pile was reduced to ashes. The ashes were then shoveled into large vats, with a mixture of quick lime and straw; water was poured on, after which a strong, dark-colored lye came off.[37] This lye was put into large kettles, often times holding several hhds [hogsheads][38] set over a furnace, [evaporating it to] a black salt or 'black salts.' The next step was to put this salt into another large kettle, [and] place it over a still hotter furnace until the salts were melted into a liquid, red and glowing. When in this state, the salts require continuous stirring with a long iron poker for three to four hours of fermentation [after which] this liquid is again drawn off into large troughs ..."[39]

The 'crude potash' was then baked at even higher temperatures in a kiln to remove impurities. The fine, white powder remaining was pearlash, which was packed into casks of a standard size, as mandated by Massachusetts law, and transported to England and France, where it commanded the highest cash prices.[40]

By 1770, the manufacture of potash became a standard part of New England husbandry, and a critical source of cash to pay taxes, buy necessities, and capitalize other industries in the depression years following the War for Independence. It was worth silver at a time when there was no specie to be had in the initial stages of settlement.[41] By 1770, Britain relied on its North American colonies for 63 percent of its potash imports. During the Revolution, the Continental Army and militias depended on New England potash for the manufacture of gunpowder, and after 1783, Britain imported more than eighty percent of its potash from the United States. The first U.S. patent in 1790 — U.S. Patent No. 1—was for an improved process to make potash. Simultaneously, local demand increased dramatically as reliance on British products attenuated and the great period of mill construction began.[42]

The landscape of the Mill River watershed was often in flames. People in the valley could see the smoke by day and the fires by night from a hundred choppings in the hilltowns.[43] Most of the forests were cleared within a few decades, and by 1840 households were only producing the ashes from the 50 cords of wood they burned each year for heating and cooking. After a long winter season, a wood burning stove or fireplace would have yielded from each cord of wood about twenty pounds of ashes, or, by today's measure, the equivalent of one five-gallon drywall pail. At year's end, this would equal a half-ton of ashes, far more than enough for household use in soap making and as a leavening agent for baking.[44]

The eighteenth-century settlers of these hills clearcut the dense, virgin stands of forest for home sites, pasture, crops, and potash. All this was accepted as a matter of sense and necessity, but records and early images reveal a landscape almost completely devoid of trees; steep hillsides and rocky tracts, suited only to woodland or sugarbush, had been all but denuded.[45] Furthermore, the demand for potash had an impact on the composition of the forest. Since elm, ash, sugar maple, hickory, beech, and basswood have the highest potash content,[46] those were the first to come under the ax or whipsaw, leaving pine, hemlock, and birch as the most prevalent remaining trees to reseed the woods. Spared from the ax were sugar maple for the cash value of its syrup, and chestnut, which resists decay and produces a lot of nutritious nuts.[47]

The skinning of the land in the Mill River watershed continued for three generations or more. By 1800, so much of the uplands had been stripped of

Fig. 2.5 Pre-Settlement Forest, Harvard Forest Diorama
Fig. 2.6 1740 Hilltown Settlement, Harvard Forest Diorama
Fig. 2.7 Height of Forest Clearance, ca. 1840, Harvard
Forest Diorama (Courtesy Harvard Forest)

hardwoods that many young people from the second generation went west to places like Oswego County, New York, or even to Pennsylvania and Ohio, where they continued to engage in the industries they had shared with their parents. Had timbering been limited to the needs of families and their livestock, forest clearance would have been far less extensive, but the potash industry demanded as much wood as townsfolk could supply. The cash value of wood ash greatly accelerated the clearing and burning of huge swaths of forest, readying it for crops and pasture.

The justly famous dioramas from the Harvard Forest in Petersham illustrate the results of deforestation on the landscape.[48]

True to life as are the dioramas, they conceal some of the impacts of clearcutting on the Mill River watershed. Hidden from view in the 1840 diorama are the deep gullies that gashed the landscape and which were filled in by debris and reforestation in the late-nineteenth and twentieth centuries. Clearcutting eliminated the carpet of the forest floor, the eighteen-inch-deep mass of mulch, which for thousands of years acted as a sponge, soaking up rain and snowmelt. Robbed of its covering, the velocity and amount of runoff coming off the steep hillsides greatly increased, carrying a slurry into the streams, eroding the landscape, and depositing millions of tons of soil, rock, and debris downstream. The turbid runoff silted up millponds and changed the bed of the Mill River as higher waters eroded away the stream banks, widening and deepening the channel.

Twenty years of forest clearing proved insufficient to dramatically transform the watershed and river. Over the next fifty years, however, the Mill River would witness such change as would open it up to frequent, severe flooding, which is one of the central stories in our next historical period. Land clearance would abate only toward the middle of the 1800s, when just about all the hardwoods had been taken, leaving stands of hemlock and pine.

We do not know the impact of clearcutting on the Mill River's fishery in the mid-eighteenth century because primary sources contain no references to fish or fishing in the Mill River. Ample commentary exists concerning fish and fishing in the Connecticut River, but not a word on the Mill. Fish were a major part of colonial life—up to a third of people's annual diet—and fishing was a vital activity: the law allowed any angler access to all streams or ponds over ten acres in the eighteenth century. Indeed, for two hundred years anglers were permitted to walk across private property, without fear of trespass, to get to streams and ponds, a right that was only revoked with the adoption of new fishery laws in the 1860s.[49]

New England journals vividly describe the great migratory runs of shad, salmon, lamprey, eels, and herring that filled the Connecticut River. Sylvester Judd, for instance, reminisced about the thirty- to forty-pound salmon that were caught in his youth.[50] Fish were particularly important during their spring migration, after salt pork in colonial larders had run out. Most of the anglers were "industrious farmers and after leaving the falls, they wound over the hills and plains with bags of shad, in every direction."[51]

Judd mentions three eighteenth-century fishing places near Northampton—two on either bank of the Connecticut in North Hadley near the mouth of Hadley's Mill River, and one on each side of Hockanum Meadows, which would have been close by the diverted (post-1720) Mill River mouth in Northampton. "The Northampton and Hadley men," wrote Judd, "were often near each other, and they bantered and joked abundantly, and sometimes played tricks and encroached upon each other... In those days, there were many coarse jokes and some harsh tricks." While Judd provides no example from the anglers, we can catch some sense of his gallows humor from an 1856 note in his manuscripts: "Killed my old cat. A beautiful cat she was, but gave us trouble."[52]

In about 1773, Elihu Warner remembered catching some forty salmon, the largest of which weighed between thirty and forty pounds.[53] Most of the fish that Northampton men caught could be found at South Hadley Falls, where salmon were picked up by dip net, while shad and other fish were caught by seine, sturgeon by spear, and lamprey by hand at night. There are, however, no references to migratory fishing spots on the Mill River itself, even at the Lower or Upper Mill dams.

Over time, of course, the fishery dwindled to a few hundred salmon and a tiny fraction of the millions of alewives, lamprey, eels, and shad. As we shall see, attempts to regulate the size of the catch would be offset by the construction of dams.

Floods

Floods, especially spring freshets, were simply part of life for all living things in the Mill River watershed. The Little Ice Age was still going strong. Winters were still long and bitter, building up thick blocks of ice, which, at ice-out, created ice dams that backed up water, often releasing it so quickly that the water and its suspended materials flooded into the rivers' secondary beds.

Although we have short descriptions of eighteenth-century floods, we will have to wait until the nineteenth century for detailed newspaper and first-hand accounts. We should remember that Northampton remained a very compact town in which only a small portion near the Manhan Meadows was subject to serious flooding. The town's small area significantly limited flood damage to any but the mills and bridges, which were subject to frequent fire and flood.

We are nonetheless left breathless in our accounting of mid-eighteenth-century floods—*nine floods in thirty-seven years, an average of one flood every four years*. Imagine what it was like to live through them. Exciting, yes, but what was it like to invest so much in building dams, bridges, and mills, knowing they could—at any time and in any season—be destroyed?

The first decade of the eighteenth century began with two major floods: one in 1704 and another in May, 1706, which set the planting of crops all the way back to June 20 (the average date of last frost today is May 10).[54] Then, in 1733, came a flood that destroyed Hulbert's sawmill and the bridge at Broughton's Meadow. Another struck in 1740, and yet another in 1744, which drowned one hundred sheep in the meadows and changed the bed of the Mill River in Broughton's Meadow (Florence).

The 1744 event was followed on December 12, 1748 by "heavy rains and great flood. The Mill river carried off the upper grist mills and sawmills, and part of Kingsley's mill dam."[55] Eight years later, Ebenezer Hunt's property was endangered by "a great Flood, about as high as that of December 1740. The water was at the height of April 1st & came within about 2 rods [37 feet] of my barn at my barnyard."[56] Two years afterward, on June 23, 1754, came a "great rain and flood. Great part of the meadow covered & much damage done to grass & grain, & many things carried off the banks down the river."[57]

There are no further records until January 5, 1767, when, after a very cold December, there arrived a "thaw and flood — carried off many mills & bridges— Hartford [Connecticut] Bridge went off. Windsor Bridge also — and our upper mill bridge. Lickingwater Bridge [Old South Street Bridge] was much disordered."[58] July 1769 and January 1770 also witnessed floods worthy of recording.

These were stormy years that presaged more and worse floods awaiting the residents of the watershed. Eighteenth-century New Englanders were already accustomed to disastrous floods and fickle weather that could scorch or freeze their crops. They responded by turning to prayer and fasting in repentance for the sins that had brought such disasters upon them. Then they rebuilt their roads, buildings, and farms and prepared for the next storms. Would they be able to handle with the same equanimity a series of even greater floods during the next century?

CHAPTER THREE

1780–1840: From Mills to Factories, From Forests to Fields and Gullies

Introduction: Life in the Mill River Watershed

Ten miles upstream from Paradise Pond, in the town of Williamsburg, is the village of Searsville, a name generally known only to the citizens of Williamsburg and then, only to those who have lived there awhile. Searsville became the first village in the town because of its mill sites on the river. Its history closely tracks the opening of America's western frontier in the eighteenth century and the vagaries of American economic life during that time.

To get to Searsville, drive up the main highway, Route 9, which is now the main road to Pittsfield, Troy, and Albany. After going through Williamsburg Center, you begin the steep climb up to Goshen and the headwaters of the Mill's West Branch. After a half-mile you go over a series of four bridges that you barely realize you're crossing. At the fourth bridge, turn right and park by the side of the road. You will easily find the trailhead that begins on the river's right bank (facing downstream) because it is a roadbed, in fact the old road to Goshen.

On an early winter's day, with enough snow on the ground to make out animal sign, you'll be in for a treat because three miles up the trail is the beautiful cascades at Devil's Den on the border of the town of Goshen. The trail begins where the original Goshen Road began in the early nineteenth century. You will shortly come to a breached nineteenth-century dam on your right, marking the site of the Searsville Reservoir that fed power to the Williamsburg mills for a hundred years. Just beyond, you'll hug the riverside while the original Goshen Road goes off to the left, and almost immediately come to a shooting range that has fitfully driven Williamsburg residents into angry exchanges about shooting regulations and private-property rights.

A beautiful little covered bridge soon appears, crossing this most modest of New England brooks: a bridge that the town's trail committee erected in the early twenty-first century. From here on, you lose the sounds of the road on your left and enter a quiet place. The West Branch Trail is as pretty a New England trail as you can find, so you lose yourself heading upstream, curving away from the brook, then back down until you reach Old Goshen Road (almost but not quite as old as the original Goshen Road). Cross it and continue another half mile until you reach Devil's Den. What a sweet section of stream this is, as reminiscent of rocks and rills as any nineteenth-century romantic poem. In winter, it gives you shapes and silence—no sound of running water, only ice plates and thick figurines that cover the pools and line the shores.

On the return, we take a loop trail off the river about a third of the way home from Devil's Den because it gives us a good quick climb up a steep slope and back down to the West Branch. Besides, we have seen a lot of deer tracks and wanted to see where they might lead us. Up toward the top of the slope, right where we might have guessed, we find the ground trampled down and oak leaves piled up in a space of about twenty by fifty feet. This is a deeryard, the spot where part of the local deer herd beds down nightly to keep warm. The deer located it far enough up the hill so they could escape either up or downhill if necessary, a good spot for a watchout. The discovery makes for a light, sweet hike back down the hill and alongside the West Branch to our car.

There used to be a mill at Devil's Den in the early nineteenth century, and a cemetery lies on a side trail nearby, with some cellar holes to mark the homesteads that disappeared well before the Civil War, for this place represents the western frontier of European New England during and after the American Revolution. The West Branch Trail has taken us back through the years between 1780 and 1840 that marked the settlement, industrialization, and deforestation of the upper half the Mill River watershed, known as the hilltown section.

Those readers observant enough to note the founding dates of New England towns ostentatiously displayed when entering a Massachusetts town, may not have noticed that the dates of incorporation are bunched together.[1] In 1760, only ten towns existed in Western Massachusetts. The number of towns exploded in the next two decades—fifteen in the 1760s and twenty-five in the 1770s, with twelve in 1775 alone. After that, the incorporation of new towns slowed dramatically—only six towns in the 1780s, five in the 1790s and eleven during the whole nineteenth century. There has only been one new town incorporated in Massachusetts since 1890. The four hilltowns of the Mill River's upper watershed were all incorporated between 1765 and 1781.[2]

The two Treaties of Paris account for the phenomenal speed of town settlement over a twenty-year span, which included more than half of all Western Massachusetts towns. The 1763 Treaty of Paris ended the French and Indian Wars (Seven Years War) in which the French ceded their southern territories of North America to the English, thus opening northern New England to English colonists. The 1783 Treaty of Paris ended the American Revolution, which was among the last wars in North America during the strife-filled eighteenth century. Colonials had been in arms for close to one hundred fifty years, whether against Native Americans or, more usually, in combination with Indian allies against French and Indian enemies. It was finally time for English Americans to settle down and carve the landscape into towns with meetinghouses and the homesteads of Congregational communicants.

The sixty years from 1780 to 1840 ushered in the Industrial Revolution and a new way of life for the Mill River. Landscapes, society and government changed so dramatically that those born in the 1770s would, in their old age, scarcely recognize the country into which they had been born. Technology transformed manufacturing. Local capitalists built dams and mills throughout the watershed even as a series of powerful floods marked the beginning of the nineteenth century.

Right after the Revolution, during the period when the new states were ridding themselves of an ungovernable compact called the Articles of Confederation, a ruckus erupted in Western Massachusetts. In 1786, Shays' Rebellion both set the stage for the calling of the Constitutional Convention and strongly influenced the debate over the role of "the people" in governing the new country. When the states adopted the Constitution in 1789, the latter ensured that a representational form of government with indirect elections, rather than direct democracy, would define the U.S. governmental structure. And of all improbable events, a paper mill on the Mill River became part of the nation's history.

The French Revolution and the Napoleonic Wars that ended in 1815 focused the attention of the new United States abroad. The European wars and shifting alliances not only had enormous consequences for the United States economy, but still lacking its own definitive culture, news of gore, glory, and heroism in Europe riveted local readers in the pages of the *Hampshire Gazette*.[3]

In 1812, toward the end of the bloody European conflicts, the United States got itself into an unfortunate conflict with Britain over the impressment of sailors, trade restrictions, British interference with Native American relations, and national pride. The British had far more important matters to settle and ended the war in 1814. This also spelled the end of the Federalist Party, the party of John Adams, which had opposed the war. A long period of new political parties and alignments began that confounds most Americans today. This politically confusing period lasted until the Civil War, after which only Republicans and Democrats remained among the major parties.[4]

A century-long Industrial Revolution began in the eighteenth century, marked by the year 1780, the first time when the annual rate of industrial growth doubled in England. The United States was not far behind in starting its own phase of the Industrial Revolution, and New England was a particularly apt perch from which to view the rapid advances in agriculture, transportation, and industry.[5] Diana Muir, in her detailed study of New England's rivers and industries, argues that investors found trade and commerce more immediately profitable than capital-intensive mill buildings. Besides, English goods remained cheap and available at the turn of the nineteenth century.[6] However, early in the nineteenth century, the pressure of a rapidly growing population in New England with few remaining agricultural opportunities spurred young people to create new ways of making a living, especially if their families had the wherewithal to support risky endeavors. New Englanders started to invent whatever tool, process, or product that could turn a profit. No better examples of such characters could be found than in the watershed of the Mill River.

With the explosion of towns across Western Massachusetts came the creation of an east-west road network between Boston and Albany. Midway along this route, Springfield became the commercial and governmental center of Western Massachusetts, relegating Mill River industries to just one spoke of the Pioneer Valley's technological and economic wheel, the hub of which was Springfield. A brief look at the population growth of Springfield, Northampton, and Williamsburg tells the story:

- Williamsburg grew slightly from 1049 in 1790 to 1309 in 1840

- Northampton's population was 1790 in 1776 and 3750 in 1840

- Springfield's population of 1547 in 1790 was smaller than Northampton's, but burgeoned to almost 11,000 in 1840.[7]

From our vantage point in the twenty-first century, accustomed as we are to contemplating millions and billions of people, one might well be surprised at the small number of people who participated in the Pioneer Valley's economic and environmental transformation over these two generations. Even Boston's 1840 population of 93,000 and Albany's of 33,000 appear tiny compared with current city populations in the tens of millions.

What was it like, living in the Pioneer Valley during this period? The historian Christopher Clark described late eighteenth-century society in the Valley as a series of interdependent networks that allowed families to support themselves and their communities through all sorts of financial and exchange instruments, which were already part of a global market.[8] By 1830, industrial mills had begun to replace household work, especially the production of textiles. At the same time, many young people began to look for work beyond their home as the Great Migration flowed into Central New York and then Ohio, Indiana, and Michigan. Instead of young people migrating solely to relieve population pressure, they left to pursue greater opportunities. As early as 1818, a Hatfield resident recalled that, of twenty families living in the vicinity, only four had children who stayed in the Valley, while six had children who went west.[9]

As new industries sprang up, women entered the work force and fertility rates declined; fewer children were needed for farm work after 1810. Women's work turned more and more toward processing dairy products or the production of specialty goods such as bonnets and brooms. Even as families continued to raise most of their own food, attention turned away from household production to the increase of household income through labor at industrial enterprises.[10] By 1840, Rolla Tryon's household factory system had given way to an increasingly industrial capitalism that would mark the rest of the nineteenth century.[11]

The Mill River watershed became the regional spoke in the Pioneer Valley's industrial wheel north of Springfield. By 1840 there were enterprises for cotton, silk, wool, and thread, as well as for buttons, woodenware, furniture, and leather. The Mill River was a true mid-nineteenth-century industrial watershed of "factory villages" from Searsville and Haydenville in Williamsburg to Shepherd's Hollow (Leeds), Broughton's Meadow (Florence), and the Upper and Lower Mills of Northampton. Almost all the entrepreneurs and investors were local men with backgrounds in capital and credit development.[12] Some, like the brothers Hayden and their recruit A. P. Critchlow, claimed artisanal backgrounds. Although factory villages in 1840 were often populated by outsiders who immigrated to find work, they were overwhelmingly Massachusetts-born.[13]

Capital investment was as risky as ever. Investors built factories in a few months and lost them just as easily to fire, flood, or, more usually, economic downturns and sheer bad judgment. We will detail some of those twists and turns in Williamsburg, the new kid on the industrial block. The most outstanding financial failure, however, came at the end of this period in the 1830s when the Mill River entrepreneurs were overeager to develop a transportation network to connect with the wider world. The only alternative to carriage road expansion was canal construction on the order of the famously successful Erie Canal built between 1817 and 1825. Inspired by the Erie, a large group of investors gathered to build a canal from New Haven to Northampton, starting in 1826 and finishing at the Connecticut River in Northampton in 1836. The enterprise went bankrupt in 1835 when the original investors lost their money, but another group reorganized it in 1836. Unfortunately for the canal, nine years later, in 1845, the Connecticut River Railroad built a rail line from Springfield to Northampton, dooming the canal as a freight carrier. In 1847 the Hampshire and Hampden Canal was officially and forever abandoned.

The canal was both an enormous engineering accomplishment and a disastrous financial failure. It could only operate ice-free from May to December, and its intricate operation was subject to flood, drought, wear, and vandalism. However, the investors must be forgiven their poor judgment or luck or both. Other canals failed, after all, and who could have foreseen railroads? The idea of the cheap transport of Mill River goods was certainly enticing, as was the tourist trade it could bring. Nor would it interfere with activities on the Mill River itself. The twenty-foot-wide, six-foot-deep canal could accommodate seventy-foot long boats with an eleven-foot beam that carried up to twenty-five tons of freight. Several small ditches mark the remains of the canal in Northampton near its southern border with Easthampton as well as a small stretch at the northern base of Fort Hill where the canal ran parallel to the Mill

River. An arched bridge carried the canal over the river near the current South Street Bridge, thence directly north down State Street, past what is now King Street and Bridge Road, and into the Connecticut River, where one can clearly see its remains at the new Northampton Boathouse.[14]

The Hampshire & Hampden Canal serves as a classic example of Mill River entrepreneurship. Engineering facility and capability were everywhere available, as were laborers. Despite the wobbly financial outlook of any investment, there were inevitably funds available to risk on alluring projects. The failure of one venture only temporarily delayed the readiness of other industrialists to invest in another. The social, cultural, and financial institutions of the old world of the River Gods had transformed into a dynamic series of forces that prepared many people in the Valley to open their arms to the Industrial Revolution. Others, however, were unwilling to pay the ethical price for economic progress, raising heartfelt concerns over the state of their souls, which, they feared, could be bought for a few dollars. Defenders of the old ways rose up in spiritual rebellion.

A series of religious revivals shook New England almost exactly one hundred years after those of the Jonathan Edwards' era. These deeply rooted historical battles pitted the morality of individual ambition against the relief of suffering. As Christopher Clark notes in *The Communitarian Moment*:

> The *Christian Almanac* for 1830, having posed the question 'Have I the right to make as good a bargain as I can?' answered firmly in the negative: 'No man has the right to do anything which causes needless suffering.'[15]

Over the course of a few decades, the instrumental view of the world won out, carried by the gospel of progress, the excitement of the new, and the lure of a more comfortable life. Northampton was in the throes of cultural change. The hard grip of Congregationalism and the River Gods had been broken; and Baptists, Methodists, and Unitarians had established footholds in town. Gross inequality in wealth created social fractures, and half of Northampton's population owned no taxable property. Homeless people had become commonplace in town.

> A floating population of strangers passed through, and unruly offspring of the propertyless who slipped through the fraying net of craft apprenticeship and the short arm of schooling malingered on street corners and patronized illegal bars. Peaceable Northampton looked more and more like a disordered city."[16]

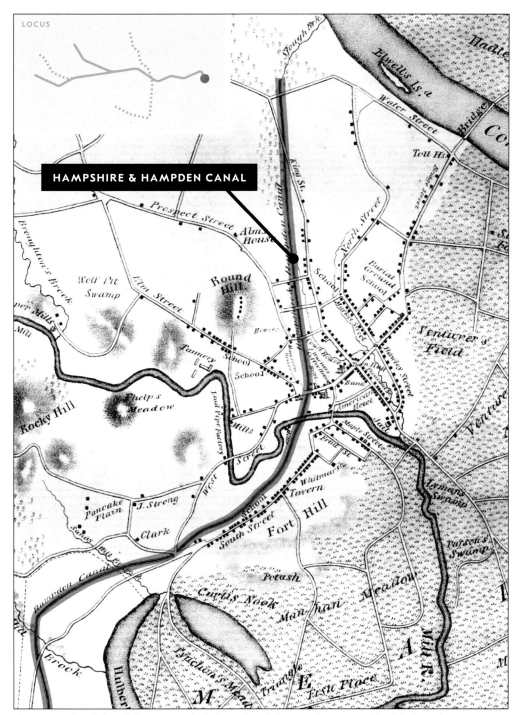

Fig. 3.1 1831 Map delineating the Hampden & Hampshire Canal highlighted by the orange line. Note that the 1831 map does not include the final connection to the Connecticut River, which was completed in 1836. (Courtesy of Forbes Library and

By 1842, a strong anti-slavery movement was centered in Florence, along with its utopian socialist community, the Northampton Association for Education and Industry, which operated a factory along the Mill. New local leaders and political parties successfully challenged the old guard as Northampton shifted away from its agricultural origins.

The Mill River remained at the center of these changes as the Industrial Revolution transformed landscapes throughout the watershed. While commerce and administration remained in Northampton proper, industrial growth shifted far upriver to the village of Leeds (Shepherd's Hollow) and into the town of Williamsburg. These changes lie at the heart of our story.

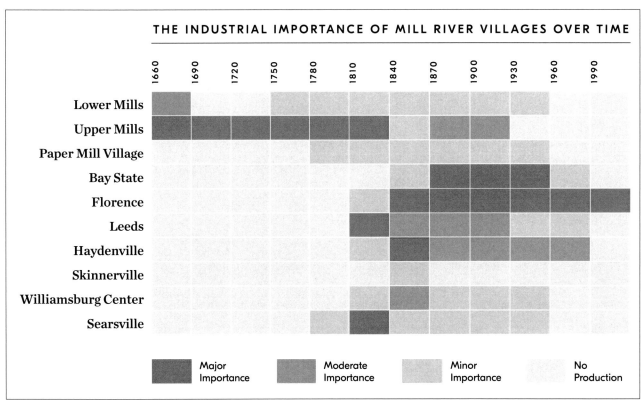

Fig. 3.2 *Chart depicting the relative importance of each Mill River village over time (Transit Authority Figures)*

Industrial Development: Dams and Mills

Industrial activity in the Mill River valley closely tracked the rise and fall of industry in New England. Each factory village contributed its share of output during different periods of history. Fig. 3.2 gives a general idea of the relative importance of each village in relation to others in the watershed and the length of time during which industries produced goods

Three signal events mark the period between 1780 and 1840 on the Mill River.

First was the establishment of the watershed's first true manufacturing facilities in the 1780s, beginning with a wood turning/lathe shop on Paradise Pond, at a site on or below the current house of Smith College's president.[17] Just upstream, William Butler established a paper mill, one of the longest continuously running factories on the Mill.

Second, manufacturing began in the village of Florence, which was to become the river's most important manufacturing center after 1840.

The third event had the greatest impact on the watershed—the establishment of the first mills in Williamsburg and Shepherd's Hollow, the village on the border of Northampton and Williamsburg (renamed Leeds in 1850).[18] During the first thirty years of the nineteenth century, it was the Mill River's most important manufacturing center. A series of new small mills were established all the way up to the Mill's headwaters in Goshen. These also contributed significantly to the watershed's industrial output, far outpacing production in the Lower and Upper Mills.

In the early 1780s, near the end of the Revolutionary War, young Timothy Jewett of Thompsonville, Connecticut, established a wood turning business at a site on the Upper Mills, the first manufacturer in the Mill River watershed to engage in mass production. He chiefly produced spinning wheels, but Charles Dean notes that this sign appeared on his building:

Linen and Woolen Wheels
Syringes and Clock Wheels
Wooden Cocks, Cheese Presses,
Distillings, Screws and Vices
By Timothy Jewett

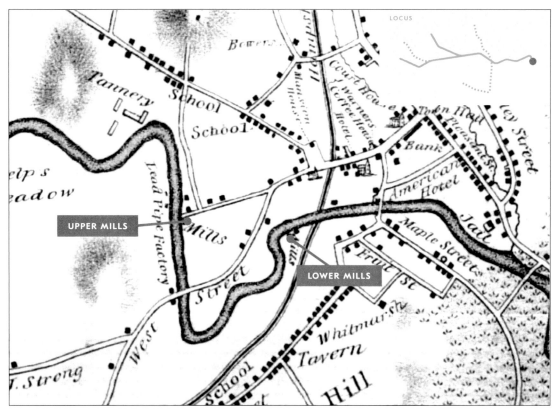

Fig. 3.3 *1831 Lower and Upper Mills of Northampton. The mapmaker has inexplicably failed to sketch in the mill ponds that would have formed behind both dams. Little is known about the lead pipe factory at the Upper Mills site. (Courtesy Forbes Library and Northampton DPW)*

How long this factory lasted and the extent to which it required water-power we don't know, nor have we any further knowledge of Timothy Jewett. [19] Jewett was a classic example of a young man in search of a future in a location with a lot going for it—an easily controlled source of power, willing lenders, and an infrastructure that could support new industry. Like so many other entrepreneurs, he disappeared as quickly as he came, leaving barely a trace.

The Lower Mills and Upper Mills

Daniel Pomeroy and the Kingsley brothers had already established their gristmill in 1791. Just prior to that, in 1789, Levi Shepherd (father and uncle of the three Shepherd boys who started the Shepherd's Hollow textile enterprise at Leeds) built the first factory in the center of Northampton near the South

Street Bridge. Connected to the back side of his home, the factory produced duck cloth, chiefly for the U.S. government. Shepherd was no River God, but rather one of the newly rich merchants who thrived on commerce, having established the town's first bank and first apothecary while dabbling in all manner of imported goods. Going by various honorifics, such as Colonel and Doctor, he made a good profit as a creditor to more than 170 local men, including Josiah Hayden and other first settlers of Williamsburg.[20]

At his death, Shepherd was declared "the wealthiest man who had ever lived in town with an estate valued at over $100,000."[21] Whether or how he used waterpower for the looms that wove flax into duck remains a question. One part of the building was for spinning and another for weaving. He also had a "rope walk," a long shed where local hemp was twisted into strands of rope. The shop, however, closed at his death in 1805.[22]

The Lower Mills site lost its importance as an industrial center for the Mill River by the early 1800s, when it became something of an industrial backwater. Only in the mid-nineteenth century would new entrepreneurs resuscitate the site.

The Upper Mills also declined dramatically in importance during the first half of the nineteenth century. While it hosted Timothy Jewett's wood-turning factory for a while, the site was relegated to a small gristmill with various ancillary uses. In 1791, for example, William Edwards built a tannery nearby, using the mill to soften hides and extract lime, as well as to roll and harden leather. Then in 1807, Joseph Burnell bought two-thirds of the Upper Mill property and got rid of the tannery, retaining only the grist mill.[23]

The 1831 map of Northampton shows a lead pipe factory on the right bank of Paradise Pond opposite Smith College. We also know that by 1840, David Damon owned the Upper Mills property, which he named Hampshire Mills, with a saw- and gristmill on it. We will follow this site's fascinating fate in our next chapter.

Shays' Rebellion and Paper Mill Village[24]

Right after the 1783 Treaty of Paris, the attention of the new United States was riveted on two events: the Constitutional Convention in Philadelphia, and the aforementioned Shays' Rebellion, which erupted in Hampshire County with implications for the Mill River. The story of Shays' Rebellion is generally told as follows: a bunch of rural ruffians rose up against the established propertied and moneyed interests, disrupting and closing down Northampton's courthouse in August 1786, culminating in the rebels' failed attempt to capture the federal arsenal in Springfield in January 1787. The rebels then fled and were later pardoned.

It is, of course, a more complicated tale. The participants, far from poverty-stricken rabble, came mostly from middle-class or well-off farmers, angry at a Commonwealth which for decades had refused to address the concerns of farmers in Western Massachusetts: Cash was scarce, and lenders and tax collectors were foreclosing on properties. Debtors were even thrown in jail.[25] After several years of petitioning the government in Boston, many Western Massachusetts men and women were convinced that the Revolution had simply replaced a British oppressor with one in Boston.

Daniel Shays, a Pelham resident, actually had a fine military record. After having fought at Bunker Hill, Lexington, and Saratoga, he resigned from the army as a captain. The Marquis de Lafayette had even given Shays a sword, which Shays later sold, presumably to help pay debts he had incurred while away from his Pelham farm. He and his cohorts never depicted themselves as rebels or Shaysites, which were derogatory terms given by the establishment, but rather as "regulators," who were fighting an oppressive state government.[26]

It turns out that family and town ties were far more important than class distinctions in determining who supported the Rebellion. For example, such towns as Pelham, Amherst, Whately, and West Springfield had contributed from 25 percent to 70 percent of their men to the Rebellion, while Northampton, Hadley, South Hadley, and Springfield contributed less than 5 percent of theirs.[27] In Williamsburg, a generational split occurred in which none of the elders, who originally settled the town, participated, but many of those from the second generation did.[28] The men with the most to lose in Northampton—mill owners, lawyers, traders, and the families of what remained of the River Gods—had a particular interest in denigrating the rebels and suppressing their uprising.

The voice of Northampton's establishment rang out from the pages of a new weekly newspaper, the *Hampshire Gazette*, founded by William Butler in the summer of 1786 to combat the rebels.[29] The *Gazette*, one of America's oldest newspapers, has never ceased publication and continues today as the *Daily Hampshire Gazette*. In the September 6, 1786 edition, Butler published governor James Bowdoin's Proclamation to "prosecute and bring to condign [appropriate] punishment the Ringleaders and Abettors of the aforesaid atrocious violation of law [the taking of the Northampton courthouse]." On September 27, Butler followed up with a classic conspiracy theory: "We are convinced that the present disturbances arise from British emissaries, residing among us, whose very wish is for our overthrow and ruin, or from the machinations of wicked and unprincipled men, who seek their own emoluments, to the destruction of their country; or from a combination of both."[30]

What does this have to do with the Mill River? William Butler needed paper on which to print his newspaper, so in 1786 he built a paper factory upstream from the Upper Mills at what became known as Paper Mill Village (now part of Bay State) on the site of what is now the defunct wire factory on River-

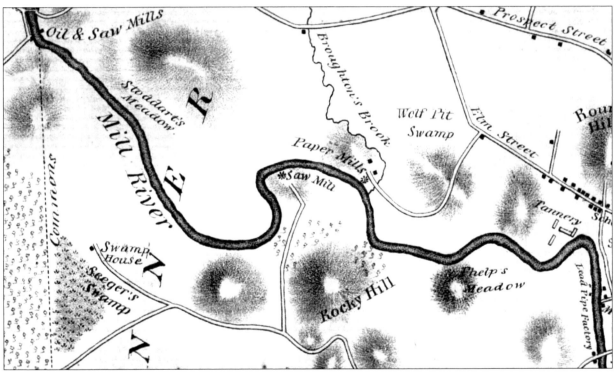

Fig. 3.4 *1831 Mills between Upper Mill and Florence. Note the site of the 1786 paper mill in the area now known as Bay State and the sawmill at the end of a long lost street on the other side of the river. Stoddart's (sic) Meadow is now Maine's Field. The oil and saw mills in the upper left were located at what is now called Nonotuck Mills (Courtesy Forbes Library and Northampton DPW)*

side Drive. Butler's mill principally manufactured writing paper until 1817, when he sold it to his brother Daniel, who continued to produce specialty paper until 1832. The mill closed briefly in the 1830s, but found a completely new life in the second half of the nineteenth century under the Eagle Mills Paper Company.[31]

So, it might be said that, without Shays' Rebellion, there would have been no *Hampshire Gazette* and no Paper Mill Village. A paper mill remained at that same site for a hundred years, and the remains of the original eighteenth-century raceway can still be seen in the section of Northampton now called Bay State.

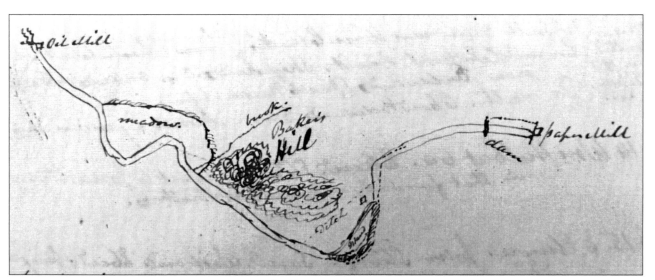

Fig. 3.5 *Sylvester Judd's 1837 sketch of the Mill River from the paper mill near Federal Street upstream to the Nonotuck Dam in Florence. (Courtesy Forbes Library)*

Bay State Village

Although a neighborhood fixture in the minds of current Northampton residents, Bay State Village was, in fact, a backwater with few inhabitants until the 1850s. Prior to that, there had been a sawmill by about 1670, followed by a fulling mill in 1702.[32] There is also mention of a rope factory that would have used hemp originally grown for use in homespun textiles and for flax seed oil.[33]

We get a wonderful glimpse of this vacant section of the river from the journals of Sylvester Judd, who wandered on foot all over the Pioneer Valley and beyond. On this particular day, July 6, 1837, Judd was exploring this reach of the Mill River and for good measure drew a sketch of it.[34]

The "oil mill" in the upper left is the linseed oil mill at the Nonotuck Dam in Florence. From there, Judd walked downriver, describing Baker's Meadow (Stoddart's Meadow on the 1831 map, and now Maine's Field) as ten to twelve acres in size.[35] Baker's Hill, named for the original seventeenth-century proprietor, E. Baker, slopes down toward the bend in the river with an island about 550 feet long. "The opposite, or Southwestern bank is high & steep much of the way from the lower end of the meadow to below the island, & down towards the paper mill." The topography of this part of Bay State has changed but little since Judd tramped the scene. And one can still retrace his steps downriver, along the top of the eighteenth-century raceway that led to the paper mill, then still in production.

Of greatest interest is the little square that Judd drew in the bottom center of the sketch, designating a house just below the dotted line indicating "the old ditch for the ancient fence," which probably fenced in livestock. This was Hezekiah Reed's house. He lived from 1723 to 1793, and the town likely built his house during the American Revolution, as "a pest house...many had small pox there."[36] In return, the town allowed him to live there for free. There is no longer any hint of Reed's residence at that paved-over site.

Seventeen years after Sylvester Judd explored this stretch of the river, Bay State came to life as a factory village, a center for bladed tools for field and household.

Broughton's Meadow (Florence)

Broughton's Meadow had only a handful of permanent settlers prior to 1800, fully one hundred fifty years after Northampton's European settlement. At a distance of three miles from the center of town, it was too inconsequential and distant to attract settlers, and remained so until the Boston-Albany turnpike was built in the 1790s.

In 1778 Joseph Warner built the first house in Florence not far from the current location of Look Park on the upland just east of the Mill River. Warner is a famous name in Western Massachusetts, and Joseph's heirs played a major role in the Mill River Valley's industrial development. Warner was of such prominence that Broughton's Meadow was often referred to as the Warner

District. Several settlers followed Warner, including Josiah White from Winchester, New Hampshire, who established "the Oil Mill," which ran until early 1829.[37] White constructed the mill on the east side of the Nonotuck Dam opposite a sawmill and used locally grown flax seed to make linseed oil, which was used in making paint, in finishing wood, and in cooking.[38] The mill and dam, located just upstream from the current Nonotuck dam, stood two stories tall with twenty- by thirty-foot dimensions, large enough for White to install a gristmill in the same building as the oil mill, a common practice of millwrights.[39]

Fig. 3.6 Josiah White's oil mill from a C.C. Burleigh, Jr. painting reproduced in Charles Sheffeld's History of Florence, Massachusetts.

After White died, his son-in-law, William Thompson, ran the mills for a few years. The latter period offers a snapshot of the variety of enterprises that could fit into two small mill buildings. According to Sheffeld, the oil mill was phasing out, but the grist mill continued to operate on one side of the dam, while on the other, the sawmill contained a machine shop with lathes and a trip hammer to manufacture butcher knives and screwdrivers, along with a planer and room for a shingle maker.[40] This was, in fact, one of the first recognizably industrial sites in the watershed.

During the first third of the nineteenth century, Broughton's Meadow was perhaps best known for the Paul Strong Tavern that stood on Main Street on the Boston to Albany Turnpike, the chief route west before the coming of the railroad in the 1840s.

> During all the time that this house was open for the accommodation of the public, liquors were sold at its bar as freely as the viands from its table. The flip-iron[42] was in almost constant use, and the 'flowing bowl' was drained with a frequency quite astonishing to the teetotalers of the present day [1890s]."[43]

Taverns, such as the Paul Strong, had been critical geographic locations at all crossroad hamlets up and down the river since the earliest days when overland travel was difficult and travelers and their horses needed frequent rest stops. They also served as local gathering places, quite similar to cafes in the twenty-first century.

In Fig. 3.7, we can locate the tavern almost next door to the school in the tiny community of Broughton's Meadow. Suddenly, things changed. Samuel Whitmarsh, who had been born in 1800 in Boston and had earned an excellent living as a men's clothier in New York City, took his savings and in 1829 moved to Northampton where he bought the beautiful property on the north end of Fort Hill, generally known as the "Lyman Estate," the site that formerly served as the center of the Nonotucks' village. Whitmarsh became enamored of the idea of silk as the next great investment in America—and not just the manufacture of silk thread. By 1835, he had convinced himself that he could create a vertically-integrated venture that went "from moth to cloth."[44]

He must have been a most charming and persuasive fellow, for he managed to attract enough money from wealthy men in Boston, Connecticut, and New York to buy everything along the Mill River in Florence from Broughton's Meadow to the oil mill site. By September of 1835 he had picked up the water privilege at Florence Dam with its ninety-acre farm, plus the oil and sawmills. He then purchased the whole two hundred acres of Broughton's Meadow itself.

Using friendly press coverage and a call to patriotism, Whitmarsh managed to convince investors to lend him the money to establish an untested American silk shop pretty much in the middle of nowhere. He paraded an array of politicians, including Daniel Webster, through Broughton's Meadow to witness his vision, which he incorporated as The Northampton Silk Company.[45] Over the next two years, Whitmarsh planted most of Broughton's

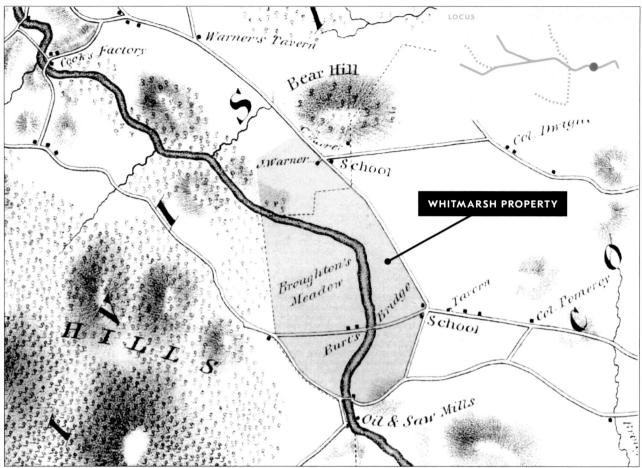

Fig 3.7 *Samuel Whitmarsh's Northampton Silk Company properties in 1837 stretched from the oil and sawmill in the lower center of the map to a line near the Joseph Warner place. (Courtesy of Forbes Library and Northampton DPW)*

Meadow with mulberry trees to feed the silk worms and to sell as seedlings; the seedlings were actually the only profitable part of the enterprise. He then built a cocoonery of two million silkworms at his lot on Fort Hill and a brick silk mill that replaced the old oil and sawmill building in Florence. In 1837, the Northampton Silk Company began producing its first silk thread on European weaving and reeling machines. Clouds began gathering that same year when, during the economic recession called "the Panic of '37," some of Whitmarsh's most important backers withdrew their money from his project. Some months after the Mulberry Tree Bubble burst in 1839, a notice appeared in the *Gazette*: "Property of the Northampton Silk Company for Sale."[46]

Samuel Whitmarsh was ruined. As a local writer recalled, Whitmarsh "had neither cash nor credit to buy a barrel of flour."[47] He sailed for Jamaica in 1840 to establish a silk factory in Jamaica, which failed too. But he was never discouraged. Sheffeld provides a poetic end to Whitmarsh's business ventures: "Though failure after failure overtook him, he was still confident that the next revolution of fortune's wheel would bring him ample recompense for all his labors and losses."[48] Whitmarsh's star rose and fell like a comet, and the comet's tail left a lasting legacy of silk making along the Mill River.

Shepherd's Hollow (Leeds)

During the first third of the nineteenth century, while Florence was still a backwater, the decline in importance of the Lower and Upper Mills helped shift the industrial scene to an improbable, hitherto unsettled reach of the Mill known today as Leeds. Charles Dean, intrepid indexer of the *Hampshire Gazette* in the mid-twentieth century, makes reference to the first permanent settler of Shepherd's Hollow. His name was Joseph Burnell. In 1800 he built a short-lived sawmill at one of the Mill River dam sites, and little more is known of him. He simply becomes one more ephemeral miller on the river.[49]

Eight years later, Job Cotton built an eponymous cotton mill on Burnell's site. In 1812, Sidney Webster established a woolen mill just downstream at what is now called Cooks Dam.[50] But it was left to the three sons and a nephew of Levi Shepherd, the wealthy Northampton businessman and local banker, to make famous throughout America the name of Shepherd broadcloth. Using part of Levi's considerable fortune, the sons and nephew took over Job Cotton's mill the year after it was built and incorporated it as the Northampton Cotton & Woolen Mfg. Co., a firm that dominated the Mill River's industrial output for the next twenty years. Although James Shepherd intended to call the place "Pleasant Valley," the factory village took the name of Shepherd's Hollow.[51]

Industrialists in the Mill River watershed were becoming adept at developing specialty items, and the textiles produced at Shepherd's Hollow are emblematic of the region's industrial strategy of turning out quality goods for small but lucrative segments of the mass market. In this respect, Northampton was more similar to France than Manchester or Lowell.[52] By 1816, the Shepherds had patented a power loom, and with it reputedly produced America's

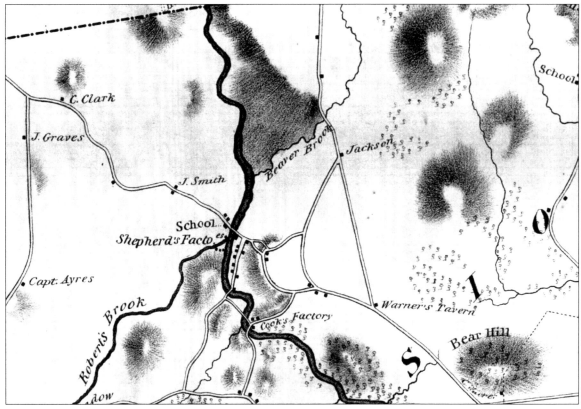

Fig. 3.8 The factory village of Shepherd's Hollow (Leeds) in 1831. (Courtesy Forbes Library and Northampton DPW)

first broadcloth. Made of wool from local merino and Saxony sheep, the cloth would go on to win awards for its quality in the 1820s.[53] But for mostly obscure reasons, the Shepherds' mills were faring poorly by the time a tariff war on textiles between Britain and the United States broke out in 1824. That was the death knell for the Shepherd factory. But in 1830, Edward Robbins purchased the bankrupt mill and brought it back to life. Within two years, the Northampton Woolen and Satinet Mfg. Co. was employing 120 men and women and producing textiles worth $175,906, a full 61 percent of Northampton's product value that year. Most of that output was sold to Robbins' wholesale house in Boston.[54]

Over the course of the next three decades, Shepherd's Hollow, renamed Leeds in 1850, continued to thrive, chiefly as part of the growing silk industry of Florence and as a manufacturer of buttons.[55]

Roberts Meadow Village

Roberts Meadow is one of two lost factory villages in the Mill River watershed, a beautiful forested site marked by a breached dam of historic significance with what was a small, shallow pond in back of it fit for a pair of hooded mergansers.[56] Few residents of the watershed even know there was a village there, with mills and a significant tannery.

The area of Roberts Meadow was named after Robert Lyman, one of Northampton's original proprietors, whose pursuit of game took him far into the hinterlands. His frozen body was found in this area, where he had fallen on one of his hunting trips.[57] As early as the 1730s, Nate Edwards, Jr., son of an original English settler in Northampton, may have constructed a sawmill at a site near the current dam. In the 1770s, a private turnpike company constructed a toll road called Chesterfield Road as part of the Northampton to Albany transportation route. The Edwards Tavern was constructed at this

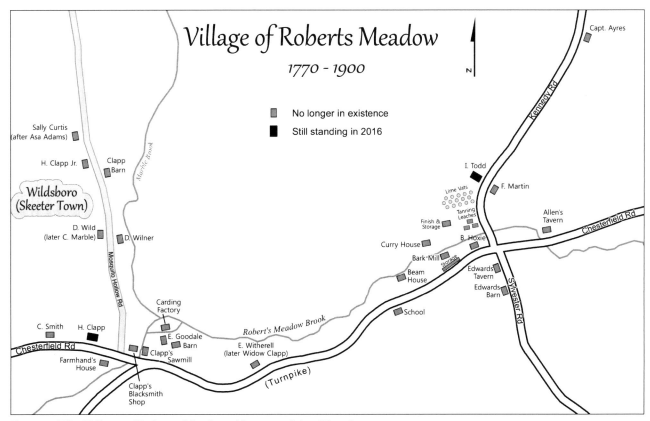

Fig. 3.9 The Village of Roberts Meadow. (Courtesy John Clapp)

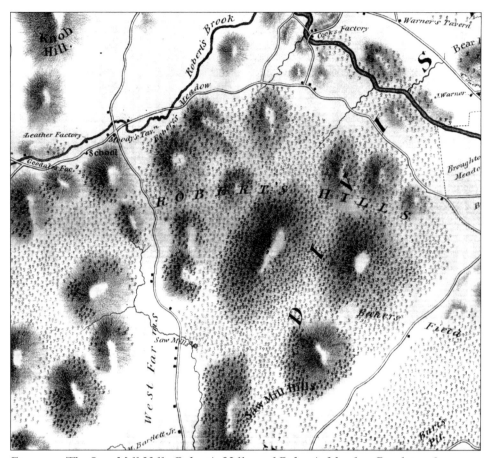

Fig. 3.10 *The Saw Mill Hills, Robert's Hills, and Robert's Meadow Brook in 1831*
(*Courtesy Forbes Library and Northampton DPW*)

site, and Nate sold his holdings in the 1790s to a relative, William Edwards, a grandson of Jonathan Edwards and an expert tanner.

Roberts Meadow became a major site for the tanning of hides during the first half of the nineteenth century. The brook also hosted sawmills and a fulling mill, and several families worked farms near the village. About twenty families housing more than sixty residents lived at Roberts Meadow at mid-century before economic life in the village died out. Only a few people were left by the time the current Roberts Meadow Brook dam was built in 1883 to provide a potable water supply for Northampton. It was breached in 2018.

The Town of Williamsburg

The families who settled Williamsburg in the mid-eighteenth century continued to farm and manufacture potash throughout the 1700s. By the dawn of the nineteenth century, however, they began to develop all the choice spots on the Mill River where there was good access to water power. A series of four factory villages grew up around these sites at Searsville, Williamsburg Center, Skinnerville, and Haydenville, at the Northampton line, which by the mid-1800s became the most industrial of the mill villages.

The reader should keep in mind that these hilltown villages to this day have double faces, one open and one closed. The closed face keeps tabs on all its residents. They quarrel and marry and have children together, care for and bury each other, and provide for their own spiritual and prosaic needs through their church congregations and town committees, which make almost all town decisions, especially those dealing with finances. The open face turns toward the wider world, which most residents know well because they have traveled widely. In the nineteenth century, raw materials such as iron might have come from Quebec or New York State, while clothing and Williamsburg's finished products would have been sold in New York City. Because few in Boston or New York know anything about Williamsburg does not mean that Williamsburg citizens are ignorant of New York or Boston.

With a premium on self-reliance, Williamsburg, much like other towns, formed a tightly knit community. Farming families worked with each other, bartering their time and skills at their seasonal chores. This agrarian ethic carried over to industrial endeavors where commodities were bartered, and there may even have been bartered brides.[58] The Hydes, Hannums, Whites, Bakers, Curts, Sears, Millers, Guilfords, Hitchcocks and Haydens, who had all arrived just before or after 1800, quickly established ties with one another. Rufus Hyde employed John White at his forge, and in 1818, John married Salome, the daughter of gristmiller J. D. Curts, who was Josiah Hannum's first cousin. When Steven Hyde married Pamela Baker in 1819, her younger brother Benjamin, Rufus Hyde employed him. In 1825, Levi Hitchcock married Benjamin's sister Phoebe, and in 1828, Benjamin wed Priscilla, a sister of Nathaniel Sears. The wife of William Guilford was the stepdaughter of John Miller, and two of Guilford's brothers married daughters of Josiah Hayden: the kind

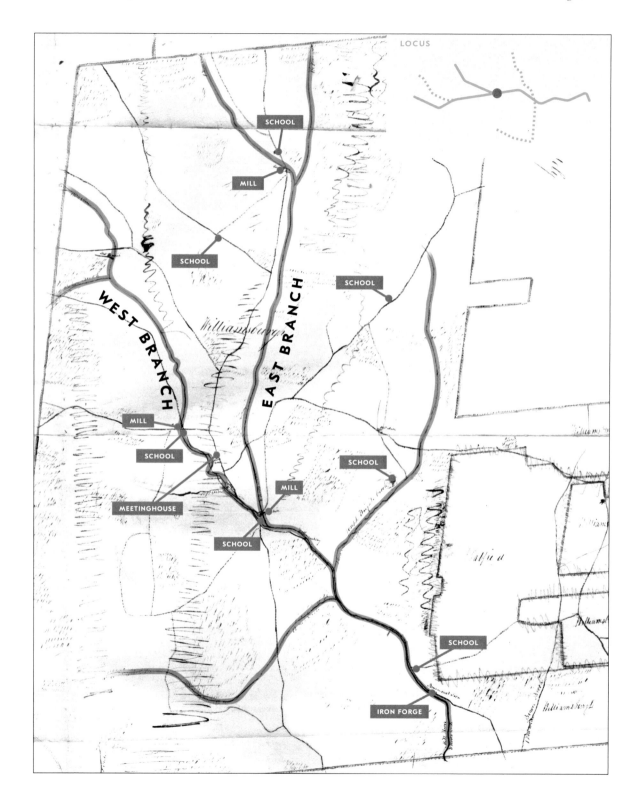

Fig. 3.11 (facing page) This 1831 Map of Williamsburg was drawn in response to the Massachusetts legislature's demand for a map from every town in the state. A poor hilltown such as Williamsburg could only afford a rather sketchy map compared to the rich components of the 1831 map of Northampton that we have been using in this chapter. The Williamsburg map illustrates some interesting features – chief among them is the large number of schools (seven in all) scattered throughout the town as was the population of about 1200. Note how the mills are clustered in the upper half of the watershed at this point in time while Haydenville in the south is barely a village in the making. (Courtesy Eric Weber and Ralmon Black. Source: State Archives)

of arrangements that inspired such folksongs as "I'm My Own Grandpa." As Ralmon Black told me, "In Williamsburg, family picnics and village festivals melded into each other."

Searsville

Rufus Hyde, Sr. settled near the Mill River in 1774, more than a mile upstream from Williamsburg Center, where he established the first long-lasting industry in the upper watershed. Working his arm and hammer, he forged axes, scythes, and other tools necessary to husbandry.[59] This happened sixty years before several famous tool factories were built eight miles downriver at Bay State in Northampton. Nearby, Josiah Hannum[60] had been making axes in the abandoned schoolhouse on Village Hill since about 1795. The ax and scythe industry grew quickly when Hyde's sons, Rufus, Jr. and Stephen, installed a trip-hammer in 1799.[61] The Hydes and Hannums merged their enterprises, and their combined efforts resulted in the widespread distribution of Hannum and Hyde scythes and axes throughout northern and western New England, New York, Pennsylvania, northern Ohio and Canada. The factory village grew quickly and noisily. "Two and a half miles distant," Prescott Williams would write in 1861, "[I] often heard the trip-hammer start at four o'clock in the morning and run till 10 o'clock in the night, when orders pressed them." Without artificial lighting, such a schedule would only be possible the month preceding and following the summer solstice.

Hannum and Hyde made many styles of edge tools—scythes, chopping axes, several sizes of hewing axes, as well as the hatchet and adze of the joiner and cooper. They bought iron wherever they could; blistered steel came from England. During the War of 1812, Hannum bought black market steel in

Quebec and drew it over the snow to Searsville with oxen. As many as 110 axes were forged a week at $1.50, a price equal to the wages for thirty hours of unskilled labor.[62]

Successful as the Hannum and Hyde enterprise was, tragedy stalked the families. Rufus, Jr. lost his two-year-old son down his well in 1812, and his wife died of consumption the next year. He soon removed to Canada, where he died in 1825, but his brother Stephen continued at the trip-hammer until he died in 1834, barely fifty years old. Hannum died the next year, age sixty-one, killed by the most common disease of blacksmiths—silicosis from years of inhaling dust off the grindstone.

In 1801, within sight of the bridge at Searsville, up the small stream near Dwight's potash works, William Guilford established a woodworking and grinding shop.[63] In 1818, Nathaniel Sears came to the place that would memorialize his name, marking the district school and factory village on contemporary maps.[64] He purchased part of Stephen Hyde's water privilege and established a fulling mill and dye shop, which burned down in the 1830s. He rebuilt and added a woolen mill with power looms that produced fulled, dressed woolen broadcloth and satinet, mostly dyed a light blue.[65] Eventually he gave up custom work to manufacture white woolen flannel, which remained viable until he retired in 1862.[66] Sears was described as

> a man of retiring but genial and friendly disposition, accommodating to his friends in business, cordial to his neighbors, diligent in business, of unimpeachable integrity, a devoted member of the Congregational Church, liberal in his benefactions... His blue satinets almost clothed the neighborhood in uniform.[67]

As Ralmon Black described it, in 1813, when the first stagecoaches began operating, travelers from Northampton passed through Searsville on their way to Albany and points west, among whom was a steady stream of mostly drunk sailors from Eastern Massachusetts, "with their bounty a-jingle in their hats," on their way to engage in the War of 1812. By 1820, the ax factory, gristmill, and woolen mill in Searsville were all prospering, as were retailing and services. In 1829, Hampshire County laid a new River Road (the current Route 9) from Florence to Williamsburg, establishing five new bridges from Williamsburg Center through Searsville and creating new road frontage for development.[68]

The families of this little factory village produced two of Massachusetts' most notable abolitionists and public figures in the mid-nineteenth century—Joel Hayden, Sr. and Henry S. Gere, both born in Searsville. Hayden was the lieutenant governor of Massachusetts in the mid-1860s and a major mill owner and investor as part of the Florence Group.[69] After the 1874 flood, his son, Joel Jr., briefly stayed on to rebuild his village and care for the workers. At the time of Joel Sr.'s death, he owned most of the village of Haydenville.

Henry Gere (pronounced "Gayer") got his start in the newspaper business at age nineteen. He went on to become publisher and editor of the *Hampshire Herald,* from which perch he plunged into politics: first as a single-issue abolitionist, then as an eclectic reformer in the Free Soil party, and finally as a member of the new Republican Party in the 1850s. In 1859, he purchased the *Hampshire Gazette* and the *Northampton Courier*, which he owned and edited the rest of his life, even through his service in the Civil War. He fought fiercely against the anti-immigrant Know Nothing Party and became a staunch Republican, who left his newspaper job after writing in 1860, "We have entered upon the most horror of horrors—Civil War." [70] Gere signed up for a nine-month stint with Company C of the 52nd Massachusetts Volunteer Infantry in 1861 and was sent to Louisiana, where he became a postmaster with time to spare wandering around Baton Rouge, taking notes and images. Gere, along with his comrade-in-arms, Marshall Stearns, was likely responsible for the photograph of Peter the Slave, "easily the most iconic image of a slave that emerged from the war, his back a mass of sores and scars emblematic of the horrors of Southern slavery."[71] When *Harper's Weekly* published the photograph, complete with a spurious story about Peter, the Union publicists had found a propaganda tool as powerful as *Uncle Tom's Cabin.*

Williamsburg Center[72]

Originally called "The Cellars" for the potash pits in this low, swampy plain, there is no evidence that more than two buildings were located in what is now called "Burgy Center" in 1780. In 1765 Thomas Fenton built a house and barn on a piece of land Hatfield granted him in exchange for building bridges that the court had ordered.[73] Samuel Bodman in about 1773 built a barn and house, which still stands, and he operated a leather tanning yard using horse power to grind hemlock bark and to agitate his vats.[74] By 1788, Jesse Wilde was running a grist mill and had deeded part of his land and water privilege to Roger Wing of Barre, Massachusetts for a fulling mill. It was

> a privilege for to set a fooling mill from yᵉ upper End of that dich I [Jesse Wilde] dug for my upper gris mill & liberty to use all yᵉ water that runs in yᵉ river from whence yᵉ dich is dug when needed for yᵉ use of yᵉ mill to still run in yᵉ dich as before...[75]

Roger Wing was not a permanent presence in Williamsburg even though the town had elected him as their fence viewer, the man who had to check the status of fencing everywhere in town.[76] But in 1790 the selectmen put him on a list of the many people whom they "warned out," a process whereby a New England town would be absolved of liabilities for the poor or unwanted. The warning out process was not uncommon, nor did it stigmatize those who were given time to leave the town either by date certain or by no date at all. Mr. Wing had done nothing to disgrace himself or the town; the selectmen simply wanted to be sure that Williamsburg would not have to pay for his upkeep or burial should he land in penury or die. There were no records of people actually forced to leave town. In 1804, Wing left town of his own accord and popped up in Adams, calling himself a "gentleman," the same year in which he sold off most of his Williamsburg holdings.[77]

The small industrial enterprises that sprang up in "The Cellars" by 1800 attracted several stores and hotels, and the place soon came to be called "Center City." Along the West Branch, from Jesse Wilde's upper mill to the Small Bridge were a cotton factory and gristmill. Another cotton mill was built near the center of Center City.[78] Across the river, on the right bank, Gross Williams had a potash works, a tin shop, and a cider mill and distillery. He improved the road, bridged the river, and gave the town a roadway connecting Main Street to Goshen Road, a section of Route 9 now called Williams Street.

By 1820, Gross Williams' nephew, Abisha Williams Stearns, had a clothing shop nearby, and a fulling mill was located just downstream. That fulling mill appears on the 1795 Williamsburg map and is mentioned in a later newspaper item as a "small mill for fulling, dyeing and dressing woolen goods... Their waterpower was obtained from the pond at Stearns' mill, by means of a penstock. The cloth dressed and colored was mostly made by hand-looms in private families."[79] This was the long-lived mill that the brothers Bodman —

Sylvester, Artemas, and Theophilus — established in 1813; it was still running in the 1850s as the Unquomonk Woolen Manufactory.[80]

Probably during the first decade of the nineteenth country, at a place called Sweetfern Plain between the Center and Haydenville, a veteran of the Revolution named Lt. Joshua Thayer started up a gristmill. The next year, a freshet washed it away, and we lose track of further developments until J. J. Lewis and J. J. Goodell took it over in the 1830s. They built a small factory that manufactured drill bits and bit stocks, after which Lewis shifted to the manufacture of spoons made of britannia metal (a tin-based alloy), harness trimmings, and faucets. Sweetfern Plain would eventually become the location of William Skinner's famous Unquomonk Silk Mill at mid-century.[81]

The small-time industrialists of Williamsburg surely had to be quick studies with several kinds of expertise. Husbandry required mechanical skills, and smithies needed to know about leather and tanning practices. Woodsmen worked with edge instruments, as did everyone in the community, for they were all house builders. When the textile factories opened up, they had the laboring hands of local girls, who already knew their way around cotton, wool, and flax. The most important general skill was literacy, and New Englanders were a phenomenally well-schooled bunch, far more so than Americans in other regions. Reading had become a necessity of life.[82] Literacy for both genders had long been a requirement in New England for religious affairs. Families read the bible around the fire and sang hymns from hymnals in church. At work, mill owners required basic literacy of their workers to ensure the proper running of industrial concerns.

Factory owners had to be able to gage swiftly changing markets, tastes, and fashions. Had textile makers been able to remain in the cotton and clothing trade, they would have done so, but cotton is a notoriously fickle product: very profitable in wartime, but subject to overproduction and falling prices in times of peace. The War of 1812, for example, created a boom for about four years and a bust immediately thereafter.

Furthermore, the social structures that hilltown people established required cooperation among those with different skills, while the political structure of the town and town meeting forced community members to rub up against each other as they made budgetary decisions. If any group of communities was ready for the upheaval of the Industrial Revolution, it would be the people of the Mill River watershed. Life was far from paradisiacal, but the ability of these nineteenth-century communities to sustain themselves and follow the changing tides was admirable.

Haydenville

In 1800, a lone sawmill could be found at the southern border of Williamsburg at the Northampton line, a mile upstream from Leeds. By 1840, however, Williamsburg's most important factories would be located at that site, which became known as Haydenville. In 1808, a Searsville native, Daniel Hayden, started a cotton mill on the land that had been a sawmill, and the rapidly growing Hayden family became the central figures in the village's dramatic growth throughout most of the nineteenth century.[83] By 1810, fifteen families had already petitioned the town of Williamsburg for a separate school district to serve, among others, the eight children of Daniel's brother Josiah, Jr. Josiah's twelve-year-old son Joel would grow up to become Williamsburg's leading industrialist and the lieutenant-governor of Massachusetts during the Civil War.

Joel Hayden was in his early twenties when he teamed up with his brother-in-law, James Condon, in 1822 to purchase the idled cotton mill, rebuild the dam, dig a new canal, and repair the building in which they began to weave cotton broadcloth. By the time they had designed a functional loom, they realized that making power looms was more lucrative than the textile trade. Within three years, they doubled the mill's size and were manufacturing various kinds of machinery. Three years after that, in 1828, Joel's brother Josiah III joined him to manufacture door locks and harness trimmings. In 1831 they turned to the making of buttons of all types, the fifth product change within ten years of operation.[84]

A disastrous fire in 1832 consumed their mill, but Joel and Josiah rebuilt it in 1833 with Joel remaining at the mill and Josiah moving on to other business opportunities. Joel experimented with various kinds of buttons. He also teamed up with Easthampton shopkeeper, future philanthropist and well-known abolitionist Samuel Williston to make cloth-covered buttons. This latter enterprise was profitable, and lasted until 1848 when Hayden and Williston dissolved their partnership, although they remained friends and mutual investors in a series of industrial concerns.

Goshen and the Headwaters of the West Branch

Simultaneous with the settlement of Williamsburg was the clearing of the woodlands at the Mill River's headwaters in Goshen. Originally part of the town of Chesterfield, Goshen already had a handful of settlers when it was officially incorporated in 1781. The center of Goshen was located on top of a hill on the Northampton-Albany road, now called the Berkshire Trail (Route 9), at the watershed divide between the West Branch of the Mill River and the East Branch of the Westfield River. Several families, chiefly from Eastern and Central Massachusetts, carved out homesteads and set to work clearing the woods along the same lines as people in Williamsburg and other hilltowns.

The first settlers appear to have been a politically active bunch. At the third annual town meeting in 1784, Goshen's nineteenth-century historian, Hiram Barrus, tersely noted that "The town had one man who evidently was not an office holder."[85] For those unacquainted with the importance of self-governance in New England, the active participation of citizens in the running of their towns may seem a bit odd, given that Goshen, like many other towns, generally had only a few hundred people. However, the pride of being one's own financial and political boss remains to this day throughout the towns of Western Massachusetts.

The first thirty years of settlement turned out to be the busiest that Goshen would ever experience, and the town's population peaked in 1800 at 724, a number regained only 180 years later. By 1830, the population had dropped to 617 and was on its downward path toward a mere 297 souls by the end of the nineteenth century. Looking back from his perspective in 1880, Barrus plaintively wrote that it was "doubtful whether the New England towns will be developed to their full power, till the West ceases to tempt her enterprising sons with the offer of richer soils and cheaper acres."[86]

During those first halcyon decades, however, several enterprising young people constructed some small mills at the headwaters of the West Branch just downstream from the Great Meadow (now called Lower Highland Lake) near the center of town. Surely the most interesting attempt to produce a niche industrial product was a spot on the West Branch where Nehemiah May and Ebenezer Putney "in about 1788 erected a mill for grinding sumac to be sent to Europe for tanning morocco. It did not pay and was given up."[87] Hiram

Barrus listed among Goshen's earliest mills "Carpenter John" Williams' saw- and grist mill near Lower Highland Lake, which he sold in the 1820s to one Abner Moore. The enterprising young Moore modified the building to run a gristmill and woodworking shop which turned out rake handles, broom handles and button molds. Downstream from Lower Highland, a wheelwright set up a gristmill at one of the Mill River's most beautiful sections, Devil's Den on the Goshen-Williamsburg line. It was a perfect mill site: its precipitous drop meant that no dam or millpond was required. Devil's Den remains one of the Mill River's most popular open secrets and welcomes public recreational use.[88]

Floods[89]

North America was at the end of the Little Ice Age during the first half of the nineteenth century, which meant that one could expect thick ice blocks on rivers. At ice-out, huge dams of ice could form, forcing the Mill and Connecticut Rivers to occupy their secondary beds—the flood plains. So long as citizens had placed no permanent structures on the flood plains, they were generally safe from damage, but some residents started building next to the meadows in areas formerly occupied by flood-plain forests. Bridge Street in Northampton,

Fig. 3.12 *Accelerated Erosion & Intensive Farming, ca. 1850 (Courtesy Harvard Forest)*

for example, which now led to a bridge across the Connecticut to Hadley, was lined with houses that bordered directly on the wet meadows. Such was the situation when the first of the major floods struck the watershed at the turn of the century, and at mid-century when the Big River changed its course, creating the Oxbow.

After two flood events in 1793 and 1798,[90] the nineteenth century began with one of the region's greatest events in historical memory—the Jefferson Flood in late March of 1801.

> As heavy a fall of rain, as was ever remembered, commenced of Tuesday night last, and continued with very little intermission until late on Thursday: The rivers and brooks were raised to a height hardly ever known before, and the damage done to Mills, Bridges, Fences and roads is incalculable. The earth near the surface, is full of water, and much inconvenience is experienced from water in cellars, which is in many places two and three feet deep, where none was ever known to stand till [this] rain.[91]

We have from the *Gazette* only a brief description of lost and damaged goods and property, but as subsequent descriptions recount, the Jefferson Flood vied for "flood of the century" status. Flood damage, however, was limited because so few residences thus far had be constructed in the flood plain.

The Jefferson Flood was accompanied by the same adventurous, festive spirit that attended all such disasters. As we read in this 1836 retrospective description,

> The water was so high, that a boat, or scow, started from Pleasant-street, not far, we understand, from the meadow gate, freighted with a goodly number of citizens of Northampton, sailed to Hadley into Front-street, and was fastened to the bar-room table of the house then kept by Mr. Elisha Cook... The crew then went in and regaled themselves with the contents of the bar, it being before the days of temperance, and then they went with their boat through the street, not by water, but probably by *steam* [original italics], launched it at Baker's ferry, and came down the river home. On the west side of Hadley street, which is lower than the other, the water flowed up nearly to the meeting house.[92]

This story, told thirty-five years after the event, is likely apocryphal. One wonders how the revelers acquired a steam engine prior to the general use of such devices. Nonetheless, the article provides a sense of the times. Such bouts of drinking and merriment accompanied all flood disasters, save perhaps the very last one in 1940.

1824 Winter Freshet

The 1824 freshet was the first flood to destroy the bridge over the Connecticut between Northampton and Hadley. This was an open bridge, built in 1804, and was replaced by a covered bridge, parts of which remained intact through the rest of the century.[93]

1828 Nor'easter

While not as high as the Jefferson Flood, the September 1828 event did extraordinary damage. There is no mention of an 1828 hurricane in the literature, so it may well have been a slow moving nor'easter. After a month of excessive heat and drought, "the windows of heaven opened," and a deluge continued almost uninterrupted for four days.

> Mill river, which flows through this village, and which had dwindled down to a placid rill during the dry weather, was swelled to a broad, deep and impetuous stream, overflowing its banks, and covering the road north of the bridge to the depth of three feet. The ruins floating on its surface indicated that extensive ravages had been occasioned by its waters... It was a fearful time in the village—it was a night of Egyptian darkness; the rain poured down incessantly and vehemently; and the angry flood raged and roared on every side.[94]

White and Thompson's mill dam at Florence was destroyed, and the factory, bridge and canal at Shepherd's Hollow were damaged. Williamsburg was hard hit when Taylor's dam was swept away and two bridges demolished. Most crops in the Northampton Meadows were destroyed when between 3000 and 3500 acres were flooded by four to eight feet of water from one to three days. This was a true "Pumpkin Flood," such as the one in the Connecticut Valley of October 2005 when the remnants of Hurricane Tammy dumped six to twelve inches of rain on the Connecticut Valley, followed a week later by a nor'easter that added another six to ten inches.[95]

> Many of the inhabitants of both sexes, went to view the Connecticut at the bridge, and the flood upon the meadows. The spectacle presented by the waters was novel and interesting, yet melancholy. On both days, a large portion of the surface of the river was covered with wrecks, carried swiftly down the muddy current. Logs, trees, boards & other lumber, ruins of fences, mills,

bridges and dams, hay, pumpkins, apples, &tc. were continually floating along, and gave plain indications of the devastations of the freshet in Franklin county, and in New Hampshire and Vermont. A part of a bridge, said to be 100 feet in length, was towed ashore at Hockanum; and a barrel of rum, found floating, was stopped near Northampton bridge; it might have been as well, perhaps, to have let it go over the falls. The pumpkins were innumerable—enough, it is presumed, to supply half the state with thanksgiving pies.[96]

1839 Winter Thaw

We now come to the first flood that Sylvester Judd documented in his manuscripts, as he followed the height of the water day by day from January 27 to January 31.[97] It began to warm up and rain on the 26th, he wrote, but the ice on the Big River was still a foot thick. While not as notable as the floods of 1801 or 1828, nor as damaging in its impacts, it nonetheless created an awesome scene.

> Mill River presented a rough, desolate aspect—the ice is piled up on its banks, many of the trees shattered & some prostrated, and the banks apparently undermined. The bed of the river is also encumbered with fragments of ice. The Connecticut presented a more grand & terrific appearance. For some distance on this side, the river & flats or beach are covered with immense masses of ice, piled up on each other at various inclinations from horizontal to perpendicular, though most of them are within 10 or 15 degrees of horizontal. These great cakes of ice are from 1 to 2 feet thick—most of them not much over a foot or 15 inches—and they are to appearance heaped up from the bottom of the river 8, 10, or 12 feet thick in all... No water is to be seen; the whole river and banks are covered with ice in all shapes. I have never seen the like, & cannot make a comparison. It reminds one of the fabled transformations of the Genii in the Arabian Nights; or one may imagine that he is viewing the ruins of Palmyra or Balbec, the wrecks of a vast marble city or a vast cemetery whose marble monuments have fallen upon the earth.[98]

What a graphic eye Sylvester Judd had! Who else could have enlivened a portrait with mere numbers? He left us with an exquisite set of observations that still rivet us in this place.

1840 Winter Thaw

"Northampton Bridge Gone!" cried out the *Gazette* headline. This was the great February flood that changed the course of the Connecticut River.

> [On February 24th] about 9 o'clock, an immense sheet of ice started above the [Hadley] bridge, came down with tremendous force against one of the middle stone piers, and swept away the top of it, to a level with the water, as though it had been constructed of pebbles. The two reaches of the bridge, of which this pier was the central support, immediately settled to the water and were carried off. The remainder of the bridge was thus far uninjured. But soon a large portion of the Sunderland bridge, together with immense masses of ice, came against the two reaches of the bridge which remained on the Hadley side of the river, and so damaged the piers, that in the course of an hour, this part of the bridge settled and went off. Two pieces of the Sunderland bridge, one quite long, perhaps 100 feet, came down in an erect position, and apparently not very much damaged. The longest struck the Northampton bridge endwise, wheeled about, and was completely crushed against it, by the floating masses of ice, the Northampton bridge apparently resisting the shock without trembling. But the concussion was too great, as the subsequent event fully proved... Three reaches of the bridge, or little less than half, remain uninjured.[99]

All the detritus in the river, including the bridge remains and blocks of ice, roared downriver, depositing much of it at Hockanum and blocking the north end of the river channel where it took a sharp right turn. The result was the closure of the river channel at Hockanum Meadow, thus creating the current Oxbow, the very one that was transfigured in Thomas Cole's famous painting *The Oxbow* (Fig.3.13). On February 25, Sylvester Judd went down to inspect. "To day [sic] the Connecticut made the long threatened inroad across the neck of Hockanum meadow a little west of the narrowest place, & where the neck is 25 or 30 rods wide, and in a few hours most of the river took that channel, & the water fell rapidly on the meadows in Mill River."[100] In the *Gazette's* recounting, "This noble stream, in her anxiety to reach the deep ocean, has shortened her course thither about three and a half miles."

Blockage of the river channel meant that some three hundred acres of land that used to be on the left bank, which Hadley farmers still owned, had moved to Northampton on the right bank of the river. Simultaneously, the Connecticut immediately began eroding Hadley's left bank, further damaging Hadley farmers. "It makes bad work for the Hockanum & Hadley people," wrote Judd, "taking away some of their land & reducing the value of all that is cut off by the new channel. The Northampton people are almost all rejoicing at the event—which is the effect of their selfishness."

The cause of the flood? "... few had expected this disastrous occurrence. There had been no storm of rain, and although the large quantities of snow had disappeared rapidly, it was almost wholly through the agency of mild weather."[101] Thus, there was no damage along the Mill River, since it contained insufficient blocks of ice to crush dams and buildings.

Only five significant floods occurred during these six decades. No doubt freshets continued to flood the meadows, but the small size of the population and limited extent of buildings and structures in floodplains not only reduced damages, but decreased runoff from impervious surfaces. However, we are about to encounter the one great land-use change that occurred during this period—forest clearance. During the next century, the frequency and severity of these floods would increase exponentially as population expanded and the land was skinned of its woodland cover.

Environmental Transformation III: *Forest Clearance*

Over the course of sixty years from 1780–1840, the combination of more powerful technologies, increasing population, access to cheap forestland, and stronger market forces initiated the dramatic landscape changes that would decimate the ecological health of the Mill River watershed by the end of the nineteenth century. All this occurred under the sunny aegis of progress, the expansion of individual liberty, and faith in a future of endless growth amid temporary financial setbacks. The countervailing gospels of conservation and preservation would appear shortly after mid-century, but for the moment, faith in inevitable progress dominated land and water use. Furthermore, a limited population and the small scale of factories rarely produced immediate or obvious environmental harm. Realization of the costs of industrialization came slowly in the latter decades of the nineteenth century.

As evidence, we can look at contemporary newspapers and novels from the early nineteenth century where one rarely finds mention of a lost paradisiacal landscape, so common in the latter half of that century. Yet we know there were dramatic disappearances, such as salmon and carnivores. By 1800, Sylvester Judd wrote that few salmon were caught, and what few ascended upriver were stopped by the new dam at Turners Falls, constructed in the 1790s.[102] Shad, however, were still caught by the thousands at South Hadley Falls.[103]

Astonishingly, in Goshen and the upper Mill River watershed, hunters and trappers, along with forest clearing, had wiped out all the big game by 1840. Goshen's historian Hiram Barrus wrote that, while bobcats were still common, a Northampton trapper had killed the one mountain lion anyone had ever seen. Wild turkeys had disappeared by 1800, and the last bear was killed in 1785. "The last deer, evidently a straggler from some northern forest, was shot in the winter of 1828." It was thrown onto a passing load of wood and "in passing the schoolhouse, the pupils, of whom the writer [Barrus] was one, were given an opportunity to see it—the first they had ever seen, the last ever killed in Goshen."[104]

The chief engine of transformation during this period was deforestation in the name of farming, husbandry, and potash production. Even as younger sons and daughters left for Western New York and Ohio, many others simply moved up into the hilltowns, where they became Jacks and Jills of all trades—raising crops and livestock for home and market, cutting timber for cash, and becoming mechanics and millwrights. They cleared the forests of timber, and their diligence and persistence created a landscape in 1840 that would have been unrecognizable in 1780. Those who settled in old-growth forest, felling 200-year old oaks and chestnuts and sugar maples, died surrounded by grasslands. They grew up listening to the songs of warblers and thrushes, and ended their days in the midst of the whistles and trills of bobolinks, whip-poor-wills and sparrows. The smell of manure replaced that of sawdust. They had physically transformed their own world and sent westward a horde of youngsters eager to repeat the process for the next several generations.

Forest clearing substantially changed the mixture of trees in the woodlands. "Pioneer" trees—the first to sprout on open, sun-filled ground—replaced the slow-growing, shade-loving trees of the old-growth forests.[105] Fast sprouting red maple, birch, poplar, cherry, pine, and ash quickly captured sites once occupied by hickory, chestnut, oak, beech, and basswood.[106] We shall see how these new kinds of forests re-occupied the landscape in the second half of the nineteenth century and their importance in a different kind of economy that was becoming increasingly dependent on industry.

Land use shifted away from forest products to field crops and livestock. At the mouth of the Mill River, farmers grew crops in the fertile Meadows, while the watershed above Florence was turned into grazing, orchard, and hay land. "New England," writes the historian Brian Donahue, "was in the midst of the rapid expansion of a commercial grazing economy [in the first half of the nineteenth century]." In Petersham, a hilltown in the Worcester hills, "cleared land jumped to 61 percent by 1831 and kept on climbing for another half century. New farm creation stumbled, while clearing went on leaping ahead. The great majority of this farmland was pasture, and most of the rest was hay. The number of acres in tillage scarcely grew at all." In some towns, like Petersham, beef and dairy cattle dominated, while across the Connecticut Valley, in towns like Ashfield in the Mill River watershed adjacent to Williamsburg, the Merino sheep boom "stripped the forests of hilltowns with lightning speed."[107]

In Chapter One we discussed the first great invasion of European plants, when the English converted both wet and dry native meadows to European fodder. We also considered the introduction of Eurasian earthworms, which thoroughly aerated the upper levels of the soil, making nutrients available to shallow-rooted forage plants instead of deep-rooted trees. The seed of English hay and clover had become available by the middle of the seventeenth century, some with beguiling names, such as Kentucky blue grass, *Poa pratensis* (*poa* = Greek for fodder and *pratensis* = Latin for meadow). All that was needed to spread these European invaders was space, and that is what quickly appeared over the course of the first half of the nineteenth century. With the clearcutting of the forest, Eurasian grasses and forbs filled in, ready as forage for the meat (i.e. oxen or castrated calves), dairy, and beef cattle and merino sheep that dotted the hillsides of the hilltowns during that period.[108]

With extraordinary efficiency, young men and women cut down most of the trees throughout the Mill River watershed. As they did so, they opened up vast areas not only to grassland, but to erosion that washed and gullied the topsoil from hillsides everywhere. With few deep-rooted trees to anchor it or the forest mulch to insulate it, the soil and rock rolled and rushed into the Mill River and its tributaries, making it more difficult for the river to accomplish its task of moving material and water downstream. Dams simply increased the river's woes, as millions of tons of soil, sand, gravel, and rock built up behind the dams, suffocating the eggs in the spawning beds of trout and minnows and robbing downstream of the materials and nutrients that fed the crayfish, crane flies, and mayfly larvae that had lived there. We saw the beginning of that process in the last chapter, but by the mid-nineteenth century, it must have devastated the small native fishery, and increased water temperatures in summer. Strange, from our perspective, is the dearth of commentary on the river's declining health. Neither newspapers nor astute observers, such as Judd, mention polluted waterways even though it had become common. Dyes from small mills and acids and heavy metals from cutleries, tanneries and ironworks poured into the Mill after the 1840s, and this appeared to have been acceptable to Americans of the time.

Fig 3.13   Thomas Cole's 1836 "The Oxbow" painted from Mt. Holyoke in South Hadley looking toward Northampton and Easthampton.

But the erosion and other damage to the land done by nineteenth-century clearing persists to this day. Take a look back at the pre-settlement forest portrayed in the Harvard Forest dioramas (Figs. 2.5 – 2.7). Then look closely at the 1850 diorama.

Note, especially in the center foreground, the gullies that have formed and the wide, eroded washes on both sides of the old lake terraces that lead down to the river. New forest growth now hides most such surface features, helping reduce erosion, yet one can still read them easily on the landscape. It's almost shocking how open is the 1850 landscape, yet, if one needs a contemporary view of the Connecticut Valley in the 1830s, there is no better witness than Thomas Cole in his 1936 painting "The Oxbow" that hangs in New York's Metropolitan Museum of Art (what extraordinary historical accident allowed Thomas Cole to paint "The Oxbow" just four years prior to the 1840 flood that changed the course of the river at that very spot?).

If the current world is tempted to curse mid-nineteenth-century society for its profligate waste of land and water resources, we hope that readers would remind themselves of the extraordinary appeal of these landscapes to the world of nineteenth-century people and their gospel of progress. Cole here evokes an Arcadian world, the Greek ideal of moderation and harmony, with its depiction of pastoral life along the right bank of the Connecticut River. On the left side of the painting, Cole juxtaposes a jumble of trees, wild and free for people to explore what the land looked like before people tamed it. Wildness and tameness are two competing landscapes of America that most Americans hold close to their hearts, even in the twenty-first century. It is almost as though the mid-nineteenth century was the last time Americans imagined that the world was "in balance."

1840–1880: Great Floods and Political Turbulence at the Height of the First Industrial Revolution

Introduction

One of the most prosaic and unprepossessing spots on the river is located on Nonotuck Street at the foot of the steep slope that leads to the center of the village of Florence, city of Northampton. Scarcely anyone visits this place, save the employees at Nonotuck Mill who must trudge the hundred yards from the drab parking lot up against the hill to the long brick factory. Nonotuck Mill houses offices, mostly nonprofits along with the local roller derby space on the old machinery floor.

The spot, however, holds ghosts and spirits that are central to this part of our story. Down the street at the junction of Nonotuck and Riverside Drive is the former site of one of America's first silk factories, which a well known utopian community ran for over four years. Sojourner Truth and David Ruggles, two of America's African-American heroes, lived and worked here in the mid-nineteenth century. William Lloyd Garrison and his fellow abolitionists gathered here to argue politics and slavery and educate their children. In sum, we stand at the center of one of America's most notable resistance movements.

Walking upriver along the sidewalk that runs next to the factory, we glance across the street to one of the few remaining white mulberry trees that fed silk worms for the silk industry. Turn left into the parking lot at the end of the factory. Stop to reflect on this place at the twenty-foot-high dam, which has occupied this site since the mid-nineteenth century. It's often quiet at this spot, but for more than one hundred years, the noise was deafening with scores of machines running off the hydroturbines and several hundred workers hurrying about. Three large factories at this site on the river employed the sons and daughters of local, hilltown, and immigrant families. Instead of River Gods, the village was looked after by the patriarchal likes of the Florence Group, wise-looking, bearded men who stare stiffly out at us from posed photographs. All that now remains of factory noise comes from a nearby ugly mid-twentieth-century industrial building that makes plastic molding, currently part of a multinational conglomerate. It emits an annoying, insistent whine at unanticipated times night or day.

Just a bit farther upstream, well within sight, is a white brick factory built somewhat later than the silk mill, so we will cross the road (Pine Street) and turn left to the bridge that crosses the Mill. This was the Pro Brush Shop (now the Arts and Industry Building), the factory that turned out all the Pro-Phy-Lac-Tic toothbrushes I found in my Christmas stocking every year. And just upriver from the bridge, across a vast parking lot, you will find the Elks Club

building on the exact site of David Ruggles water-cure hospital which was followed, after his death, by a fancier Victorian spa that burned down in 1865.

You should easily find the old iron footbridge behind the Elks Club that crosses over to the A&I building. Now search for the path along the river at the derelict side of A&I. It is difficult to find, but persistence will pay if you just scramble through the brush. Find the path near the riverbank that was labeled "Lovers' Lane" on an old postcard. The path will end at the bridge on Meadow Street. Turn left over the bridge. Across the street, behold the Ross Farm, an early nineteenth-century farmhouse that served as a stop on the Underground Railroad. The fields that stretch beyond the farmhouse are Broughton's Meadow, now called Florence Fields, the westernmost arm of Lake Hitchcock in our watershed. The fields, and the Mill River that runs through them, tell many sto-

Fig. 4.1 Nonotuck Silk Company, ca. 1875. Note the deforestation in the background of rolling hills. (Courtesy Florence History Museum)

ries, one of which concerns the Williamsburg Dam Disaster, which will figure prominently in this chapter.

The forty years from 1840 to 1880 marked a turbulent time for the Mill River: rapid industrial and population growth throughout most of the watershed, the zenith of forest clearance, the emergence of Florence as the center of Mill River industry, the introduction of steam power and railroads, eight major floods (an average of one every five years), the most deadly dam disaster in American history to that point,[1] and the Civil War—all this within half the span of a human life.

We begin at a time of momentous technical discoveries and inventions. The use of coal to fire high-pressure steam engines made machinery of all sorts possible, including the locomotives that revolutionized transportation and the steam-driven turbines that massively increased textile production. Coal from Northeastern Pennsylvania's anthracite region transformed metal making, providing a reliable supply of iron that helped expand the nation's industrial base.[2] New nineteenth-century technologies changed the scope and scale of industry, similar to the way global capitalism and information technology have done in the twenty-first century. Great dams, canals, and locks on big rivers replaced the little crib dams on streams. Industrial cities —Lowell, Lawrence, Holyoke, Fall River—answered the rapidly increasing global demand for goods, leaving New England's little factory villages to vie for the leftover crumbs of capital investment and markets.

In 1813, the newly formed Boston Manufacturing Company, part of a group of entrepreneurs called the Boston Associates, built its first textile mill in Waltham on the Charles River, followed a decade later by the first mill on the Merrimack at Lowell, and then mills in Lawrence, Massachusetts and Manchester, New Hampshire. By 1850 these mills were more than two hundred fifty feet long, fifty feet wide, six stories high, supplied by water from many miles of canals, and staffed by thousands of operators, chiefly girls from the New England countryside.

But at the height of their influence in 1850, the Boston Associates found themselves almost inundated by a second wave of industrialization that relied on coal to produce steam power. "Tucked away in the southeastern part of [Massachusetts], Fall River offered a bold new challenge to Lowell's industrial hegemony... [By using coal-fired steam engines] the Fall River mills doubled their number of spindles between 1855 and 1865. By 1875, they led the nation with over 1.2 million spindles, almost twice the number operating at Lowell."[3] The First Industrial Revolution had dwarfed the world of small mills and local investment banking.

A new financial system arose in tandem with novel technologies and transportation, and the changing concept of "corporation" provided the financial muscle to make large corporate investment attractive. Most manufacturing enterprises prior to about 1810 were partnerships that did not require state charters, while corporations generally referred to quasi-public agencies that served public functions, such as colleges or libraries. In the first decade of the nineteenth century, the Massachusetts legislature granted fifteen corporate charters; from 1810 to 1820 the state chartered 133 new corporate entities. Historian Theodore Steinberg observed that over the course of the century, corporations would be transformed from public agencies to private ones that promoted individual gain.[4]

Fortunately, the nimble entrepreneurs in the Mill River watershed, funded by local investors willing to support industrial enterprises, had already become adept at manufacturing high-quality products for niche markets.[5] While small in size, Mill River industries found a sweet spot in American manufactured goods, namely agricultural tools, silk thread, woven cloth, and buttons produced in the shops in Bay State, Florence, Leeds, Haydenville, and Williamsburg. In 1860 there were more than sixty such enterprises on the Mill River.[6] Far from being overwhelmed by big industry, Mill River manufacturers surfed the waves of the rising and falling American economy, adjusting to circumstances by tweaking technologies or marketing, reducing production during panics but sometimes building to excess during periods of jubilation. Nowhere was this more clear than with the entrepreneurs of the Civil War era, who thrived during the conflict, overbuilt in the ebullient aftermath, and crashed during the 1873 Panic.

The First Industrial Revolution brought with it both population growth and depopulation in different parts of the watershed. Northampton almost quadrupled in size from 3750 people in 1840 to more than 12,000 in 1880, while Williamsburg grew from 1300 to 2234. Meanwhile the big industrial cities on the Connecticut River grew at the same rate as Northampton, but had larger populations to begin with. Holyoke, incorporated in 1850 as one of America's first planned industrial cities, started with 5000 people and ended in 1880 with 22,000. Springfield, Western Massachusetts' largest city, grew from about 11,000 in 1840 to 33,000 in 1880.[7]

Most hilltowns in the watershed experienced dramatic depopulation. Goshen lost more than a third of its inhabitants, starting at about five hundred in 1840 and dipping to 327 in 1880. Westhampton and Ashfield experienced similar declines after the economic bust of the merino sheep craze in the 1830s and 1840s when hilltown famers in New England grazed hundreds of thousands of merinos.[8] Many young hilltowners either moved down into the factories or west into New York and the Old Northwest states of Ohio, Michigan, Indiana, and Illinois. Hardscrabble farmers in these towns turned to dairy products and orchards for local sale just so their few score families could subsist.

As the population grew in mid-century, a mix of various foreign-born inhabitants—first Germans and Irish, then Quebecois, Italians, and Poles—changed the ethnic composition of the old Yankee towns and villages. In 1855, Northampton suddenly found that 24 percent of its inhabitants were foreign born. Of these, 66 percent were Irish and 15 percent were German and Dutch. Williamsburg at that same time was 13 percent foreign born, of whom 70 percent were Irish, 13 percent German, and 10 percent English.

This was important on at least two levels: First, foreigners both filled the immediate needs for labor in the mills and provided expertise in the silk and cutlery enterprises. William Skinner, for example, a London arrival in 1845, turned his silk dyeing skills into a fortune on the Mill River. Second, foreigners fed the nativist fears of local residents, who were convinced they were losing control of their own leading role in the new republic. A new anti-immigrant political party erupted—the American Party, generally called the Know Nothings, which became a part of an unprecedented political fluidity that verged on chaos.[9]

Northampton found itself in the maelstrom of the turbulence, which was a messy amalgam of political parties that reflected the social and economic tensions of the nation. In the 1840s and 1850s parties appeared and disappeared with alarming speed, save the Democratic Party of Andrew Jackson (president 1829–1837), which supported working men and slavery. Since slavery was anathema to almost all of New England, many Mill River residents favored the new Whig Party, which was the party of business, morality, and strong government. "But the soft antislavery of Whiggery was not sufficient for political abolitionists in Northampton...who in 1840 formed the Liberty Party, the nation's first third party devoted to abolitionism."[10] By 1850, the Liberty Party had morphed into the Free Soilers, who soon disappeared into the new Republican Party that elected Abraham Lincoln.[11]

Fighting against the anti-immigrant tide, Northampton was one of the few spots in Massachusetts that refused to vote for the Know Nothings in the election of 1854, which swept Know Nothing Governor Henry Gardner into office for four years, along with every seat in the Senate and 380 of 390 House seats. Northampton, writes Bruce Laurie, "stood fast against the Know Nothings, a patch of green in a vast landscape scorched by blazing fires of nativism."[12]

Anti-slavery and abolitionist sentiment, rather than anti-immigration, infused life in the Valley as America sped toward the breakup of the Union. Florence became the center of a strong abolitionist movement with its utopian socialist community called the Northampton Association for Education and Industry (NAEI). The Association ran a factory and fed its members from the lands it owned at what is now called Florence Fields, the Mill River's floodplain off both Meadow and Spring Streets. Safe houses for runaway slaves dotted the City, and Sojourner Truth, fresh from her stay in New York City, became an NAEI member, as did several of what would become Northampton's most prominent citizens. Ironically, tourists from southern states found this center of abolitionism a popular destination as well because of its lovely summer weather, plus such accommodating attractions as Mt. Holyoke and water cures in Northampton and Florence.

Northampton: Industrial Development and the Factory Villages

Industry boomed in the Mill River watershed during the middle of the nineteenth century as this Arcadian valley took on the appearance of a series of factory villages—industrial beads on the Mill River necklace. A tourism guide to Northampton recommended a visit to the new cotton mills at Haydenville, and "Sylvester Judd noted the noise from the fourteen triphammers of the Bay State Tool Company, which rang out across Northampton after the factory opened in 1855."[13]

The character of the industrial sites along the length of the river varied significantly. The largest concentration of diverse industries was centered in Florence during much of this period. Downtown Northampton became a cultural center and began calling itself Paradise City, a name reputedly suggested by the opera singer Jenny Lind (the "Swedish Nightingale"), who spent several months at the water cure resort on Round Hill.[14] We will never know whether

Mme. Lind truly pronounced Northampton a paradise, but the nickname became a marketer's dream and has clung to the city since that time.[15] Meanwhile, the mill pond at the Upper Mills, which would soon be named Paradise Pond on the Smith College campus, had a late-nineteenth-century fling with a large tool factory. A new factory village arose at Bay State, while Florence became both a manufacturing center and a village that experimented with utopian socialism, whose adherents left a legacy of philanthropy. Leeds, Haydenville, and Williamsburg retained their original small-factory character until 1874, when the Williamsburg Dam Disaster destroyed all but two or three of the factories between Williamsburg Center and Florence Fields.

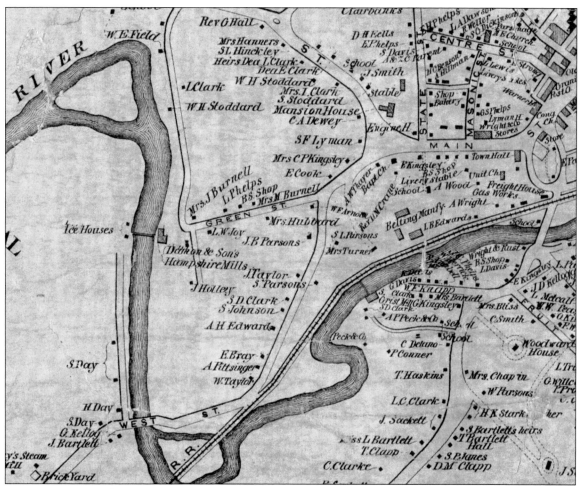

Fig. 4.2 *1860 Walling Map showing the Lower Mills with Silas Clark's grist mill and dam near the center of the map and Damon and Sons' Hampshire Mills at the end of Green Street on Paradise Pond. (Courtesy Forbes Library and Northampton DPW)*

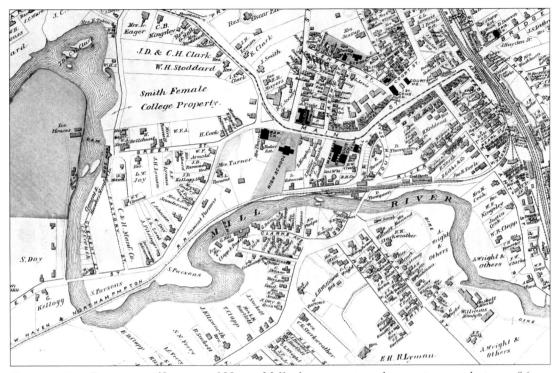

Fig. 4.3 *1873 Beers map of Lower and Upper Mills showing extraordinary city growth since 1860. Note how islands have accumulated between the lower and upper dams suggesting a build-up of sediment between the two dams. (Courtesy Forbes Library and Northampton DPW)*

A network of local Mill River entrepreneurs continued to dominate their communities' enterprises until the 1870s, when outside capital finally began to buy up the silk, textile, and cutlery firms that characterized the Mill River.[16] Factory owners were acutely aware of market trends and traveled to Europe to learn new technologies and to lure expert machinists and artisans back home. Such men as J. P. Williston, Samuel L. Hill, and Joel Hayden became wealthy enough to afford to risk capital on experimental products such as vegetable bone buttons and early plastic formulas. They also left a trail of charitable institutions in their wake: the Hill Institute in Florence and Easthampton's Williston Academy are two prominent examples. Residents throughout the watershed accomplished all this while remaining on the periphery of the enormous changes in the size and complexity of American manufacturing. Even though a coal gasification plant in Northampton lit gas lamps in town beginning in the 1850s,[17] Mill River industries did not convert to steam power until a decade after the Civil War, and it was not until the turn of the twentieth century that electricity overtook steam as the chief energy source for industry.[18]

The Lower Mills—The Collapse of the Wire Mill and Miraculous Survival of its Workers

The only thing left at the Lower Mills by 1860 was Silas Clark's grist mill, as shown on the "Walling" map. At the height of the Civil War in 1863, Horace Lamb from Central Massachusetts rented space from Clark to install a wire-making enterprise on the second floor of the mill's wood-frame building.[19] The old building could not withstand the weight of the new machinery on the upper floor and the 5500 bushels of grain on the ground floor. It collapsed in no time, prompting this October 1, 1863 *Hampshire Gazette* headline: "Falling of the Lower Mills; Four Men Buried in the Ruins; Their Wonderful Escape From Death." Undaunted, the mill owners refurbished the dam and rebuilt the building, again in wood, and the grist mill and wire factory continued to conduct their businesses under water power until the end of the century.[20]

Events, however, continued to stymie any chance of effortless success. In a quick re-run of the Lower Mills vs. Upper Mills court fight of the mid-eighteenth century, a newly constructed factory at the Upper Mills brought suit in 1869 against Clark's mill, charging that Clark, in reconstructing his dam, had increased its height "causing the water to set back and injure the privilege of the [new] hoe factory." The plaintiff's case was judged without merit and Clark prevailed.[21]

As one can gauge from a glance at the 1860 and 1873 maps, Northampton grew quickly after the Civil War as new streets were cut and families and businesses thrived. There remained, however, only the one factory at the Lower Mills. In addition, one large firm on the lower Mill River set up shop in the 1860s: a basket manufacturer downstream from the Lower Mills near the crossroads of Conz (Maple) and Pleasant streets. The factory never used waterpower from the river, but started out with a fifty-horsepower steam engine to prepare materials for handwork. The location was chosen more for its proximity to the railroad than to the river. From 1863 to about 1930, the Williams Manufacturing Co. made baskets of all shapes and sizes, using bamboo, oak, hickory, elm, ash, and beech, which were sent chiefly to New York City but as far away as California. By 1880, Williams Manufacturing, with two hundred hands and 75,000 square feet of floor space, claimed to be the largest basket maker in the country. By 1900, with financial problems and technological change, they were down to sixty workers and much reduced output. Reminiscing about his forty years with the company, one employee remarked on the change in the work-force:

> When Charles Spring entered the employ of the Williams company [in 1858]...most of the employees were native born Americans, i.e. Yankees. A change came over the scene after a time and the Irish people were in the majority in the factory. This condition of things ran along for some years, when another race crowded in and the sons of Erin got out. This time it was the French-Canadians, and at one time the help was almost wholly composed of that race. But more was to come, and a few years ago the Poles began to take a liking to Northampton...and now [in 1898] constitute a majority of the employees.

The mill was badly damaged in a 1910 fire and sold off in the 1920s.[22]

The Upper Mills and the Maynard Hoe Shop

In 1840, the only building left on the Upper Mills was David Damon's saw- and gristmill. Sadly, as had occurred so often over Northampton's first two hundred years, fire and flood made life miserable for the mill owner. In 1844 Damon's mill building burned, and he rebuilt it. Then the 1854 and 1859 freshets damaged the mill, after which Damon once again rebuilt. The mills finally gave up the ghost when fire destroyed them in 1864 near the end of the Civil War.[23]

The war's end brought an enlivened entrepreneurial spirit to the Mill River watershed, and within two years the Upper Mills were given amazing new life with the construction of the famous Hoe Factory built in 1866 by the three owners of the former Bay State Tool Company. They found their perfect site at the Upper Mills, where they constructed the Clement & Hawke Mfg. Co. on David Damon's seven acres of land and buildings that they had bought for $11,000. This was a substantial five-story structure in which most of the space was used to make cutlery and the rest was rented out to other manufacturers.[24] They most likely built the current rock-faced dam at the same time, although it has been refurbished several times subsequently.

The factory had a colorful fifty-year history. Shortly after its beginnings as a maker of household cutlery, it shifted to the manufacture of agricultural tools, namely hoes, shovels, and rakes. The enterprise almost went bust in the 1873 Panic, but Ebenezer Maynard saved it and changed its name to Maynard's Hoe Factory. Fires damaged it in 1871 and 1886; the 1874 flood damaged the dam

Fig. 4.4 Photograph ca. 1895 showing dam repair in front of the Maynard Hoe Shop at Paradise Pond. (Courtesy Forbes Library)

and raceway, and the 1878 flood took out part of the dam. When Smith College opened its doors in 1875, Maynard's Hoe Shop would be its noisy neighbor until the latter's demise in the early twentieth century.

We cannot leave the Upper Mills without mentioning the major landowner on the other side of the river from the Hoe Factory, the Northampton Lunatic Asylum with its half mile of Mill River frontage opposite what would become Smith College's property.[25] It opened in 1858 with the avowed purpose of curing "the insane in the Moralist tradition, a branch of Heroic Medicine, which focused on placing the ill in beautiful environments to stabilize the mind. At its heart, the Heroic Moral system posited that mental illness was generated from an imbalance of the four humors: blood, phlegm, black bile and yellow bile." This just prior to the discovery of germ theory when disease was believed to be caused by "miasma," bad air from fetid wetlands.[26] At the turn of the nineteenth century the institution's name was changed to The Northampton State

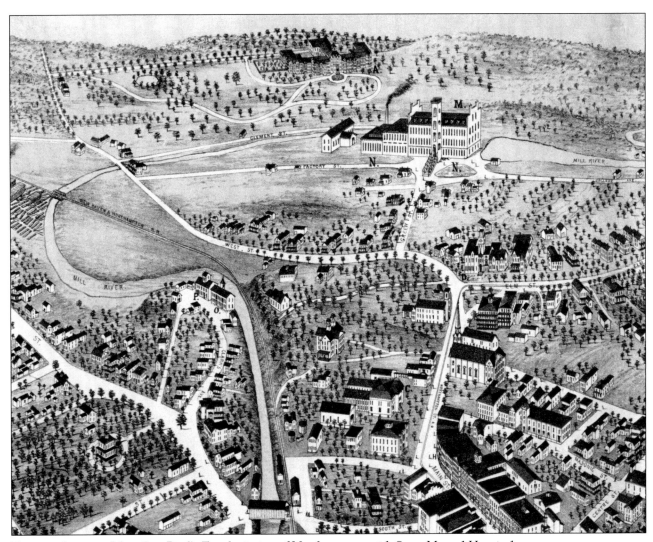

Fig. 4.5 *Section of the 1875 Bird's Eye depiction of Northampton with State Mental Hospital top center, an outsized Maynard Hoe Factory at Paradise Pond and upper Main Street with the South Street covered bridge at the bottom center. (Courtesy Forbes Library and Northampton DPW)*

Hospital, and at the end of the twentieth century the hospital itself emptied out, leaving the legacy of a landscape filled with hints of something evanescent, its demolition celebrated in 2006 with a recording of Bach's *Magnificat* blasting from the window frames. MacArthur award winner Anna Schuleit, creator of the event, made a video of it in ten of the most arrestingly emotional minutes one can experience.[27] The Nonotuck corn-hills became the farm fields for the State Hospital, which finally became the athletic fields for Smith College toward the end of the twentieth century.

Before moving on to Bay State Village, we should mention that the paper mill in Paper Mill Village, which had been started by William Butler during Shays' Rebellion, continued its successful operation during the middle of the nineteenth century as the Eagle Mills Paper Co. Although it burned down in 1860, its owner, William Clark, rebuilt it in 1863 and sold it seven years later to the Vernon Paper Company, which manufactured colored paper. It burned down again in 1878 and was rebuilt once more, this time using both water and steam power. Its paper-making days ended in 1887.[28]

Bay State Village

The empty stretch of the Mill River that Sylvester Judd had tramped in 1837 became occupied just three years later when George Hill, otherwise unremarked upon and no relation to Samuel Hill, built a dam just downstream from Stoddard's Meadow (currently called Maines Field) along with a factory to manufacture rope and other articles from hemp.[29] In 1854, a group from Waterbury, Connecticut bought the property, dam, and water rights to build a factory to manufacture farm tools under the Bay State Tool Co. name. Their main product was a "planter's hoe" for sending to markets in the southern cotton regions.[30] A factory village grew up around the mill, and the neighborhood expanded quickly as other factories relocated to the neighborhood. The Bay State Company quickly failed in the Panic of 1857, but another group of investors—William Clement, C.A. Maynard, and C.W. Hawke—took it over as the Bay State Hardware Co. The company expanded during the Civil War, adding cutlery and gun barrels to its product line. The owners ran into financial trouble after the war, and in 1871, local judge Samuel Hinckley became an investor in a group that took it over, changing its name to the Northampton Cutlery Co. Northampton Cutlery had a long life and only closed in 1987.[31]

A screw factory moved into the section of land at the bend in the river where Hezekiah Reed's Revolutionary War pest house once stood. The New York owners of the International Screw Nail Co. bought an eight-acre parcel of land from Bay State and constructed a three-story brick factory in 1866 that still stands.[32] The screw company failed in the late 1870s, and the expanding Northampton Cutlery enterprise took over and expanded the factory in 1880. A tightly knit neighborhood grew up around the factories. Residents of Bay State to this day take pride in their village, which retains some of New England's finest remnants of industrial factories and housing.

Florence Takes Center Stage

The bankrupt and peripatetic Samuel Whitmarsh, whom we met in the last chapter, left Northampton for Jamaica in 1840 at the instant when the little settlement of Broughton's Meadow was about to burst into industrial bloom. The silk industry was to become one of Northampton's most enduring and profitable manufactures, lasting into the first quarter of the twentieth century, and a series of other enterprises followed, including sewing machines and a plastic molding company that became one of America's foremost hair- and toothbrush makers. Florence became the center of Mill River industries, which lasted far

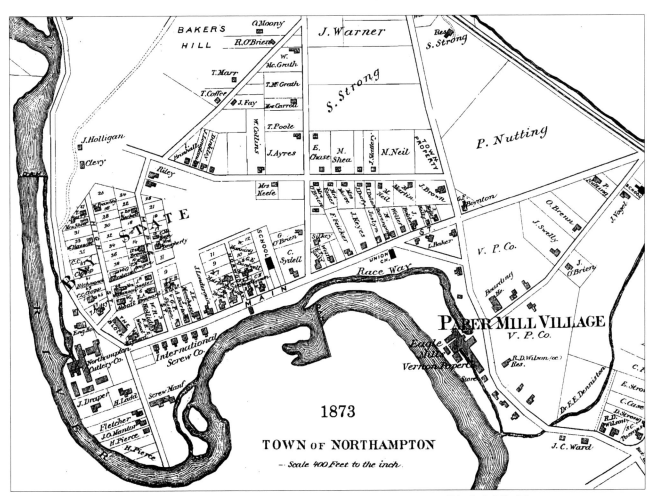

Fig. 4.6 1873 Map of Bay State. Note that the paper mill continues to operate as "Eagle Mills, Vernon Paper" and the cutlery as "Northampton Cutlery Co." A new building at the bend in the river houses the "International Screw Co." (Courtesy Forbes Library and Northampton DPW)

longer than those in other factory villages and spawned a series of other mills upstream in Leeds and Williamsburg. As manufacturing expanded, an experiment in communal living arose simultaneously.

What an extraordinary chapter in American history this turned out to be, the exact point in time when the Northampton Association for Education and Industry was founded. This was, in Christopher Clark's term, "the communitarian moment" during the 1840s when at least fifty-nine utopian communities were established in America.[33] The idea for the NAEI was conceived in 1841 when three men—George W. Benson, Samuel L. Hill, and Hill's friend Hiram Wells — arrived in Northampton from Connecticut. All three were abolitionists and experienced businessmen, well acquainted with the vicissitudes of running a farm or an industry. Although they were still recovering from the economic depression that dogged America after 1837, they pooled their resources to buy Whitmarsh's defunct Northampton Silk Co. and farmland. The trio immediately set about to gather like-minded men, and formed the NAEI in 1842.

In the 1840s, Florence's abolitionists lived cheek by jowl with Northampton's conservative Calvinists and southern visitors who frequented Northampton's tourist spots.[34] The well known anti-slavery activists David Lee Child and Lydia Maria Child had arrived in 1838 and moved to Florence in 1840, determined to compete with producers of slave-grown cane sugar by raising sugar beets for the first time in America. Lydia Maria's two years in Northampton reflect the battle of ideas and passions that raged in the city and the nation in general. She had become a confirmed abolitionist by the time she moved to Northampton where she, ironically, found herself living in a boarding house

> within earshot of the former slave owner and auctioneer, Thomas Napier... Her exposure to slaves, brought to Northampton by vacationing Southerners, cemented her opinion that 'the South will never voluntarily relinquish her slaves, so long as the world stands. It must come through violence. I would it might be averted, but I am convinced that it cannot be.'[35]

She hated Northampton. "I never was in a place that I liked less than Northampton... Nature has been lavish of beauty, but the human soul is stagnant there." She moved with her husband to Florence to expand and develop his dream of a sugar beet industry, but left for New York in 1841 before the flowering of the Community.[36]

The NAEI founders, all of whom came to Florence within a year of 1841, were eager to start a profitable business that would challenge slave-harvested cotton. Silk seemed to them not only a good business decision, but one with anti-slavery implications. One of the founders, Joseph Conant, had been involved in establishing a silk company in Manchester, Connecticut, and he had worked at Whitmarsh's Northampton Silk Co. Samuel L. Hill, another founder who had experience with textile mills in Connecticut, knew Conant. Austin Ross, who came to manage the NAEI farm in 1845, arrived after his Congregational Church in Chaplin, Connecticut rejected his anti-slavery pleas. Other members invested capital, so the enterprise began with a communal passion, technical expertise, and enough capital to commence business, though nowhere near enough to ride out economic roller-coasters and the demands of creditors.

The Community, as it came to be known, adopted principles in which "the rights of all are equal without distinction of sex, color or condition, sect or religion." Women, African-Americans and specifically self-emancipated slaves had equal pay and voting rights. During its four-and-a-half-year lifespan, NAEI welcomed at least 240 men, women, and children into its fold, although a maximum of 120 lived there at any one time, turning the upper floors of the silk mill into a boarding house and dining commons. [37]

Fig. 4.7 Late 19th-century photo of the original combined factory and boarding house that Samuel Whitmarsh built ca. 1837 and which the Northampton Association of Education and Industry occupied from 1842 to 1846. Subsequent owners expanded it over the next century and it was not demolished until 1968. (Courtesy Historic Northampton)

The Community's potential was never realized. They could not make a go of raising silk worms and had to import expensive raw silk, nor could they find markets sufficient to sell the amount they needed to sustain the group. Shortly after their founding, Joseph Conant's cohort left, taking their capital and expertise to establish their own silk enterprise nearby. Samuel Hill originally projected a need for $50,000 in capital, but it turned out to require $100,000. And the hard winter of 1842–43 killed many of the mulberry trees. "The community was locked in a descending spiral from which it could not escape," wrote Christopher Clark.[38] It disbanded on November 7, 1846. Florence remained a factory village apart from almost all other factory villages, a place imbued with a sense of individual responsibility for the commonweal and devotion to the causes of abolitionism and equal rights. Many of the Community's members stayed on in Florence after its dissolution, establishing religious and philanthropic institutions such as the Free Congregational Society and the Hill Institute.[39]

The NAEI made Florence a mandatory stop for radical abolitionists. Some passed through, others stayed for years. Visitors included such notables as Frederick Douglass and George W. Benson's brother-in-law William Lloyd Garrison. Sojourner Truth, formerly enslaved in New York state, found her voice in Florence. Her biographer, Nell Irvin Painter, noted that, "after thirty years in slavery and fifteen years of making herself free through the power of the Holy Spirit, Sojourner Truth ... launched the career of antislavery feminism for which she is known to this day."[40] In 1844 she gave what was perhaps her first antislavery speech. While living at the Benson's house between 1846 and 1848, it is likely she began working with Garrison's friend Olive Gilbert to develop her *Narrative of Sojourner Truth: A Northern Slave.* Four years after the Community disbanded, she bought her own house on Park Street in Florence from the proceeds of sales of her *Narrative.* She left Florence in 1857 to join a spiritualist community in Michigan, spending her final years in Battle Creek.

After an active life in New York City, David Ruggles joined the Community. He was one the nation's first black publishers and a crucial Underground Railroad figure, who had helped more than six hundred former slaves, including Frederick Douglass, escape to freedom. In 1842, Ruggles, almost blind and in poor health, moved from New York City to the Community and regained some of his health by using hydrotherapy. He opened his Northampton Water Cure in 1846, where a who's who of the antislavery movement sought health cures until Ruggles' death in 1849.[41]

Among the many immigrants who stayed in Florence were a number of fugitive slaves, such as Basil Dorsey, who owned a house and worked as a teamster for the local mills for almost thirty years. In 1850, Florence's black community constituted about 10 percent of the village's six hundred people. By that time, the great tide of Irish immigrants had brought destitute Irish families to join the labor force in Florence as well. Of the 129 residents living on Nonotuck Street across from the factories on the river, 63 percent were either African American or Irish American. At the end of the Civil War, Irish-born James O'Donnell, who lived on Nonotuck Street, formed the Eagle baseball club, the first racially integrated organized baseball team in the U.S.[42]

The next decade laid the groundwork for Florence's rapid expansion during the last half of the nineteenth century. First among equals was the silk industry. Samuel Hill led the effort to divvy up the remnants of the Community and to account for all the assets and liabilities. He helped Austin Ross purchase the farm and joined with former members of the Community to organize the Nonotuck Silk Co.[43] The Mill River industrialists became known as the "Florence Group," with names like Hill, Joel Hayden of Haydenville and the Williston brothers based in Easthampton. They combed England and Germany for expert advice and workers, whom they lured to the banks of the Mill in the 1840s and 1850s. In 1843, while traveling in England, Joel Hayden met a young Englishman named Alfred Critchlow from Nottingham and convinced him to help establish a button factory.[44] Critchlow worked for Hayden for a couple of years and went on to invent a material based on shellac that was a forerunner of plastic and played the major role in manufacturing molds for brushes, an industry that dominated Florence for most of the twentieth century. Another young Englishman, William Skinner, who had learned the silk dyeing trade in London, came to Florence in 1845

Fig. 4.8 Statue of Sojourner Truth erected by the Sojourner Truth Memorial Committee at the corner of Pine and Park Streets around the corner from her house on Park. (Courtesy Waymarking.com)

in search of his fortune. Skinner did indeed make a fortune, lost it to the 1874 flood, and regained it shortly thereafter.

In the 1850s, with the invention of the Singer sewing machine and the invention of the "machine twist" that created a much stronger silk thread, Florence's silk industry boomed.[45] Florence began to produce both sewing machines and increasing amounts of the highest quality silk.[46] By 1850, it had become clear to the local citizens that their place needed a new name befitting an important village. On a winter's day in 1852 they met to decide on a name. At the 1852 meeting, German-born Dr. Charles Munde, who expanded the water cure and its hotel, offered an evocative European name for his village.

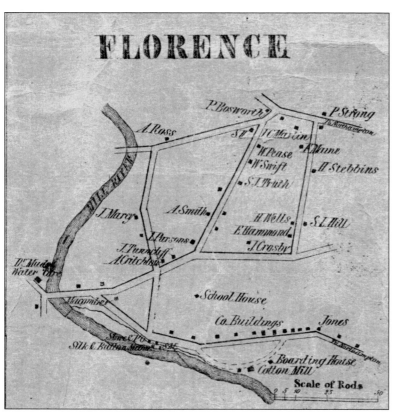

Fig. 4.9 *W.J. Barker's 1854 map of Florence showing the former Whitmarsh/NAEI silk mill as the Greenville cotton mill. The Nonotuck silk mill is upstream shown as "Silk & Button Manuf." with a store and the Florence post office. Dr. Munde's water cure is on the left. Sojourner Truth's house is in the center and the Ross farm is along the river on the upper left. (Courtesy Boston Public Library, Leventhal Map Collection)*

"The pretty village, the clear stream, the silk mill, all suggested to his vivid imagination the propriety of naming the village 'Florence,' and the stream 'Arno.'" The locals adopted Florence unanimously and just as quickly rebuffed the attempt to rename the Mill River as the Arno.[47]

Despite its inauspicious start and its location in what seemed to be a backwater, Florence's silk industry became a phenomenal success. In the 1860s, the silk industry expanded rapidly upriver from its beginnings at the NAEI factory and boarding house. New investors came aboard, adding an imposing brick factory just upstream from the NAEI building in the 1850s.

Simultaneously, the Dimock brothers, part of the Florence Group of investors, took over a defunct textile mill in Leeds a mile upstream from Florence, turning it into the Leeds branch of the Nonotuck Silk Company, which became nationally famous for producing a new brand of silk named Corticelli (the Nonotuck Silk Co. only changed its name to the Corticelli Co. in the 1920s, toward the end of its life). Three miles upstream from Leeds, in the town of Williamsburg, the ambitious young Londoner William Skinner had already opened his new silk mill (in 1854) at a dam site that would soon be known as Skinnerville. Skinner's enterprise was just as successful as the Nonotuck Co. By 1860, three major silk factories were employing several hundred workers along the Mill River.

FLORENCE WATER CURE ESTABLISHMENT NEAR NORTHAMPTON MASS.

Fig. 4.10 Etching of Dr. Charles Munde's Florence Water Cure Establishment, which replaced that of David Ruggles on the same site. (Courtesy Forbes Library)

Florence's second most important industry began flourishing as well. From its roots as Alfred Critchlow's Florence Compound (made from wood fibers, resin, and shellac) this proto-plastics industry developed into a manufacturer of cases to hold daguerreotype and ambrotype images, as well as cases of all sorts for which molding machines were needed. Members of the Florence Group organized the Florence Manufacturing Co., which built a new factory on the Mill River in 1866 upstream from Nonotuck Silk. Florence Manufacturing quickly became known for producing high quality toilet brushes (hair brushes, in today's terminology) and elegant mirrors, all using Florence Compound.[48]

Fig.4.11 Nonotuck Silk Building, which in this 1860s iteration is Littlefield, Parsons Company. Women outnumber men many times over and children form a considerable number of workers. (Courtesy Historic Northampton)

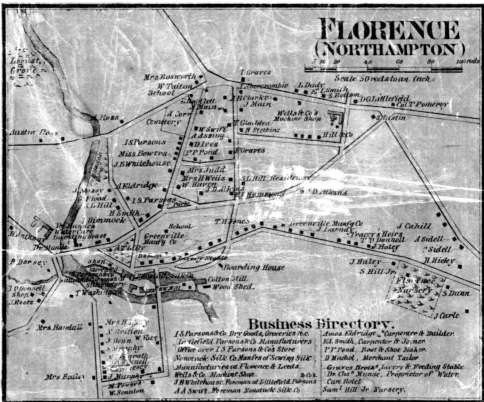

Fig. 4.12 *1860 Walling Map of Florence, which shows explosive growth since 1854. The NAEI silk mill has become a cotton factory and both Littlefield Parsons and the Nonotuck Silk Co. occupy the site of the current Nonotuck Mills. Factory housing and boarding houses dot Nonotuck St., and what is now the center of Florence on Main St. is just beginning to develop. Note "Locust Grove" in the upper left on the Ross Farm, mentioned as a gathering place for abolitionist sympathizers. (Courtesy Forbes Library and Northampton DPW)*

Fig. 4.13 View of the Florence Manufacturing Company, which became the Pro-Phy-Lac-Tic Brush Company, from the bottom of Nonotuck Silk Dam ca. 1890. (Courtesy Florence History Museum)

From the start, hairbrushes became Florence Manufacturing's leading product: everyone needed one, and they tended to be quite costly. "The shape of a hair brush," wrote the author of the company's anniversary brochure, "is one of the things which the ages are not likely to see changed. The oval brush-part—the length, shape and curve of the handle are right. They can no more be improved than the shape of the violin."[49] As medical science improved dramatically in the late nineteenth century, dental hygiene quickly followed, and Florence Manufacturing developed new ways to engineer and market what would become the Pro-Phy-Lac-Tic tooth brush. That same unknown author described its origins:

> The first tooth brushes made here were made by a man sitting at a chuck, a piece of bone before him, boring one hole after another, gauging by his eye the distance apart these holes would be... The curved handle, one of the most distinctive features of the Pro-phylac-tic brush is cut from thigh bones of cattle. No other bone has this curve.[50]

The bristles came from swine raised semi-wild in Russia and Eastern Europe, and the factory cleaned, sorted, bleached, and sterilized them. By the late nineteenth century, labor was replaced by a machine and bone by celluloid, although bone-handled brushes were made well into the twentieth century.

At the end of the nineteenth century, the plastics molding industry challenged silk for primacy of place in Florence. The "Brush Factory" would become Northampton's most important industrial employer shortly thereafter.

What happened to the fields of Broughton's Meadow itself, that ancient arm of Lake Hitchcock with its fertile soils? Samuel Hill had lived in the farmhouse during the heyday of the Community, and after its dissolution, the farmhouse and land passed into the hands of Austin Ross. The farmhouse remained a haven for fugitive slaves for several years, and the house and land stayed in the hands of the Ross family for the remainder of the nineteenth century, chiefly as a dairy farm.

In 1874, the dam on the East Branch of the Mill River in Williamsburg gave way, leading to a disastrous flood, an event of enormous consequence to the watershed, which we will describe as we approach the end of this chapter. The Ross Farm became the terminus of the flood that tore through the upper watershed and dumped its ghastly remnants on Florence Fields, where it spent its force. It severely damaged the Ross Farm as well. Towns from around New England sent volunteers to help search through the six-foot-high piles of wreckage for the forty-two bodies that were eventually found. Then the debris had to be cleared off, and underneath, reported the *Gazette*, "some of the most productive soil in the neighborhood was buried under a stratum of sand and gravel from two inches to two or three feet in depth." Austin Ross, sixty-two years old in 1874, restored the farm with the help of his family and continued to live there until his death at the age of ninety.[51]

By the time the flotsam of the Mill River Disaster ended up on Florence Fields in 1874, Florence had become the centrifugal and centripetal center of the Mill River Valley. The entrepreneurial energy of this cramped geographical space pulled in laborers, inventors, and investors, while it dispersed its force into new enterprises up- and downriver through its auxiliary silk, button, machinery, and textile enterprises. It pulled in immigrants from both the hilltowns and abroad to work its factories. It attracted money from local and regional investors as well as construction workers; inventors of plastic, buttons and silk thread; utopian dreamers; and philanthropists. Florence extended its force

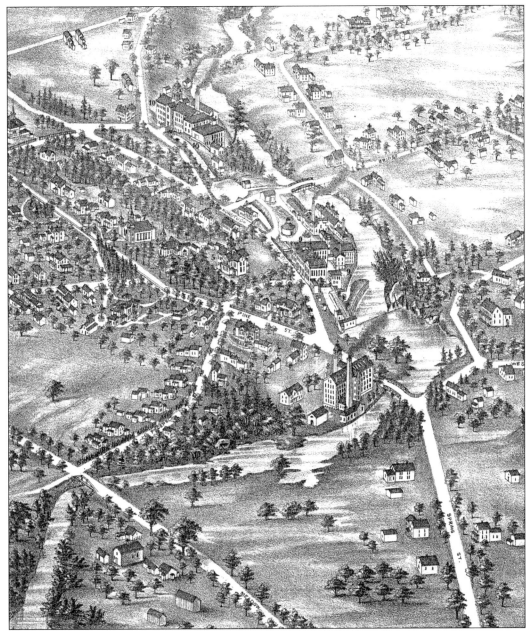

Fig. 4.14 Section of the 1879 Galt & Hoy bird's eye view of Florence. This map shows a flourishing factory village at the height of the First Industrial Revolution. At the bottom left corner is the Ross Farm. In the center stands the Florence Manufacturing Company with the Nonotuck Silk building just downstream below the dam. At the dam is the gatehouse with the headrace directing water into the factory and then out the tailrace into a pond to the left of the bridge. The millrace then runs into the Greenville building of the silk company and back into the river behind the factory at the top of the map. (Courtesy Florence History Museum)

Fig. 4.15 Photo taken shortly after the 1874 Williamsburg Dam Disaster of volunteers searching the wreckage for bodies in Florence Meadows. (Courtesy Forbes Library)

upriver when the Florence Group picked up factories during economic downturns, and helped create reservoirs to ensure a steady source of waterpower ten miles upriver to the headwaters in Goshen. In so doing, Florence became the industrial center of the Mill River, the fulcrum between the Meadows and Highland Lakes. It was the anti-slavery response to conservative Northampton Center. It packed people into company housing, and its factories dumped toxic, concentrated industrial materials into the Mill River.

In short, Florence reflected many of the raging countercurrents in mid-nineteenth-century America. Florence at its peak could substitute for so many villages in mid-nineteenth-century America if, perhaps, it was a bit more colorful, ambitious, and technically advanced. Many readers will find parallels with their own towns, especially if they are old enough to have experienced the rise and decline of small-town life on the periphery of urban regions.

Leeds

During the two decades between 1820 and 1840, the textile industry in Leeds (formerly Shepherd's Hollow) played the leading role in Mill River industry. The village's broadcloth became so renowned that when its first post office opened in 1840, it changed its name from Shepherd's Hollow to Leeds—a reference to Leeds, England, legendary for its own textiles. With the growth of Florence and Haydenville, however, Leeds receded in importance although it remained a vital industrial community with three manufacturers in the third quarter of the nineteenth century—silk, buttons, and emery wheels. These shops were all offshoots of factories that began in Florence with the Florence Group of investors.

The village's leading factory in the 1830s, the Northampton Woolen Co., ran into problems in the 1840s, including a rain burst in 1846 that brought the road down upon the mill in a landslide, tearing away one wall of the building.[52] At last, in the Panic of 1847, the company failed, and members of the Florence Group took over the buildings in the 1850s. Nonotuck Silk picked up two of the mills as an outpost of the Florence factories, and Lucius Dimock and his brother Ira moved from Florence to Leeds and managed the button factory successfully through the end of the century.

The inventive Alfred Critchlow, having moved on from his Florence Compound days in Florence, shifted his activities to Leeds, where he established the enterprise that everyone

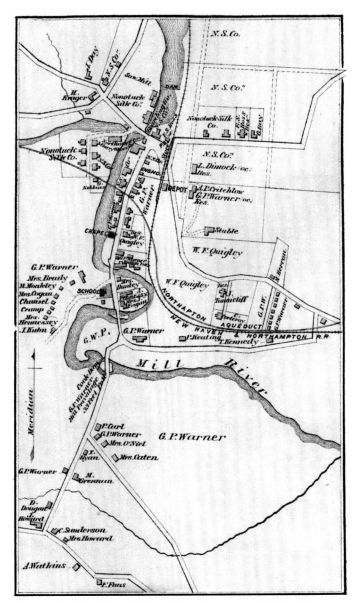

Fig. 4.16 1873 *Beers Map of Leeds one year before the Williamsburg Dam Disaster. The Warner (Critchlow) Button Factory is at the top of the U-shaped river bend in the center of the map, and the Nonotuck Silk Mill is near the top of the map. The Emery Wheel Co. at the confluence of the Mill and its tributary, Roberts Meadow Brook on the left, had moved to Leeds from Florence in 1870. (Courtesy Forbes Library and Northampton DPW)*

called The Button Shop. Its claim to fame was vegetal ivory buttons, made from the ivory-like seeds of tagua palms—washed, dried, hand-carved on lathes, dyed, etched, drilled, and polished.[53] Critchlow was nothing if not creative and had moved into a community that seemed to fit his need for no-frills living. A very short man with a trim gray beard, he was an unusual presence in the village of Leeds. Although an abolitionist with egalitarian values, he lacked any interest in the kind of community social activities that marked Joel Hayden's Haydenville. Sharpe writes tellingly of the condition of Leeds Village:

> As a result [of Critchlow's disinterest in town affairs], Leeds had the reputation for being less inviting, and a little dirtier, than the other mill villages along the river. The road down the middle of the village was a dusty or muddy path, depending upon the season, lined with houses whose front doors opened on to the street. There were no sidewalks, fences, or granite horse-mounting blocks as there were in Haydenville and Williamsburg.[54]

A third factory, the Emory Wheel Company, came to Leeds in 1870, established by one J. L. Otis, a Civil War hero born in Lyme, Connecticut. The company, located at the confluence of Roberts Meadow Brook and the Mill River, focused on grinding wheels and machinery for buffing and sharpening tools and lasted until the early twentieth century.[55]

Williamsburg: Industrial Development and the Factory Villages

Haydenville

From 1840 to 1860, when Florence's industries were still developing and Leeds' were in eclipse, Haydenville became the most important factory village on the Mill. The water power came from the river, but the entrepreneurial power came from the Hayden family, and chiefly from Joel Hayden, Sr. Born in 1798, Joel was the grandson of one of Williamsburg's original settlers, Josiah Hayden.[56] According to Sharpe, Hayden's impact on his village was quite the opposite of Critchlow's on the village of Leeds.

> If you had lived in Haydenville between the 1830s and 1870s, you couldn't have worked, worshiped, banked, belonged to a club, or voted in an election

without encountering Joel Hayden, Sr, his money, or his politics. Hayden was the richest man, largest employer, biggest landlord, and greatest [benefactor in the town of Williamsburg]. He owned a brass factory, a cotton factory, a foundry, and a gas works... He was the Haydenville Bank president, a director of the railroad, the [Master] of the Masonic lodge, the head of the cemetery association, and a member of Hope Engine Company, the local firefighting squad... His political career as selectman, county commissioner, and state legislator culminated with three [one-year] terms as lieutenant governor, as a Free-Soiler and, later, as a Republican.[57]

As a social and political creature, Joel Hayden was everything Alfred Critchlow was not. In an uncrowded world, individuals could shape the culture of any community. Hayden gave Haydenville pride of place in the upper watershed and a presence in the statehouse in Boston.

In the 1840s, Joel worked alongside his brother Josiah and his partner Samuel Williston at the Button Shop, a cotton mill, and a foundry that produced power looms, door locks, harness trimmings, and cast buttons. When Williston moved the Button Shop to Easthampton, Joel Hayden and A.D. Sanders began to manufacture plumbers' goods on a small scale inside the button factory. In 1851 Hayden built the largest factory on the Mill River at that time, named the Brass Works, which employed a hundred workers. It sat at the upstream end of the village, while his cotton mill and gas works were located downstream near the Northampton town line.

By 1870, Haydenville was a thriving, compact factory village with several hundred citizens and all the services a village could want, from doctors and barbers to a grocery and bank. It stood second only in industrial importance to Florence in the Mill River Valley, while Northampton remained the commercial and administrative center. Joel, Sr. had taken on partners in his various enterprises including his son Joel, Jr. and Edward and Collins Gere, brothers of the *Hampshire Gazette* owner/editor Henry Gere. Factories and houses jammed the banks of the Mill River beginning with the impressive Hayden Gere & Company's Brass Works on the left bank with Joel and Josiah Hayden's mansions up the hill opposite the factory. Downstream, the workers' housing lined the right bank along with shops and offices while uphill on the right bank were the Congregational church, hotel, and foundry near the mill pond. Farther downstream were the tobacco works at the dam and below that the cotton mills.

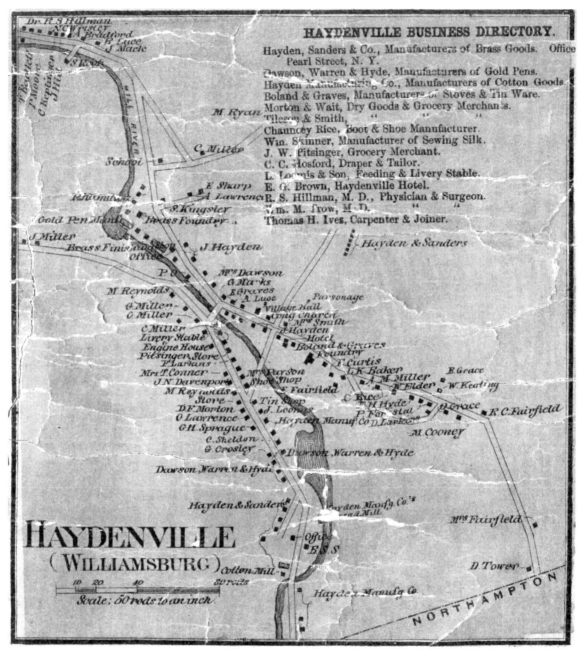

HAYDENVILLE BUSINESS DIRECTORY.

Hayden, Sanders & Co., Manufacturers of Brass Goods.   Office Pearl Street, N. Y.

Dawson, Warren & Hyde, Manufacturers of Gold Pens.

Hayden Manufacturing Co., Manufacturers of Cotton Goods.

Boland & Graves, Manufacturers of Stoves & Tin Ware.

Morton & Wait, Dry Goods & Grocery Merchants.

Tileson & Smith,   "   "   "

Chauncey Rice, Boot & Shoe Manufacturer.

Wm. Skinner, Manufacturer of Sewing Silk.

J. W. Pitsinger, Grocery Merchant.

C. C. Hosford, Draper & Tailor.

L. Loomis & Son, Feeding & Livery Stable.

E. G. Brown, Haydenville Hotel.

R. S. Hillman, M. D., Physician & Surgeon.

Wm. M. Trow, M. D.,   "   "

Thomas H. Ives, Carpenter & Joiner.

Fig. 4.17 *Walling's 1860 Map of Haydenville presents the picture of a busy factory village with the Brass Works and gold pen companies at the north end of town and Hayden's woolen mill at the south end. A "Village Hall" and Congregational Church stand down the street from the Hayden brothers' houses and a full complement of village needs were met by local commercial enterprises. (Courtesy Eric Weber)*

Life in the mills was difficult for many of the workers, who earned about six dollars a week while sitting at a bench twelve hours a day, something "none but a strong constitution can stand [for] long." As one of the workers at a pen point factory in Haydenville put it,

> the people of this village [are] of the most mixed character you ever see. They are composed mostly of Irish, Germans & English. What Yankees there are mostly foremen & overseers in the factories, of which there are three. There is no social or neighborly feeling, none in the least. Hayden (who owns the mills) is better than Dawson [pen point factory owner]. Dawson looks down on the overseers, overseer down on the foremen, they down on the hands generaly, & so on. Of the Irish there are two classes, Protestand [sic] & Catholic. Germans detest te tam [the damned] Irish."[58]

So, it seems like the vision of a happy, patriarchal village that one finds in nineteenth-century novels was not as close to the truth as the factory owners would have liked. There must have been a lot of tension in the air, and how could it not have been otherwise? Money was always tight, the world of the workers essentially depended on the generosity of the factory owners, who, no matter how generous, lived in a world made fragile by flood and ill fortune. Immigration and jealousy created quarrels, and the future could have only been uneasy, given the vagaries of financial life.

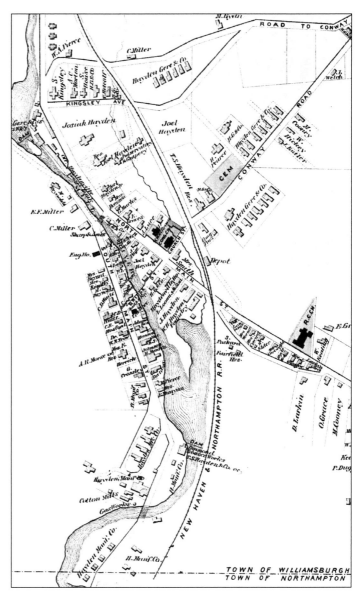

Fig. 4.18 Beers' 1873 map of Haydenville shows how quickly Haydenville had grown in just a dozen years. Here it is at the height of its importance with a new Catholic church for the immigrant workers and a rail line. The Haydens now own the Brass Works, a foundry, a tobacco mill and cotton mill as well as many workers' cottages.

Fig. 4.19 *This is a sketch of the Unquomonk Mills that William Skinner built in 1854 to manufacture and dye silk thread. (Courtesy Eric Weber. Original source is unknown.)*

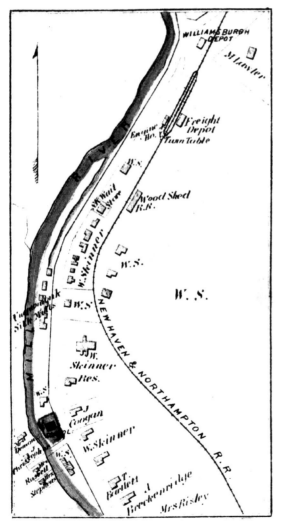

Skinnerville (aka Sweetfern Plain)[59]

William Skinner fit the definition of a self-made man. He exemplified the startlingly rapid pace of life during the mid-nineteenth-century's First Industrial Revolution. He was born in Spitalfields, the silk-weaving district of East London, and, having learned the invaluable secrets of dyeing silk, he emigrated to America to join a fellow Londoner in Northampton, where he shortly became one of the partners in a Florence silk concern. Eight years later, Skinner found a site a mile and a half upstream of Haydenville, at a place called Sweetfern Plain, where in March of 1854 he bought the S.S. Wells Blacksmith Shop and opened his locally-renowned Unquomonk Silk Mill.[60]

Williamsburg Center and Searsville

Williamsburg Center was a center only insofar as it was located at the confluence of the East and West Branches of the Mill River, and centered between Searsville and Haydenville. By 1870 "Burgy" had become a pleasant village with a meetinghouse, some fifty houses, two cemeteries, two churches—Congregational and Methodist—two gristmills, two sawmills, a tannery, a woolen mill, and two button mills. Two of the village residents (Onslow Spelman the button-shop owner, and Lewis Bodman) became men of substance and investors in the Williamsburg Reservoir Company that built the ill-fated Williamsburg Dam on the East Branch. Bodman was a grandson of one of the first settlers of the district and had come to own the Unquomonk Woolen Mill in the mid-1800s.

Fig. 4.20 *Beers' 1873 map of Skinnerville depicts the small 20-year-old mill community that had become the terminus of the railroad up the Mill River. It was a one-industry town of some two dozen houses that lasted only until 1874 when it was utterly destroyed by the Williamsburg Flood. (Courtesy Eric Weber)*

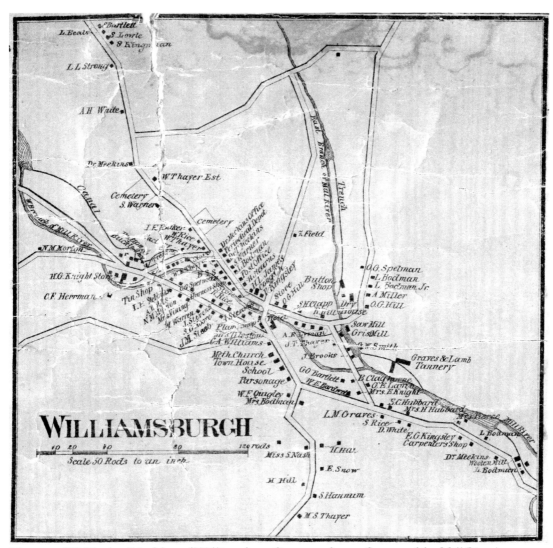

Fig. 4.21 *Walling's 1860 Map of Williamsburg Center at the confluence of the Mill River's East and West Branches depicts a village of streets crowded with homes, a Congregational and a Methodist church, several stores, and small factories including two button shops, sawmills, gristmills, a tannery, and a woolen works. Four small dams control the flow of water for the mills. (Courtesy*

Searsville, Williamsburg's original village, changed little during these forty years, ceding its early importance to villages downstream. The Sears woolen mill continued to function, employing a considerable number of local residents.[61] Searsville factories produced the bricks used in building factories downstream as well as edge tools and buttonmolds that were made at the small dam sites, which also housed saw- and gristmills.[62]

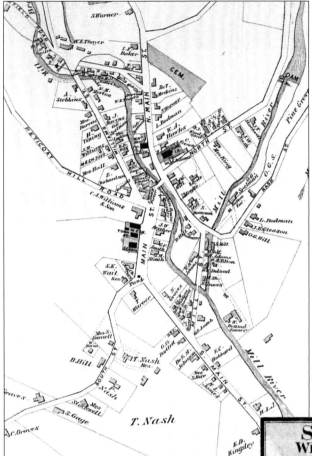

The little factories often had short lives. Failure might come in the form of bankruptcy, but most often as fire, such as the one in the spring of 1872.

When the sawmill at Searsville Reservoir was found to be a fire, well agoing, in a wind blowing strongly from the west, flying embers quickly caught in the leaves and under brush, causing a running fire by wood fences and through grass lots. In a few moments it attained startling proportions, filling the air with burning flying cinders from Searsville over the hill so that buildings as far down as the old Parsonage, on Village Hill, were in danger.[63]

Occasionally the factory owner himself set the blaze, as is the case when Searsville's Levi Bradford set fire to his gristmill in 1878. He had just switched his power source from water wheel to steam, so we are left to wonder why he would have taken such a measure, especially since he continued to rebuild thereafter.[6]

Fig. 4.22 Little had changed in Williamsburg Center between 1860 and 1873. The Beers map has most of the same property owners and enterprises as one finds on the Walling map. (Courtesy Eric Weber)

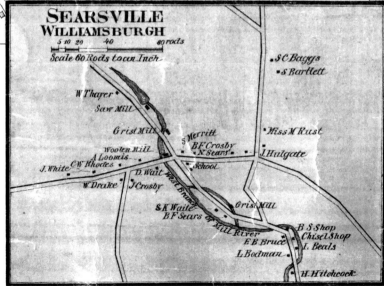

Fig. 4.23 Barker's 1854 Searsville map depicts several mills crowded together along this short stretch of the West Branch: a sawmill, gristmill, the Sears woolen mill, and an edge-tool shop. (Courtesy Eric Weber)

Floods

As Northampton's population quadrupled to more than 12,000 people between 1840 and 1880, the severity of damage from flooding increased commensurately. Five major floods occurred in just the first twenty years of this period, caused by a variety of weather phenomena—spring freshets, a nor'easter, a hurricane. Northampton had yet to expand into the meadows, but a denser building pattern in low-lying sections (Fruit and Maple Streets and the section encompassing Valley, Holyoke, and Hawley streets) meant greater risk of property damage. By the 1850s, the town of Northampton finally saw fit to construct a dike along Lickingwater, running from upstream of the Old South Street Bridge down to Pleasant Street. What follows are tales of the most significant floods during these forty years.

1843 *Flood Spring Freshet*

While the 1840 flood changed the course of the Connecticut River, the one in 1843 did greater damage along the Mill. It started raining on April 14 and continued for several days, prompting the *Hampshire Gazette* to report that

> we are in the midst of a flood, such as has no parallel within the range of forty-two years, if it has any period within the memory of any now living. The lower parts of the town are almost immersed. Maple and Fruit streets are covered with water, to a depth of from one and a half to three feet. All the houses are completely surrounded, and are inaccessible except by boats and horses and carriages. All the cellars are full of water, and barns and out-buildings are so flooded, that it has been necessary to remove many animals to higher ground.[65]

The *Gazette* called for community support as it continued, "But the worst part of the story remains to be told. Early yesterday afternoon, the cellar wall to the valuable brick house, in Maple Street owned and occupied by Messrs. Warren and James Reed, began to give way." After describing the dire condition of the place, the author wonders, "What will be the fate of the house?" One never finds out.

1845–1850 *Spring Freshets*

A series of reasonably large freshets marked the years between 1845 and 1850, floods that barely hit the pages of the *Gazette*, but which Sylvester Judd reported as sufficient to cover the railroad bridges. The usual flooding occurred in Wright, Maple, and Fruit streets as well. Judd noted that in 1847 "a lot of musquash [muskrat] hunters were out."[66]

At decade's end in April 1850, Judd remarks that the "Mill River is high; it is probably higher than the Connecticut, for it has considerable current... At the brick culvert made for the brook between Hawley & Pleasant streets... the water is within 8 or 9 inches of the interior of the arch." Contrary to common sense, people were still building down Maple (Conz) street, and, of course, those houses were flooded, as were the adjacent meadows where the muskrat hunters "were about in small boats or skiffs. They are commonly 2 in a boat with a dog and gun."[67]

As these mid-nineteenth century flood stories began to unspool, a sense of foreboding crept into the author's head. I could hear the river warning the townspeople: "Stay out of my floodplain." At first I heard it as a whisper, but I knew that inevitably the river would raise a cry. Yet as I continued to read and transcribe the stories, I turned away from the river's voice and habituated myself to the inconveniences of floods. I had begun to anticipate the exhilaration of "the Big One," whenever that might occur. I shut out the anxiety and closed my ears to the river's cautionary words. I simply awaited the next exciting account of pigs, cows, rafts, muskrats, and paddling in the streets. When would events become serious? I will let the reader decide.

1854 *Nor'easter*

"The greatest flood ever experienced in this part of the country occurred on Sunday and Monday last," reported the *Hampshire Gazette* on the May 2, 1854.[68] "The damage in all quarters is immense," continued the reporter, who was particularly adept in writing what could be called the Victorian Superlative Voice. This rare May flood was caused by an unceasingly heavy four-day downpour that fell on already soaked ground. Farmers had already plowed the meadows, which had to be allowed to drain before replanting could begin, a fact that severely delayed the growing season.

Excitement, disaster stories, recreational activities, and the customary calculation of comparative flood heights ensued. Sylvester Judd was among those with measuring instruments.

> Men dispute about the heighth [sic] of the Jefferson flood in 1801 and no one knows certainly, though some make confident assertions, on mere conjectures. The general belief is that the present flood is higher than the Jefferson— opinions vary from 3 inches to 6. 9. 12 & 15 inches. I think 6 inches is enough, if not too much.[69]

Once again, Fruit and Maple (Conz) Streets were inundated. As the *Gazette* noted, "Mill River, as a matter of course, followed the lead of its superior, and 'backed up' by the Connecticut, 'spread itself' in all directions." For the first time we have an inkling that residents would not heed the river's warning to stay off the flood plain. Maple and Fruit Streets were navigable only by boat, and houses at the lower end of the streets had to be abandoned. A certain Mr. Tribus was unpleasantly surprised in his newly-bought house to find that his cellar wall had pretty much fallen. On the same street, Mr. Wilcutt was obliged to greet his guests as they "sailed into the parlor through the front door." And Mr. Ansel had to ferry his cows and horses over to higher ground after he had stashed his calf in the attic.[70]

There was major damage all up and down the Mill River. The top of the dam at the Lower Mills (Clark Avenue) disappeared from sight, and the dam at the Upper Mills (the Hampshire Mills) was partially destroyed. Florence sustained considerable damage, and Dr. Munde's famous Water Cure Establishment near the current Arts and Industry building was flooded out. There were reports that many of the bridges from Paper Mill Village upstream had been washed out, but no one died in this flood, despite the stories of near drownings.

Sylvester Judd, as was his custom, noted assorted oddities that attended the flood.

> People were out in abundance today to see the flood, male & female in the mud & in good going. Boys amused themselves by making rafts of boards and other things, swimming about, & sailing about on their rafts... Hunters were out after muskrats. One skiff with 3 men brought in 10 large muskrats. They shot them on the flood trash, among trees... Birds were about the meadow, on the railroad, on trees & on the trash, some were singing in the midst of desolation.

Sylvester Judd often provides us with a window into the mentality of mid-nineteenth New Englanders, and there is no better example than his straightforward observations on this flood. Insistent as he was on accuracy, measurements, and comparisons, he combined it with a keen sense of ordinary enjoyment, beauty, and sadness. "Birds about the meadow, some singing in the midst of desolation." Judd, in his working life and most of his notebooks, remains a no-nonsense Yankee, and the poetry of his writing derives from his gimlet-eyed observations.

1859 *Spring Freshet*

The decade ended with a huge spring freshet that destroyed part of the Northampton-Hadley Bridge, which the *Hampshire Gazette* reported in detail on March 22.

> The ice breaking up, accumulated at 'the bend' above the great bridge, which held until about noon of Wednesday, when it gave way, and in its progress swept off about one-third of the bridge. About one half of this portion was secured at the lower end of Hadley street, and the remainder went down the river, some of it lodging at South Hadley and the residue going over the great dam at Holyoke. A portion lodged at Springfield and served as a bone of contention to sundry Irish people there, who contended stoutly against each other for its possession.[71]

The portion of the bridge that ended up in the hands of the "sundry Irish" of Springfield was the part that had been repaired after the 1840 flood, which created the Oxbow. The Big River was changing its course. In the 1830s, the river channel ran close to the Northampton side of the river; the 1831 map shows a very small Elwell's Island. Over the next twenty-five years the channel shifted east, as Elwell's Island grew, and the Hadley side eroded, a problem the Corps of Engineers continues to try to alleviate to this day.[72]

The Mill River, "always an 'early riser,'" as reported in the *Gazette*, wreaked havoc with the Lower Mill Dam in Northampton proper, where thirty feet of the dam's woodwork was carried away. Meanwhile, at Damon's Upper Mill on Paradise Pond, the right bank of the pond itself gave way at the very same place where it would in the first decade of this century: at the Smith athletic fields. "In a very short time," reported the *Gazette*, the water had forced a passage around the dam, through an embankment three feet above the high-water mark. In its passage it undermined about a third of the ice house of Messrs. Wright & Rust, sweeping off portions of both house and ice. The damage here cannot be less than $2000. It is believed that holes made by muskrats caused the water to cut this new channel. The stone dam stood nobly, a credit to its builders.

One hundred fifty years later, in 2013, muskrats were again at work, undermining the banks, forcing Smith College to partially drain the pond and stabilize the banks. The dam, rebuilt in the 1860s, still stands as an iconic part of the landscape.[73]

In the 1859 flood, we get the first mention of a dike near the South Street Bridge, and its first appearance on a map in 1860. Since there is no mention of a dike in the 1854 flood, it is likely that the people of Northampton had a dike built by a private company after that damaging event.[74] The new dike, constructed just downriver from the South Street Bridge, ran parallel along the Mill to a railroad bridge at the current junction of Conz and Pleasant Streets. It was in danger of collapse in 1859 until local volunteers spent two days and nights shoring it up. These heroic efforts attracted a crowd of some 3000 visitors from the town, according to the *Gazette*.

Newspaper coverage of this flood ends with a clue about Northampton's parsimonious nature when it reported that "the town yesterday appropriated $200 towards repairing the culvert near South street bridge." Almost all efforts to beat back flood waters and support recovery and rescue efforts were voluntary in nature. Citizens expected little help from the local government, and the town obliged. Northampton had never been known to be generous.

1862 "The Lincoln Flood," a spring freshet

In the midst of the Civil War, this flood swept across Northampton like Confederate troops over the Union infantry at the First Battle of Bull Run. "The Greatest Freshet on Record," shouted the *Hampshire Gazette* banner headline of April 22, contending that the flood was two feet higher than that of 1854 and two-and-a-half feet higher than the 1801 Jefferson Flood. Emergency flood crews immediately focused on the new dike, and the *Gazette* reported the fight for the dike as if it were coming from the field of battle.

"Will [the Dike] stand?" was the question asked by all... The afternoon wore away and as each hourly record of the rise was reported—"two inches an hour"—the faces of the most sanguine grew more and more serious. Inch by inch the enemy advanced and at five o'clock it had reached the top of the old embankment. "Shall the fight be continued, or shall we surrender?" was the question. A "council of war" was held at about half past 5 o'clock, at which it was decided to have an alarm. People now rushed down by hundreds. Most of the residents within the dike had taken up their carpets, removed their furniture up stairs, driven away their cows, hoisted their pigs to barn scaffolds, [and] cleared their cellars... Nothing but miraculous power could prevent it from overflowing. It came! At half-past seven a small break occurred directly in the rear of Mr. Josiah Dickinson's house. At first it was about the size of a quart measure, but it increased rapidly. In one or two minutes another stream began to pour over a few feet east of the first break. The earth was swept away as if it were meal. All was lost! The alarm was sounded along the dike, now lined with people, and a perfect stampede occurred. Each man for himself took the highest land with an alacrity and fleetness which would have done honor to rebeldom.[75]

The Lincoln Flood was odd insofar as its cause was solely snowmelt unaccompanied by rainfall. The temperature had reached eighty-two degrees on April 16, melting a considerable snow pack from the winter. Coupled with the backup of water from the 1849 Holyoke dam, the flood's impacts were considerably greater than might have been expected. And because no storms accompanied the melt, the flood's effects were hardly felt upriver from downtown Northampton.

The flood, however, did serious damage to the Maple and Fruit Street neighborhood, which the dike could not protect. For example, the house in which the estimable historian J. R. Trumbull was then living was inundated throughout the first floor and "fifty or more volumes of valuable books were submerged; also bedding, clothing &tc." The *Gazette* also mentioned the Meadows, which were cleared of "snakes, mice, muskrats, woodchucks, skunks, and all other animals. Large numbers of field mice were found on Sunday by exploring parties. A dozen or more were found on one limb."

1869 Hurricane

On October 5, a Category 2 hurricane hit New England, dumping about a foot of rain on the Connecticut Valley over two days, and this time the Mill River was not spared damage, for "it was never known to be higher in the memory of the oldest inhabitant."[76] The storm arrived at a terrible time for farmers, just after harvest when all the corn had been cut and both stalks and cobs were waiting to be picked up in the fields. William Field, who lived on the banks of the Mill near Paradise Pond, was nearly drowned when, in trying to secure his cornstalks, he ventured too near the dam of the Hoe Factory. His boat was swept over the dam, but, just at the top of the dam "he leaped out and fortunately cleared the undertow and was saved by a rope thrown from a window of the factory."[77]

While Bay State factories and canals barely escaped major damage, Maynard's Hoe Shop at Paradise Pond had flooding in its forge and grinding departments. Downriver, Clapp and Pomeroy's gristmill at the Lower Falls was undermined and fell in. King Street Brook overflowed, inundating all the basements along that street. The dike, however, held for the most part, thus protecting Maple and Fruit Streets.

Upriver, Florence appeared to have escaped major damage, and Leeds only lost a section of its railroad track. Williamsburg, however, with its bare hills, was caught in a flash flood when the river rose two feet in just a few minutes, carrying off eight bridges and buildings. "The roads were fearful washed and the total loss will run up many thousands."[78] The Searsville Reservoir broke out into the road, and downstream, William Skinner's dye house and other out buildings were swept away, and the factory's foundations endangered.

1874 The Williamsburg Dam Disaster

In 1874 the dam on the Mill River's East Branch gave way, leading to America's deadliest industrial accident up to that point.[79] "It was one of those appalling calamities such as rarely visit any community, and is calculated to leave its dread memorials in the hearts and brain for long years afterwards."[80] To the point, it was the defining moment in the history of the upper Mill River.

The story of the 1874 Williamsburg Disaster has been given thorough treatment by Elizabeth Sharpe in her 2007 *In the Shadow of the Dam: The Aftermath of the Mill River Flood of 1874* that we will only briefly describe some of its highlights. In Sharpe's telling, the disaster becomes not only a story of death and destruction, but a fable for our time. Who was responsible, who bore the cost, and who, if anyone, paid the price? These are questions of accountability that haunt our current era. William Skinner's great-great granddaughter, Sarah Skinner Kilborne, added colorful context to stories of the Disaster along with details that fill out the character of some of the villages and the reasons why some factory owners rebuilt and others did not.[81]

As industry expanded in the villages along the Mill River, the demand for more reliable waterpower increased. Joel Hayden had purchased a mill site and land for a reservoir at the headwaters of the West Branch in Goshen in 1839 and had then rebuilt and substantially enlarged it in 1854. (It is now called Lower Highland Lake.) Factory owners up and down the valley were eager to invest in another reservoir. In 1864, Joel Hayden initiated the formation of the Williamsburg Reservoir Company with such notables as Lewis Bodman and Onslow Spelman of Williamsburg, William Skinner of Skinnerville, Alfred Lilly, Lucius Dimock, Samuel L. Hill of Florence, the owners of the Bay State Cutlery, and Northampton's J. P. Williston. Two years prior, Joel had found a suitable dam site on the East Branch of the Mill three miles upstream from Williamsburg Center on the back acreage of Simeon Bartlett's farm. The dam was designed to be forty feet high, creating a hundred-acre reservoir that contained over seven hundred million gallons of water. Work began under the supervision of a number of Reservoir Company members, but Joel, who had supervised the building of the Goshen dam {Lower Highland Lake) in 1840 and its reconstruction on the West Branch in 1854, was preoccupied with his office as Massachusetts' lieutenant governor and could barely keep an eye on the work as it progressed. In trying to save money in design and construction, the company ignored the advice "to have the work looked over carefully" by a competent engineer and instead made some crucial errors: reducing the size of the outlet pipe, failing to tamp down the earthen embankments of the dam, and basing some parts of the core wall on gravel rather than bedrock or hardpan. The builders did not even fully mortar the core wall.[82]

Problems of leakage and slumping occurred from the very first, and despite

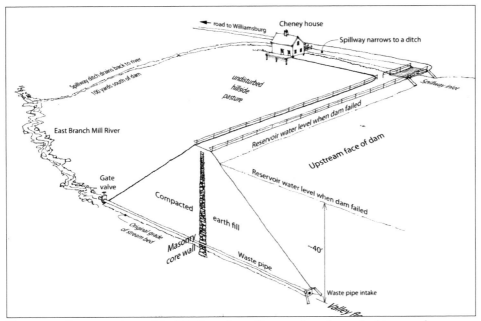

Fig. 4.24 Cutaway view of the Williamsburg Dam and environs, looking southwest and downstream, from original stream bed to west end. (Eric Weber illustration)

improvements, the integrity of the dam was always problematic. Joel, who had supervised the reservoir's operations from 1866–1873, kept a constant eye out on its condition, never allowing the reservoir to become more than about half full. "A half-full reservoir holding 300 million gallons of water was better than no reservoir. Coaxing and coddling a lame dam was less costly than removing it and building a new one."[83] To increase reservoir capacity, Joel and the Mill River Reservoir Company started construction on another reservoir in 1872 just above the Lower Highland Lake in Goshen. The latter, predictably named Upper Highland Lake, is now located in the DAR Sate Park. This appeared to alleviate the demand for water to run the mills downstream.

But Joel had taken ill that same year and, while he was able to inspect the Williamsburg Dam to his satisfaction one last time in the spring of 1873, he died in November. One of Joel's partners, Onslow Spelman, secretary-treasurer of the Dam Company and owner of a button shop in Williamsburg, took over as informal dam supervisor. In Elizabeth Sharpe's words:

> Spring 1874 arrived late. During the last two weeks of April, four big storms dumped so much snow that Williamsburg residents took sleighs to church the last Sunday in April... When warm weather finally came a week later, as if

Fig. 4.25 Remains of the dam with the caretaker's house unharmed. Note the highlighted stone in the photo. It marks the edge of the road today. (Courtesy Williamsburg Libraries)

to make up for lost time, Spelman instructed gatekeeper George Cheney to close the gate pipe to fill the reservoir, and keep it closed. Cheney complied. The reservoir seemed to fill all at once. Within a week, 600 million gallons of water pressed against the earthen dam, from the base to within a few feet of the crest.[84]

On the morning of May 16, 1874, Cheney noticed a forty-foot-wide section of earth slough off the dam face. He immediately went down to open the gate valve of the wastepipe. Then, leaping on his horse bareback, he pressed his mare down the river road barely fifteen minutes ahead of the imminent flood to warn downstream villagers. Others heroically carried on, warning mills downriver in Skinnerville, Haydenville, Leeds, and Florence.

Meanwhile, back at the gatekeeper's cabin, Cheney's wife Elizabeth positioned a chair on the porch where she could watch the dam. About twenty minutes after the slide on the east bank, she saw and heard the eastern half of the dam explode upward.

Elizabeth Cheney would later testify at the county coroner's inquest that it "seemed to burst all at once, from the bottom, where the earth seemed to be lifted up," as though someone had inserted a giant shovel under the base and thrown the dirt skyward.[85] As the ground heaved, a column of dirt and rock rose in the air, but instead of falling back to earth, it was pushed forward by the great surge of reservoir water, suddenly freed of the dam. She said it "made an awful noise, like an earthquake."[86] A *Gazette* reporter told the sad story:

> Hardly had the warning been announced when the deluge was upon them, wild, impetuous, resistless and terrible as fate. The first rush of the advancing flood was formidable as a tidal wave, sweeping everything before it. It rolled onward in a billow from six to ten feet in perpendicular height, laden with a mass of flood wood composed of dismantled houses, bridges, factory buildings, fences, uprooted trees of enormous size, dead animals, and, fearful to relate, human bodies,—men, women, and little children,—rent, bruised stripped of their clothing, and battered almost beyond the power of recognition.[87]

In fact, the reporter underestimated the height of the flood wave as it approached Williamsburg Center. Although it is true that the height of the flood varied widely, Eric Weber, president of the Williamsburg Historical Society and expert on the Dam Disaster, has no doubt that the leading wave was at least 20 feet high where it entered Williamsburg Center at Spelman's button shop.[88]

> [The wave] knocked all the walls out from under the factory's heavily built, rigidly triangulated roof, then floated the intact roof three hundred feet downstream. Just below the confluence of the East and West Branches, where the valley widened to more than 400', the flood spread out and obviously grew shallower, but it was still deep enough to carry two dozen houses and other buildings entirely away before it reached where the pharmacy is today. A large pine tree at the confluence of the two branches had all its bark battered off to a height of about 20'.

The flats at Skinnerville were probably covered by no more than seven feet of water, rubble, and debris, but through the narrows between Haydenville and Leeds it was up to twenty-five feet in depth. "Everywhere it went, it was pushed this way and that, piled against one obstacle and diverted away from others, by the underlying topography, by structures that resisted, and by temporary dams of flood-borne debris that changed from moment to moment."[89]

Fig. 4.26 Bird's-eye view of the Williamsburg Dam Disaster from Harper's Weekly, 1874. (Courtesy Eric Weber)

One observer wrote that

> the floodwave looked like a hayroll, but instead of strands of hay, the roll was comprised of trees, timber, roofs, boulders, mill wheels, furniture, animals, and people, with no water visible... Most of the factory workers escaped, and the majority of the dead were women, children, and older people at home eating breakfast or doing morning chores. Half of the victims were immigrants, mostly from Canada and Ireland. Within an hour of the dam break, 139 were dead, 740 were homeless, and the villages of Williamsburg, Skinnerville, Haydenville, and Leeds were washed away.[90]

Every factory village from Williamsburg Center to Florence felt the fury of this awful series of stupid mistakes and misjudgments that ended the existence of one village and destroyed much of three others. When George Cheney rode pell-mell into Williamsburg, he stopped first at the house of Onslow Spelman, the dam supervisor, to warn him of impending disaster. The men argued. Spelman couldn't believe the dam had given way, but Cheney insisted, and finally Spelman ordered Cheney to get a fresh horse and ride downstream to warn Skinnerville and Haydenville. According to Sharpe, "It had taken Cheney [about fifteen] minutes to ride to reach the village and several minutes for him to convince Spelman that the dam was breaking."[91] While Cheney was getting his horse at the stables, Collins Graves, a local farmer, who was delivering his milk that day, drove into the yard. He saw the stricken Cheney, got news of the dam break, and took off with his mare and wagon downstream.

As Graves drove down toward Haydenville, Cheney rode past the Williams House hotel, warning residents along the way of the flood, but before he could get far downriver, high water cut him off and he returned home to look after his family. Word of the coming flood at first only reached residents along the West Branch from one person to another as each ran down the road. By the time the church bells rang, the waters were already upon the lower part of the village.

Graves continued down Main Street, crying out warnings to those along the road, heading directly to Henry James' woolen mill with its fifty workers. Meanwhile, Spelman stood waiting on Potato Hill opposite his shop between North St. and the East Branch, watching the flood as it carried away Sarah Bartlett's house along with Sarah and her daughter, the first to die in the flood.[92] Spelman then watched his button factory disappear. As Sharpe described it, the flood tore down the dam, then the torrent pounded the mill building with such force that it swept the mill out from under the roof, which floated four hundred feet downstream. All that remained was the rocky ledge the factory had sat on and two wooden sheds... Spelman's workers had escaped unharmed.[93]

The churning mass of the flood next picked up William Adams's sawmill and gristmill and then took more lives. Adams found his wife and children safe, but in trying to cross back to his sawmill, was knocked down, and the water "carried his body a mile downstream where it was covered so deeply with sand that only two fingers protruded."[94] The river took the lives of more than a dozen people between the gristmill and Hayden's cotton mill. Back upstream, at James' cotton mill, Collins Graves was, fortunately, taken at his word, so many of the workers escaped, but seven were killed. The dead at Williamsburg Center numbered fifty-seven, a grievous toll indeed.

Fig. 4.27 After the flood, Rev. Gleason of the Congregational Church, put up crude signs in Williamsburg indicating the locations of vanished houses to help disoriented survivors find their way among places that had once been familiar. This one read "Dr. Johnson's—six drowned." (Courtesy Williamsburg Libraries; caption by Eric Weber)

Fig. 4.28 Empty riverbank where William Skinner's Unquomonk Mills had stood. Skinner's damaged mansion is seen behind the site of the former mill. The house was moved disassembled and rebuilt in Holyoke and is now Wistariahurst Museum. (Courtesy Williamsburg Libraries)

On the evening May 13 just over forty-eight hours before the dam broke, William Skinner, then a board member of the newly-formed Silk Association of America, was at the Association's annual dinner at Delmonico's in New York City, giving a speech full of optimistic predictions for the future of the American silk industry. On the fifteenth, he was on the 3:00 p.m. northbound train from Grand Central Station headed for Skinnerville, where he was expected at 9:05 that evening on the train called "the Burgy Flyer."[95] In Sarah Skinner Kilborne's words,

> As he walked up the steps to his front door, there in the middle of Skinnerville, with the river flowing reliably behind him, the mill at rest across the way, the houses of his neighbors and employees all around, and a reunion with his wife and children just seconds ahead, there wasn't one clue, nor any sign, that the very next morning nearly everything in his world would be swept away.[96]

In the early morning of May sixteenth, nothing seemed amiss in the half-mile-long string of about thirty-five buildings, home to two hundred people, most of whom worked at William Skinner's Unquomonk Silk Mills.[97] Suddenly

Collins Graves raced into Skinnerville, warning residents of the impending flood, pleading with the superintendent to evacuate everyone before he continued downstream to Haydenville. One Skinnerville resident, when he looked upriver toward Williamsburg, saw "what looked like a huge cloud of thick smoke and remarked to his companion that 'they are all burning out up there.'" He had mistaken the torrent's spray cloud for a fire.[98] The millworkers quickly emptied out of the factory, streaming up the railroad embankment on the other side of the road behind Skinner's mansion while Skinner joined in helping everyone to get to safety, shouting "To the hills! To the hills!"

> The water had taken fifteen minutes to pass through Skinnerville, and when it was gone, so too was Skinnerville...Where half an hour before had been an enviable industrial village, busy with orders of colorful silk thread to be filled, there was now a mud-swept landscape strewn with timber and rocks, raked utterly clear of [any] trace of life.[99]

Onward rushed Collins Graves from Skinnerville, barely ahead of the flood, and found himself trying to convince Samuel Wentworth, supervisor of the Brass Works, that Haydenville was about to be inundated. Wentworth, convinced he knew more than the farmer, maintained that it would take four

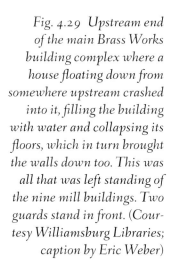

Fig. 4.29 Upstream end of the main Brass Works building complex where a house floating down from somewhere upstream crashed into it, filling the building with water and collapsing its floors, which in turn brought the walls down too. This was all that was left standing of the nine mill buildings. Two guards stand in front. (Courtesy Williamsburg Libraries; caption by Eric Weber)

days for the water to get there, thus losing valuable time to evacuate the factory. But another rider, who had tried to return upriver to Skinnerville, hurried back down to warn the residents of Haydenville of what he had witnessed. In his interview with a newspaper, the reporter wrote that Wentworth estimated the height of the flood at thirty feet, not ten feet as in the previous description:

> Once he looked behind, the air seemed to be full of flying timber. Great trees were turning end for end; now their enormous roots were in the air, and then he would see their trunks and branches whirling round. At the top of the perpendicular wall of water, advancing down the valley, 30 feet high, were seen houses and barns turning over.[100]

Nothing, save the noise and darkness of the flood, could convince Wentworth of the danger. But the workers, having heard whispers of disaster, rushed out of the Brass Works across the road to higher ground.

> The rush of water emptied all nine buildings of machinery, raw materials, patterns, molds, and finished goods, and then dissolved the buildings. One writer said that the brass works melted away 'like a pyramid of sugar in hot water, sinking out of sight almost instantly.' All that was left was the center section of the brick upper shop and a smokestack from the boiler.[101]

The flood enveloped almost everything downstream of the Brass Works—a dozen or more tenement houses, one boarding house, the barbershop, tinshop, stove shop, the grocery and boot shop, the blacksmithy, stables, factory buildings and all four iron bridges. After crushing the foundry and tobacco mill, the flood took a direct path across the curve in the river, avoiding the cotton mill, one of the few factory structures that remained. "In less than eight minutes, Hayden's monument, which had taken him a lifetime to build, was a wasteland."[102] Twenty-seven villagers had died, most of them Canadian women and children who lived near the bottom of Haydenville.

The flood struck Leeds a little after 8:00, taking out all of the dams, injuring the upriver mills and houses, and decimating Main Street, sweeping away all factories and buildings save for three small homes.[103] The terrible wave of water-borne mud, buildings, and drowned animals and people grazed the Nonotuck Silk Mill, then "broadened to almost the entire width of the village, so that nothing and no one could escape its embrace." The Silk Mill's boarding house on the east side of the river was picked up and tossed across the road, careening into buildings and killing two women who could not escape. The flood's onslaught carried one building after another downstream, houses smashing against each other, whole families either carried away or saved by happenstance. Walter Humphrey, clinging to the roof of his floating house, managed to grasp his neighbors' helping hands and landed safely inside the Quigley house. Fred Howard, a boxmaker at the Button Mill, got most of the workers out of the factory, dragging one girl up to safety and hauling another worker up by his collar while watching others disappear in the waves. Howard described what he saw in a letter to his brother:

> ... all this time other houses were falling or sailing down the stream only to be dashed to pieces a short distance below. The whole valley was a wild torrent filled with men, women, and children, horses and cattle, trees and broken houses, the former waving their hands and crying for help till some timber struck them and either killed them outright or pushed them under and drowned them... You must remember that all this occurred in a very short time, probably in one minute after I first saw the water... I was on the railroad [track] and in another minute both shops were gone and in less than ten minutes from the first warning the water had begun to recede.[104]

William Skinner was left with nothing except his debts and the questions of where to rebuild and how to lend a hand to everyone in his community. He quickly set about soliciting the general public for the precise supplies his villagers needed. "He sent one request to Springfield 'for clothes for seven boys ages

Fig. 4.30 Searching for brass goods downstream from the remnant of the Brass Works (Courtesy Eric Weber)

6, 10, 11, 14, 15, 17, 20—and six girls—ages 16, 6, 5,4, 3, 2—and some baby clothes." He established a bank account in New York to collect money for a relief fund to help his workers through hard times.[105]

While he was finding relief for the villagers, at the same time he had to make immediate plans to pay his debts, which meant going back into the silk business. He moved quickly, choosing to rebuild his business in the new planned-industrial city of Holyoke rather than remain in the Mill River Valley.[106] On October 2, William Skinner's son, Will, Jr., wrote in his diary, "Pulled up stakes and left Haydenville. Bill & I drove down in buggy."[107] The Skinner family moved to Holyoke, shipping the disassembled Skinnerville mansion there, mostly by rail, where it remains today as Holyoke's Wistariahurst Museum.[108]

Over the course of the next quarter century, William Skinner enjoyed a meteoric rise, and, by the time of his death on February 28, 1902, his estate was worth $3 million, about $475 million in current dollars.[109] As part of his legacy, he left to his family the William Skinner & Sons Silk Mill, with its central building a thousand feet long stretching over three city blocks and more than five acres of floor space. It was considered the largest silk mill under one roof in the world.[110]

As for Skinnerville itself, it became a lost village, and only locals now know the name. Hidden away on a roadside berm across the highway from the river, in a commercial area called the Village Green, an unobtrusive marker stands as sole witness to Skinnerville's existence.

At the time of the Disaster, Joel Hayden, Jr. was the managing partner of Hayden, Gere, and Co., owned by Hayden, Collins Gere (Henry's brother) and Sereno Kingsley, who plays no major part in this story.[111] Joel posted a notice the day after the flood that he had plans to rebuild an even larger factory than the one his father built.[112] He doubted, however, that he could convince the railroad company to build a branch line to him for free, and began receiving offers to relocate from far (Brooklyn, Bridgeport, Jersey City, Providence) and near (Holyoke, Hartford, Chicopee, Springfield). Joel began to dither, but, unlike Skinner, he had deep roots in the Mill River Valley and owned a great deal more property. Businessmen throughout the valley jumped in to help persuade Joel to remain. Contributions for survivors flowed in from all parts of the country, and fifteen Northampton men agreed to lend Hayden, Gere & Co. $100,000—a third of the total required—to reconstruct the Brass Works, and Henry Gere, the *Gazette's* editor, wrote a passionate plea in the newspaper:

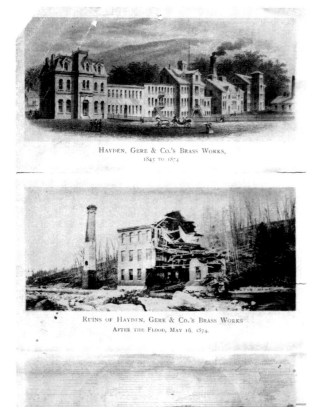

HAYDEN, GERE & CO.'S BRASS WORKS,
1845 TO 1874

RUINS OF HAYDEN, GERE & CO.'S BRASS WORKS
AFTER THE FLOOD, MAY 16, 1874.

NEW MANUFACTORY OF HAYDEN, GERE & CO.
HAYDENVILLE, MASS.

WAREHOUSE,
84 BEEKMAN STREET,   1875.   WAREHOUSE,
NEW YORK.   17 & 19 UNION ST.
                                           BOSTON.

Fig. 4.31 Commemorative card of Haydenville Brass Works before and after the 1874 Flood. (Courtesy Forbes Library)

It is not a light undertaking to remove a large business from its birth place and the place of its mature years, to a new locality. In Haydenville, the people employed in the works were a community in themselves. The company there has complete control—it can make and unmake its own laws. In larger places it must do more as others dictate... we speak the voice of the people for miles around, where we express the earnest hope that the company will not leave the spot where it has flourished so well.[113]

Joel did start rebuilding in late 1874, but was struggling to keep up with payments to construction workers and tradespeople. By 1876, he was in such financial distress that he began reducing the wages of all his workers and staff, some of whom went on strike or simply left. In 1877, Collins Gere withdrew from the partnership, marking the end of Hayden, Gere & Co. Joel, Jr. left to search for his fortune in Lorain, Ohio, where he remained until 1890, after which, he returned to Northampton. By 1905 he had relocated to Boston. His sad story ended when he died penniless in 1918.[114]

The Brass Works managed to survive under several different partnerships, even through the financial troubles of the 1890s. In 1899, the Hills brothers—Christian, Albert, Henry, Reuben, and Jacob—local boys who grew up within a mile of the Brass Works, bought the factory and ran it successfully through the first half of the twentieth century. It closed in 1954.

Of the 139 lives lost in the disaster, fifty-one died in Leeds. General John L. Otis, whose Emery Wheel shop was not heavily damaged, was put in charge of the post-flood rescue and relief efforts. Dimock and Warner quickly rebuilt and repaired their factories in 1875, and Nonotuck Silk and the Emery Wheel works continued in business. Leeds memorialized her dead on a plaque in a stone by the side of the Mill River on Main Street in 1999.

What sadness there was following the flood to find the majority
of the dead were women and
children. One must remember that
the huge wave of mud, trees, bodies,
and buildings passed through in
only ten or fifteen minutes, and
the riders had barely had time to
warn the factories. The women and
children, caught at home in their
factory housing were often taken
by surprise unless they had heard
the cries of alarm or had family or
neighbors warn them. The forty-two
bodies recovered at Florence Fields

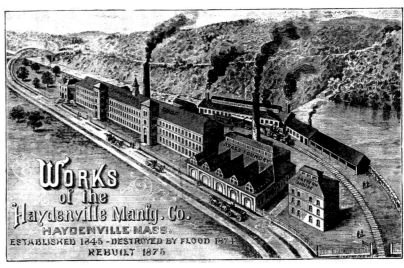

Fig. 4.32 *1890 Illustration of the Brass Works, known then as the
Haydenville Mfg. Co. (Courtesy Eric Weber)*

testified to the broken dreams of the families who had made the factories run.

Who was responsible? Who was charged with negligence? Those questions were left to an inquest that the Hampshire County coroner conducted immediately after the disaster.[115] The inquest jurors quickly returned their verdict
in July, charging five parties with abrogating their responsibilities: 1. Massachusetts lawmakers for lax legislation; 2. Proprietors of the reservoir for placing prof-

Fig. 4.33 *Photo taken from
the railroad bed in Leeds
showing part of the oxbow
bend below Warner's
button factory, of which
only the smokestack and
part of the steam engine
remain. To the right of
the mill site, William
Quigley's large white
farmhouse and one or
two others remained near
their foundations; a dozen
or more others had gone
down the river. (Courtesy
Williamsburg Libraries;
caption by Eric Weber)*

Fig. 4.34 *Looking upriver in Leeds from the present site of the brick mill that was built after the flood. Behind the two men in the left foreground is the ruin of the emery shop dam. Men in the middle distance stand on an improvised footbridge where the vanished Mulberry Street Bridge had been. The silk mill buildings stand at left on what is now the Chartpak parking lot, and in the distance at center is the ruined silk mill dam. The silk mill boardinghouse, where many of the mill girls lived (and some died), had stood just to the left of the surviving building at far right. (Courtesy Williamsburg Historical Society; caption by Eric Weber)*

it before lives; 3. Engineers for their poor design; 4. Contractors for poor construction, and 5. County Commissioners for failure to exercise oversight and discharging their most important duties in the most superficial manner.

The jurors had accurately nailed the culprits, who had neglected their moral responsibility. Still, no fines were paid, no penalties levied. "Survivors [writes Sharpe] didn't react, protest, storm anyone's house, or hang anyone in effigy... If villagers gossiped or fumed about hostile actions...the papers didn't mention them. Rather than expressing malice or powerlessness, villagers were shocked to think that their local manufacturers had caused the flood."[116]

Public outrage did, however, result in one positive outcome. A year after the disaster, Massachusetts enacted the state's first dam safety regulations, which required approval of designs for new reservoir dams.

After the flood, a few factories managed to rebuild, although most of them encountered severe financial headwinds. Some, like the James Woolen Mill, struggled for a decade or so and then went out of business. Spelman rebuilt his stone dam and button works, which he sold to Frederick Crosby in 1882, after which Spelman left for Westfield.[117] Others in Haydenville and Leeds were taken over by Northampton and Florence enterprises, such as Nonotuck Silk. Factories in Florence and the Nonotuck Dam were only slightly damaged. But, in Sarah Kilborne's words, "the northern portion of the valley lost its industrial pulse forever."[118]

A Coda: The 1878 Freak December Storm

Just four years after the Williamsburg Dam Disaster, a strange and terrible flood visited the Mill River watershed, dealing another blow to Williamsburg, although no lives were lost. The 1878 Flood is the only major December flood on record. Its cause was a freak storm that dumped a half-foot of snow on the area followed by a warm south wind along with rain that fell unceasingly in sheets for the next twenty-four hours.

Everywhere there was water. Down the hillsides it came with rushing force, filling the streams with surprising rapidity, and causing them everywhere to overflow. Hundreds of bridges were carried away. Many buildings were destroyed, the roads were badly washed, and along every stream there was a fearful scene of disaster and ruin.[119]

> The river from Williamsburg to Florence was once again hit hard, while the area downstream into Northampton suffered minor damage. The snow held in place until the afternoon of Tuesday, the 8th of December when ... it began to rise uncommonly fast at Williamsburg. At four it was alarmingly high, and shortly after that it had flooded the street in front of James' store and the church, and from that point to the brass shop at Haydenville, the valley was covered with a foaming torrent, which was a more terrifying sight to the inhabitants than the great flood of 1874, as it lasted longer. Nearly every house on the river banks was surrounded, and it was thought that more damage would be done than was occasioned by the reservoir flood.[120]

The main street of Williamsburg Center was devastated and the roadbed almost entirely swept away. "The road is gouged the deepest in front of the brick hotel and close to the bridge, in some places, six, eight, and even ten feet." For every gouged-out location, one could find a field or yard filled with sand, rocks, and stones. One of the Center's bridges left standing had no river running under it. "The river runs west of the bridge, and cannot easily be turned back again."[121] Only one of five bridges in Searsville remained, and the floodwaters took out seven bridges at Williamsburg Center and Searsville.

Downriver in Haydenville, however, less damage was done. The dams remained intact, as did the bridges, although parts of roadways and bridge abutments needed repair. On the other hand, Leeds was hard hit. River Road from

Haydenville to Leeds was "nothing but the bare, yellow, shelving rocks," and the railroad track was washed out.

> But the greatest loss on the stream was just below the button shop... There were too many winds and turns here for the tumultuous waters to follow, and they made their first strike for a straight, untrammeled way, by breaking the escape-way of the button shop pond and cleaning the earth away to solid rock.[122]

The new riverbed cut off road access to the houses on "shanty row" on the west side of the river, necessitating the construction of a new bridge, known as the Hotel Bridge.[123]

Florence and Northampton escaped major damage from the flood. Once again, the Ross farm was underwater. Water "stood a foot deep in the kitchen of his residence, and three feet deep on his barn floor, reaching nearly to the backs of his cows as they stood in their stables." A wooden structure in the back of the Nonotuck Mill was badly damaged, but the dam, built in 1873, withstood the force of the water.[124] In downtown Northampton, people gathered on the old South Street Bridge to see whether the Mill would overtop the dike as it had done in the Lincoln Flood, but once again the dike held.

Environmental Transformation IV: *Deforestation*

Deforestation reached its apogee in the middle of the nineteenth century in most of the Mill River watershed, resulting in greater and more disastrous floods. As the forests disappeared, Americans began to feel the loss of their wilderness heritage, while simultaneously migrating more and more quickly toward the excitement of industrial cities and their promise of wealth and progress. Just as industrial and urban pollutants increased, a discovery was beginning to revolutionize the health sciences: germ theory, which proved that water could carry disease. It was also a time when Americans began to define their attitudes and values toward nature and urban landscapes—a set of visions, which have remained with us up to the present.

The scramble for wood to make potash had denuded many hillsides of their tree cover well before mid-century. By 1840, a growing population and the demand for grazing lands, housing, and factory construction simply overwhelmed the local supply of timber. Steep hillsides, stripped of their tree cover and open to downpours, led to soil erosion, severe gullying, and rivers clogged with sediment that destroyed habitat for fish and aquatic insects.

Terrible flooding ensued. The sixty years from 1780–1840 had witnessed four significant floods. Then, over the next forty years from 1840–1880, six major floods occurred, not counting the 1874 disaster. Some of this may have been due to the end of the Little Ice Age and warmer spring times that caused quicker snowmelt. But the chief culprit was deforestation, which eroded the steep-hilled upper watershed, especially during the floods of 1869 and 1878. Goshen's Hiram Barrus described the sad state of Goshen's brooks by the end of our time period in 1880. None of the streams in Goshen, he wrote,

> are as valuable for mill purposes as they formerly were. When the country was covered with forests, and the swamps and meadows were undrained, evaporation was much less rapid than now, the rains were retained as if by an immense sponge, to flow off gradually. Now, the heavy rains flow off rapidly, the springs consequently receive a more scant supply, and the brooks being more exposed to the direct rays of the sun, their rocky beds become heated, and the evaporation of the passing water is greatly accelerated. The result is that many of the mill brooks are not usually more than about half their former size.[125]

The phenomenon of deforestation varied chronologically, with some areas stripped as early as 1830 and others only in 1850 or 1860. Most of the forests in the watershed had been cut over by 1830 to provide for asheries, housing construction, and cleared ground for grazing and tillage.[126] Most cut-over sections, however, reverted immediately to woodland in the early nineteenth century, and the 1831 town maps of Northampton and Williamsburg show a considerable amount of

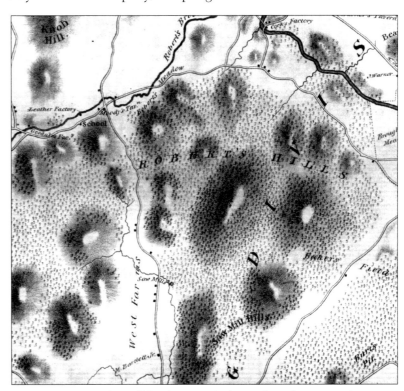

Fig. 4.35 *1831 Map of Northampton's forested northwest quadrant of Robert's Hills and Saw Mill Hills, then called the Long Division. The dotted areas denote forested land. (Courtesy Forbes Library and Northampton DPW)*

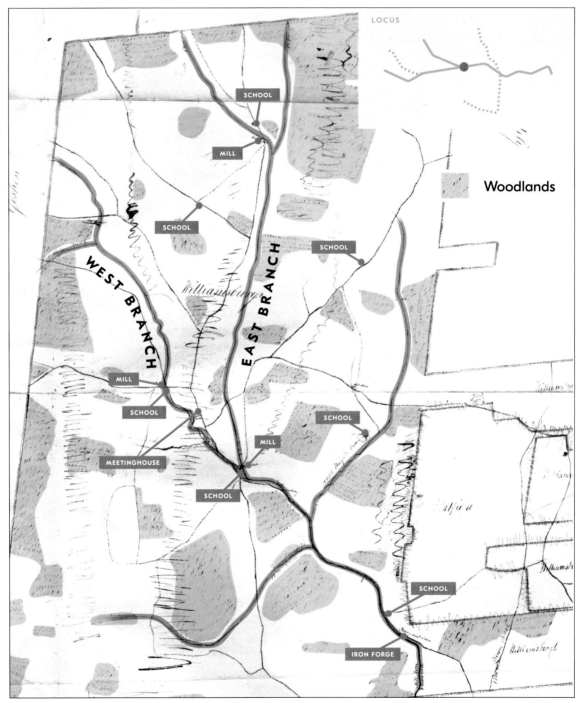

Fig. 4.36 *1831 map of woodland (shaded areas) in Williamsburg. Timber was located in scattered blocks throughout the town, mostly second growth. The squiggly lines delineate steep topography, some of which is open and other sections not. (Courtesy Ralmon Black and Eric Weber)*

woodland. Northampton's original Long Division in the town's northwest quadrant showed woodlands covering "Roberts Hills" and the Saw Mill Hills (Fig. 4.35), while timber still covered many scattered patches in Williamsburg.

In 1840, woodlands consisted predominantly of evergreens and sugar maples because the potash industry had claimed most of the deciduous trees. Sugar maples, however, were often spared for sugaring purposes, and most of the cutover sections were left in pine and hemlock. Huge swaths of open land provided pasturage for both sheep and cattle during the "Merino Craze"[127] of the 1820s and 1830s. Even after wool demand collapsed, families continued to strip their woodlands, which were their only remaining cash crop. Sylvester Judd wrote that "thousands of farmers in Massachusetts could not live from their farms, if they did not sell wood and timber... The time seems not very distant when many farmers not only will have no wood to sell, but none to use."[128]

In the mid-nineteenth century, pine found a ready market as saw timber, boxboards, and railway construction. Not only were the white pines of the hillsides being harvested, but landowners were clearcutting the yellow or pitch pine of the sandy pine barrens as well.[129] Judd left a clue that pine was in serious demand in 1850:

> The millyards [in 1847] are full... The large trees are all disappearing. Much of the timber is used here, and much is sold to other places... The greater part of the timber is White Pine; a good deal of chestnut and yellow pine. The chestnut is for shingles, much of it. ...I noticed several white pine logs 3 feet in diameter, and one about 3½ feet... This large log had between 150 and 160 concentric rings.[130]

In the late 1840s, sufficient forest could still be found to harbor game, even though all the big game, namely deer and bear, had been hunted to extirpation. We have a snapshot of the kind of animals in the region from a hunting competition in 1848 that Sylvester Judd captured "not on account of the hunt, but to show the kinds of quadrupeds & birds that are about in this vicinity on the 1st of November."[131] After shooting and trapping more than 19,000 birds and animals—from squirrels, chipmunks and weasels to jays, hawks, and woodpeckers—"the hunters closed their 'campaign' with a grand supper at the Nonotuck House, about 125 people." Red squirrels turned out to be far and away the most significant game species killed—6000 as compared to 2300 gray squirrels and 2600 blue jays. Red squirrel habitat is pine and hemlock forest. Gray squirrels live in deciduous woodlands. Throughout this time period woodlands became more and more scattered and dominated by almost pure stands of pine.

The mid-nineteenth century farm economy in the Mill River watershed and throughout much of New England was marginal. "The stripping of the woodlands symbolized the fragility of the upland economy," noted historian Christopher Clark. In 1841 Northampton's woodland covered 25 percent of its total land, but only 11 percent by 1860. Williamsburg's woodland, which was only 11 percent in 1841, dropped to 8 percent in 1860.[132] The resulting hillside erosion devastated the Mill River and its tributaries and prompted a region-wide reaction that evolved into the roots of the American environmental movement.[133] In response to the loss of old-growth forests, the decline of game animals, a growing scarcity of timber, and soil impoverishment, Americans became nostalgic for their wilderness birthright and frightened about the future. The last third of the nineteenth century witnessed the rise of scientific resource management, embodied by Gifford Pinchot; and the wilderness preservation movement led by transcendentalists H. D. Thoreau and John Muir.

Bridging both these movements, a Vermonter named George Perkins Marsh raised his call to arms in *Man and Nature; or, Physical Geography as Modified by Human Action*. "Man is everywhere a disturbing agent. Wherever he plants his foot, the harmonies of nature are turned to discords."[134] Marsh then went on to describe the processes by which New Englanders had skinned the hills of timber, thus allowing soil to wash into streams, killing the streams' biota.

> We have now felled forest enough everywhere, in many districts far too much. Let us restore this one element of material life to its normal proportions, and devise means for maintaining the permanence of its relations to the fields, the meadows and the pastures, to the rain and the dews of heaven, to the springs and rivulets with which it waters down the earth.

Whether this ringing cry reached the hearts of subsistence farmers is doubtful, but the founding in 1863 of "Mass Aggie," the Massachusetts Agricultural College at Amherst, certainly appealed to their utilitarian bent, and the rural children of Northampton and the hilltowns took advantage of the new scientific education available to them. In other words, the farmers and loggers of the Mill River region did not need to know anything about transcendentalism or John Muir to recognize that they needed to husband their resources. At the most basic level, it was more useful for local landowners to adopt a utilitarian ethic that preached resource conservation for sustainable use than Muir's preservation ethic that urged non interference in ecosystem management.

Pollution and Sewerage

Sediment and rubble from the hillsides were only one source of pollution. As the density of factories and population increased, runoff from filthy streets and septic systems fouled the Mill River's water, as did industrial effluent. The Mill River continued faithfully to perform its job—to carry and deposit its load downstream—but now it was transporting materials dangerous to its fish and frogs, and to its human inhabitants as well.

Concerned about increased flooding, Northampton town fathers had stormwater sewers constructed in the center of town, first along Market Street Brook (aka the Towne Ditch or Governor's Brook) to carry off surface water from Market Street and King Street.

The sewer looked like the one in Fig. 4.37. It was a four-foot wide by five-foot deep stone box covered with bricks with a brick arch and a wood-plank floor. It carried only stormwater, in essence, serving as the brook's overflow flood plain. The idea of "combined" sewer systems that mixed household

Fig. 4.37 A 1981 photo of one of the oldest sections of the Market Street Brook sewer dating from about 1860. (Courtesy Doug McDonald and Northampton DPW)

sewage with street overflow only became possible with the general acceptance of water closets, or toilets, in the late nineteenth century.[135]

Before 1870, the general perception was that rivers were capable of diluting whatever pollutant they carried downstream to some indeterminate spot where they regained their health. Further, it was generally thought that disease was spread through "miasma," or noxious air that usually came from rotting organic matter. As historian John Cumbler pointed out, "almost all tort cases involving water that made it to the Massachusetts Supreme Judicial Court were about quantity. Indeed, there were only three cases relating even vaguely to pollution" prior to 1860.[136] Plaintiffs complained of damage to their economic circumstances, not their deteriorating health.

Pasteur's and Koch's experiments on microbial activity led to germ theory, and suddenly rivers became a subject of scientific study. By the late 1860s, scientists and health-care professionals had accepted that water-borne microbes caused cholera, typhus, yellow fever, and dysentery; therefore polluted water posed a serious health threat. Massachusetts was the first state to pass public health legislation in 1869, proclaiming that "All the citizens have an inherent right to the enjoyment of pure and uncontaminated air, water and soil, and this right should be regarded as belonging to the whole community."[137]

Pollution control in cities and towns rested on three pillars: water supply was addressed in the 1870s, wastewater treatment in the 1880s, and solid waste management only in the twentieth century. In 1860, the 6700 citizens of Northampton got their drinking water from the Mill River or its tributaries and from cisterns. They dumped their wastes into cesspools or privy vaults (mere holes in the ground, lined or unlined).[138] There is no hint from newspapers or journals that the general public was aware of the dangers of water-borne disease, at least in our watershed. But having recognized its responsibility to care for the public's health, the town of Northampton built its first drinking water reservoir in Leeds in 1871, and by 1880, the 12,000 citizens of Northampton had secure drinking water supplies.[139] Although the public enjoyed the health benefits of the new system of reservoirs, the Mill River became ever more loaded with pollutants that flowed from the increasingly numerous factories, particularly in Florence, Bay State, and the Upper Mills. The situation would only become worse over the next half-century, until water treatment plants and new sewer systems were built after the Second World War.[140]

Contending Visions of the American Landscape

Two separate environmental movements emerged in mid-century. The first was rooted in the conservation of natural resources based on science, and featured such names as G. P. Marsh and Gifford Pinchot. The second derived from the aesthetics of transcendentalism and the Hudson River School of painters along with nostalgia for wilderness, as can be seen in the paintings of Albert Bierstadt. These new movements, which coalesced into the twentieth-century environmental movement, came as a reaction to industrialization with its attendant concentration of capital and power in the hands of investors and factory owners and its ugly impacts on waterways, landscapes and health. The transcendentalism of Thoreau and the Hudson River School allowed millions of Americans to tap into their nostalgia for Arcadia Lost and to create the myth of the Great American Wilderness. American Wilderness is, in fact, a most peculiar concept that has few parallels in other societies. It is a state of nature, which can only be achieved by extirpating or removing the Natives, who had lived there for more than 10,000 years, then harvesting most of the timber, followed by reforestation.[141] Nonetheless, American wilderness became a powerful force in shaping the American psyche, and remains to this day a battle cry to defend nature.

In 1872, the federal government actualized the early land preservation movement by establishing the nation's first national park, Yellowstone, "as a public park or pleasuring-ground for the benefit and enjoyment of the people."[142] Philanthropists, who were eager to beautify their towns and cities, subsidized the creation of parks and open spaces. Central Park in New York City opened its gates in 1858, and Hartford's Bushnell Park was created in 1861. In Boston, America's great landscape architect Frederick Law Olmsted spent much of his time in the 1870s and 1880s on Boston's Emerald Necklace of parks. Wealthy New Yorkers set aside vast tracts of forestland for their private Great Camps in the Adirondacks, leading to the Adirondack Park in 1892.

Both the scientific and aesthetic vision of American nature came hard up against the realities of the Industrial Revolution, with its incredible inventions and the promise of endless technological progress, its hope for limitless profits, and its devastating impact on land and water. As Ted Steinberg wrote,

The attempt to impose order on the land and waterscape is among the most striking and powerful features of industrial transformation. It is also a vital component of the quest to maximize productive potential, to efficiently capitalize on the earth's natural resources. The control of nature, whether for economic interest or leisure pursuit, underlay the advance of industrial capitalism.[143]

Factory owners and power brokers demanded control over natural resources—skinning the mountains of their timber, then damming major rivers, and using the rivers' physical dynamics to move their effluent downstream. "The temptation to cast into the moving water every form of portable refuse and filth, to be borne out of sight, is too great to be resisted," wrote the pollution investigators for the Massachusetts State Board of Health in 1873.[144] Textile mills poured out organic dyes such as madder, logwood, peachwood, and indigo, which had to be fixed with mordants, such as muriatic and sulfuric acid, and arsenate of soda. Paper mills dumped caustic alkali solutions used to break down raw materials as well as the bleaches and dyes used for different types of papers. Cutlery and tool factories added lubricants, acids, and heavy metals—chrome, nickel, silver, lead, copper, and zinc.[145]

How did these contending forces play out in the Mill River Valley, long dominated by local commercial interests? The voices for industry, inventiveness, and economic growth rang out through the pages of the *Hampshire Gazette,* in which one would be hard put to find support for conservation or preservation. After all, most families had jobs at one of the sixty or so manufacturing establishments on the Mill River, and most of those enterprises found the river a convenient place in which to dump effluent.[146] However, neither the damage done by dumping nor the culpability of mill owners for the 1874 Williamsburg Disaster were sufficient to incite a public outcry or provoke legal action. Historian Elizabeth Sharpe, in her telling of the 1874 Flood story, explained why there were no serious repercussions for factory owners, whom the investigators had found guilty of poor judgment and negligent behavior. Elizabeth Sharpe, as we noted, explained that citizens in the Mill River Valley were loathe to react violently toward the dam and factory owners

> to whom they were indebted for the churches, schools, and social institutions, [and, therefore,] could not be cast out as evil men...Americans in 1874 lived in a complacent moral climate in which steam engine explosions, bridge and building collapses, and train collisions occurred with alarming frequency.

While Americans saw the Mill River flood as a terrible calamity, it was but one incident out of thousands for which no one was held accountable.[147]

Meanwhile, in the sphere of agriculture, farmers on the rich meadows of Northampton and Florence generally made a good living from whatever crops were most in demand, chiefly broom corn and tobacco, which gave good returns in the mid-nineteenth century. Furthermore, they now had the services of Mass Aggie across the Connecticut River for guidance in scientific farming. As for farmers in the hilltowns of Williamsburg, Goshen, Chesterfield, Ashfield, and Westhampton, they were simply struggling so hard to survive that they found it difficult to take G.P. Marsh's advice to "restore this one element of material life [the forest] to its normal proportions." Brian Donahue, an environmental historian, argued that farmers knew perfectly well what they were doing in continuing to cut timber and allowing much of their open land to return to scrub and second-growth timber without reforestation plans. Farmers had few options open. Many of their children had left for the West or enlisted in local and regional factory work. Hilltown farmers, therefore, developed a pattern of providing for local needs, chiefly dairy products, such as those which the heroic Collins Graves of Williamstown sold throughout the Upper Valley. Well into the twentieth century, farm families focused on the choices they had, whether to support three or four cows or six or eight of them, which all depended on the amount of fodder they could store, the number of children on hand, and the condition of the land.[148]

Looking back from our twenty-first century perch, we can well understand Americans' attitudes toward the technological and natural world in 1870. After all, we compartmentalize our attitudes in the same way as did our forbears. The most dramatic inventions were yet to come, and today we are still captives of a kind of nineteenth-century American imagination. Growing environmental awareness co-existed with the necessity to dump effluent into waterways. The quest for natural beauty accompanied the scarification and destruction of aesthetic landscapes. Communities came to depend on income from the very sources of food and clothing that fouled the environment. Conservation and exploitation went hand in hand.

The contending passions for different landscapes—wilderness, arcadia, village and city—remain with us today. More often than not, those passions are expressed in lobbying efforts and political broadsides, but there used to be voices celebrating America's landscape diversity as reflected in it contentious needs.[149] Walt Whitman wrote one of his most famous poems in praise of America's many faces of work and nature.

"Give Me the Splendid Silent Sun" 1865

> *Give me the splendid silent sun, with all his beams full-dazzling;*
> *Give me juicy autumnal fruit, ripe and red from the orchard;*
> *Give me a field where the unmow'd grass grows...*
> *Give me nights perfectly quiet, as on high plateaus west of the Mississippi,*
> *and I looking up at the stars;*
> *Give me odorous at sunrise a garden of beautiful flowers, where I can walk*
> *undisturb'd...*
> *Give me to warble spontaneous songs, reliev'd, recluse by myself, for my own*
> *ears only;*
> *Give me solitude—give me Nature—give me again, O Nature, your primal*
> *sanities!...*

Here is the world of nature that would have thrilled the Nonotuck sachem Umpanchala and the Reverend Jonathan Edwards. These ingredients in the common pot will appeal strongly to those who live in this valley, where nature is often close enough for bear, deer, and coyote to inhabit their place. But Whitman is not finished, and will not turn away from what made many American landscapes so distinctive—the mix of natural scenes and noisy, crowded factories and streets.

> *Keep your splendid, silent sun;*
> *Keep your woods, O Nature, and the quiet places by the woods;*
> *Keep your fields of clover and timothy, and your corn-fields and orchards;*
> *Keep the blossoming buckwheat fields, where the Ninth-month bees hum;*
> *Give me faces and streets! give me these phantoms incessant and endless along*
> *the trottoirs!*
> *Give me interminable eyes! give me women! give me comrades and lovers by*
> *the thousand!...*
> *Let me see new ones every day! let me hold new ones by the hand every day!*
> *People, endless, streaming, with strong voices, passions, pageants;*
> *Manhattan streets, with their powerful throbs, with the beating drums, as now;*
> *The endless and noisy chorus, the rustle and clank of muskets, (even the sight*
> *of the wounded;)*

Manhattan crowds, with their turbulent musical chorus—with varied chorus,
and light of the sparkling eyes;
Manhattan faces and eyes forever for me.

While not quite Manhattan, the Mill River Valley certainly contained crowded village sidewalks and plentiful factory noise. The common pot had been redefined; the Industrial Revolution had upset the balance of its contents by adding unimagined technologies and numbers of people, which increased the speed of life. This transformation risked tipping over the pot. It would take the next one hundred fifty years to regain some equilibrium, tentative though it might currently be. After great efforts to right the pot during the last half of the twentieth century, will global warming challenge any hope for the future of the people of the *wlôgan?*

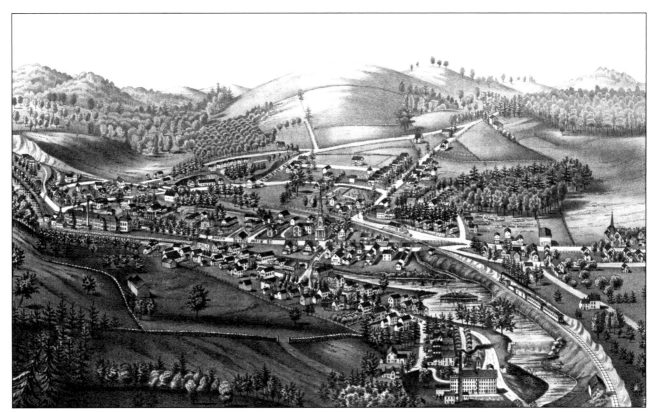

Fig 4.38 An 1886 bird's-eye view of Haydenville. Here is an example of the landscapes described in Walt Whitman's "Splendid Silent Sun." Note both the extensive open land and blocks of forest that surround the village, and its mills, churches, and houses with the river and railway running through the heart of town. (Courtesy Library of Congress)

CHAPTER FIVE

1880–1940: *Flood, Contamination, and Diversion*

Introduction

We have come to the last chapter of our Mill River story and the final reach of the river. This time, we will need a canoe or kayak, which we will launch near the river's confluence with the Connecticut at a place known as Hulbert's Pond, where the Massachusetts Audubon Society's Arcadia Sanctuary is located. One cannot walk this reach but only paddle it at high water, usually in March or April during the spring freshet. In this season, the Connecticut River is often running at about 50,000 cubic feet per second (cfs), enough to back water up onto the lowlands of the Oxbow, flooding the forests of Hulbert's Pond. The flood stage will last perhaps three more weeks, after which come the low flows of summer that run about 8000 cfs.

We have chosen a warm April day. The surface of the water appears quiet, with little hint of the quicker current that runs a few feet below us. We have paddled this stretch so often that it no longer seems odd to be cruising between trees, passing signs that say "No Parking." It is, however, a rare treat, for there remains only a pittance of the extensive flood plain forests that once lined many of the banks of the Connecticut River before they were drained. The trees, mostly silver maple with red maples, sycamore, cottonwood, and American ash mixed in, are all about fifty feet tall and maybe fifty or a hundred years old. Many arch over the banks, forming a canopy in some places. Ostrich fern line the banks.

You will hear so little noise in this place—maybe the splash of a painted turtle popping off a submerged log or a pickerel hunting a sunfish near the surface. If you come upon a beaver, it may slap its tail, but that may be all you hear. Muskrat and mink make no noise. It is too early for the song birds to arrive to nest, and they are many—veery with their lilting notes that descend slightly, contrasting with the harsh double notes of great crested flycatchers. At dawn and dusk, a cacophony of sound comes from warblers, flycatchers, and vireos.

Other wonderful birds make homes in this forest. A great horned owl fledgling sits on a half-submerged log, blinking. Wood ducks nest in boxes and perch on limbs nearby. American mergansers and mallards will be arriving shortly to nest by the banks. Not far from us, but unreachable by boat, is a heronry with about two dozen huge great blue heron nests in the crowns of maples or white pines that grow just above the flood line. On a tall pine at one end of the herons is the even larger nest of a bald eagle couple.

Our destination on this paddle is the bridge over South Street at the south end of Fort Hill. You get there by keeping more or less river right, and it's difficult to find the main channel of the Mill hidden beneath tree falls. On this trip, we will barely make it past a big tree fall that bars the way to the bridge. We reach the bridge, which is, sadly, an ugly sight—just a low wall of concrete that hides the river from the roadway. Even worse, the concrete blocks that hold the bridge have prevented further passage upstream. It is frustrating because the dam at Paradise Pond beckons just another mile upstream. On the other hand, the noise of Northampton's traffic is not why we've taken this paddle, so we turn back into the forest.

It's been a worthy trip. This quiet place so full of life has calmed our most anxious thoughts. It's good to give oneself over to the end of the Mill River.

Our last chapter covers six decades, from 1880 to 1940, less than the span of an average person's life. This era coincides with the Second Industrial Revolution with its transformational inventions, and the subsequent world population explosion that wove people and places into global networks and changed most aspects of life. Home heating, lighting, and sanitation created comfortable homes; farms and fields produced enough to support an expanding population that grew as childhood mortality declined; and medical miracles increased life expectancy due to public health breakthroughs. A host of mass-produced products transformed luxury items, such as automobiles, into common goods. For those who have played the game of "Which Generation Has Experienced the Greatest Changes During Its Lifetime?" clearly those born in the 1880s and deceased in the mid- to late-twentieth century win the grand prize.

The economic historian Robert Gordon has argued that five great inventions between 1870 and 1950 created the conditions for economic growth that society will likely never see again. Those inventions were electricity, urban sanitation, chemicals and pharmaceuticals, the internal combustion engine, and modern communications. As Paul Krugman writes,

> From the beginning of human ancestors 3 million years ago to the rise of cities 10,000 years ago, through the Middle Ages, to the beginning of the Industrial Revolution around 1800, living standards doubled. Another doubling took place over the subsequent period to 1870. Then...the world economy took off.[1]

Gordon argues that "some inventions are more important than others, and the unique clustering of the Great Inventions in the late nineteenth century will never recur. The economic revolution of 1870–1970 was unique in human history, unrepeatable because so many of its achievements could only happen once."[2]

What would become of the Mill River in this new world? For one thing, the Second Industrial Revolution doomed the local in just about every way. Almost all stand-alone shops and banks and businesses and farms became part of a network. Geographical isolation was no longer an option as small-gauge railroads reached into the corners of every valley that could promise some prized mineral or timber product. During the first two hundred years of their existence, Mill River villages had played an outsized role in national affairs. Their industries and people had become famous in the American colonies and the New Republic, but as the nineteenth century turned into the twentieth, the Mill receded in importance. By 1930, it had taken its place among the many little watersheds of the Northeastern United States. So integral to the lives of Northampton citizens, it simply disappeared from sight in 1940 in downtown Northampton, while the city's industrial presence remained chiefly in Florence. The industries of the upper Mill River never recovered from the disastrous 1874 Flood.

Had one been living in Northampton in 1900, however, one would have never discerned the dark shadows of the mid-twentieth century. The city prospered during the last two decades of the nineteenth century and the first two of the twentieth century. Cutleries were in full swing at Bay State, and the silk industry was at its height from 1880 to 1920.[3] The Florence Manufacturing Company came up with inventive ways to make plastic molds, becoming the major producer of toothbrushes in the country. Tourism thrived in this stronghold of Republican politics, as did the legal and financial sectors.

The city's most famous resident for the first three decades of the century was Calvin Coolidge, who graduated from Amherst College in 1895 and began practicing law in Northampton, where he immediately got into politics. By 1910, he was elected mayor of the city and two years later went into state government, becoming governor in 1919. Coolidge's presidency lasted from 1923 at the death of Warren Harding until 1929; on retiring, he returned to Northampton. The no-nonsense, conservative utilitarianism of the thirtieth President reflected Northampton's centuries-old focus on commercial and administrative success.

These old values lived on in the village. Radical traditions of antebellum Florence continued after the Civil War with the establishment of the free-thinking, anti-clerical Free Congregational Society with Charles C. Burleigh as speaker; the Florence Kindergarten, the first free, endowed kindergarten in the U.S.; and the Workingman's Savings Bank, now Florence Bank, today's most prominent bank in Hampshire County. Philanthropy continues to thrive there. The wills and testaments of such leading lights of the Florence Group as Frank Look, Alfred Lilly, and Samuel Hill provided for the legacies of Look Park, which became a regional draw; Lilly Library and the Lilly Hall of Science at Smith College; and the Hill Institute, which continues its kindergarten and inexpensive semester-long crafts programs.

In 1883, Northampton became the second city in Western Massachusetts to replace its town meeting form of government with a mayor and city council. The *Hampshire Gazette* began daily publication of the *Daily Hampshire Gazette* in 1890.[4] Population dynamics in the lower Mill River Valley tracked the general trend in the Northeastern United States. Northampton's population, which had quickly doubled in the twenty years from 6700 in 1860 to more than 12,000 in 1900, doubled again over the next sixty years to almost 25,000 in 1940 (the city's 2016 population was 28,549). Immigrants made up about a quarter of Northampton's citizenry, with French Canadians and especially Poles accounting for most of the late influx. In comparison, Springfield's growth dwarfed that of Northampton—from 33,000 people in 1880 to almost 150,000 in 1940, about 25 percent of whom were immigrants throughout that period.[5] Springfield in the late nineteenth and early twentieth century was a true national industrial hub, an outpost of Westinghouse and Rolls Royce, Monsanto, Mass. Mutual Insurance, Diamond Match, and myriad smaller enterprises. The Great Depression, however, marked the beginning of Springfield's economic decline, although its location as a transportation hub and its industrial diversity left it better off for a longer time than many other New England cities.

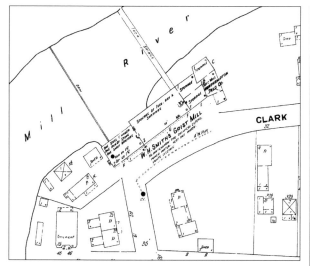

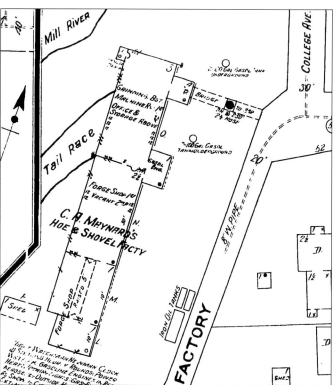

Fig. 5.1 *The 1910 Sanborn Map (fire insurance map) depicts a factory with two mills in it – Smith's Grist Mill and the Northampton Talc Co. The gristmill had a steel grinder, a set of grinding stones, a smut machine to clean the wheat, and storage rooms. The gristmill was probably using a water-driven turbine for power. The small talc factory ground talc from the nearby Berkshire Hills that was used in many industrial processes and for talcum powder. (Courtesy Northampton Department of Planning and Sustainability)*

Fig. 5.3 *The 1910 map of the Maynard Hoe & Shovel Factory shows the large building occupied by the hoe and shovel shop. Most space is devoted to the forge rooms with grinding room and offices standing at the upstream end of the building. Waterpower was still being used but with gas engines in reserve.*

Fig. 5.2 *Postcard view (ca. 1920) looking upriver from New South Street Bridge to the Lower Falls Dam. The railroad on the right is now part of the local rail trail for bikers and walkers. (Courtesy Steve Sauter)*

Industrial Development, and the Factory Villages

The Lower Mills and Upper Mills

Only three industrial concerns on the lowest end of the Mill River lasted into the early twentieth century—the Williams Basket Factory at the south end of town, a gristmill at the Lower Mills, and Maynard's Hoe Shop at the Upper Mills. The Williams Basket Factory limped along until about 1930,[6] and the small factory at the Lower Mills on Clark Avenue changed hands and reverted to its original function as a gristmill in the early twentieth century. On June 21, 1890 Horace Lamb sold off the Grist Mill portion of the property to Richard P. Smith, who continued in that business for several years. Two fires in 1899 and 1900 damaged the brick building but it survived. The Lamb wire business, however, did not. On March 14, 1902 the property was sold at auction and the wire industry in Northampton ceased to be. Richard P. Smith, presumably William H. Smith's son, acquired the wire mill shortly after

Fig. 5.4 Northampton Hosiery Company, ca. 1915. Plant was still driven by water power. Bridge connected building with train tracks on opposite shore of Mill River.(Courtesy Forbes Library)

the auction. He appears to have improved the dam and rented out the property to the Northampton Hosiery Company. This concern occupied the building until around 1935 by which time most of the local silk industry had come undone. In 1955, The Gehenna Press was established here by artist Leonard Baskin. With pressman Harold McGrath and editor Sydney Kaplan, Baskin produced limited edition books of high artistic merit.[7] The little dam became a quaint postcard scene during the early part of the century and was only torn down after the Second World War. Some rubble from the breached dam lies in a brush-filled ditch, unnoticed by walkers and bikers on the rail trail up a steep bank on the north side. Establishing an oft-repeated pattern, the former Lamb wire mill saw reuse in the 1980s as artist studios and light industry, finally being converted to residential condominums in 1988.

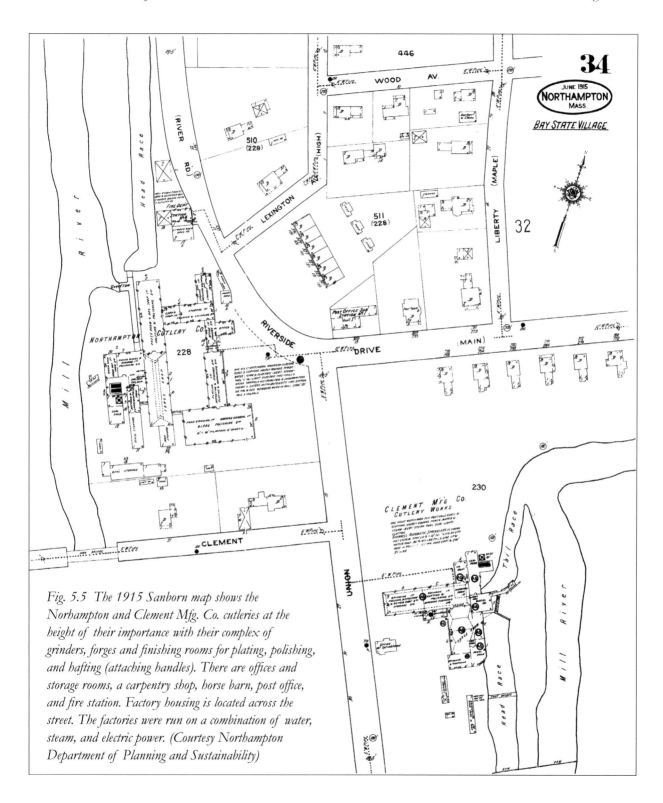

Fig. 5.5 The 1915 Sanborn map shows the
Norhampton and Clement Mfg. Co. cutleries at the
height of their importance with their complex of
grinders, forges and finishing rooms for plating, polishing,
and hafting (attaching handles). There are offices and
storage rooms, a carpentry shop, horse barn, post office,
and fire station. Factory housing is located across the
street. The factories were run on a combination of water,
steam, and electric power. (Courtesy Northampton
Department of Planning and Sustainability)

The Maynard Hoe Factory at the Upper Mills carried on a robust trade for the last two decades of the nineteenth century, but ran into trouble after 1900. One of Northampton's few labor strikes hit the Hoe Shop in 1906, by which time the factory's second floor was vacant. Its signature tower was torn down in 1914, and fire destroyed the remainder of the building in 1919. The remnants were carted away in 1922. Only a flat piece of cement remains above the dam to memorialize the factory.

The Flourishing Bay State Cutleries

The tool industry had found a solid home at Bay State in the mid-nineteenth century and continued to employ several hundred hands throughout much of the twentieth, during which outside owners took over running the factories. Three concerns were located at Bay State—Northampton Cutlery and Clement Manufacturing at Bay State; and Rogers, Ltd., which had taken over the defunct Vernon Paper building in the 1880s. All these businesses were tied to larger industrial firms in the region and could respond to changing instructions from owners, whether in Connecticut or, as the case with Rogers, in Canada. Sometimes the factories focused on handles, other times on plating, sharpening, or forging for both wholesale and retail markets.

The cutleries were among the few factories in the watershed that continued to use the Mill River for its original purpose—to turn water turbines that powered some of the machinery. The 1915 Sanborn map shows the dams and raceways that the plants used at that time.

Florence and Leeds Remain the Industrial Center of the Mill River

The glory days of Nonotuck Silk came after the 1874 flood, as the company achieved full employment in Florence and continued its practice of caring for its workers. By 1920, Nonotuck Silk owned more than

Fig. 5.6 Nonotuck Silk Co. advertisement in 1899 for its proprietary Corticelli silk. (Courtesy Historic Northampton)

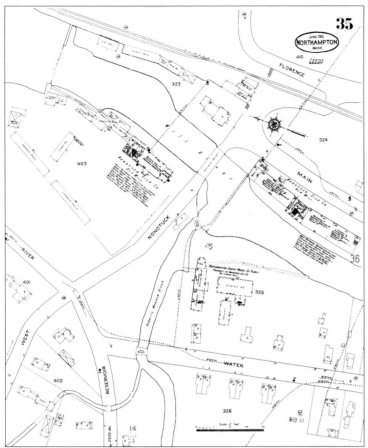

Fig. 5.7 *1915 Sanborn map of the two Nonotuck Co. silk factory buildings in Leeds – the "Old Factory" on the left at the present-day ChartPak lot and the "New Factory" on the right in the former Button Shop. The mills ran on water, steam, and electric power. In the center of the map at the confluence of Roberts Meadow Brook and the Mill River stand the vacant Northampton Emery Wheel Company's buildings. The firm had failed in 1913 (Courtesy Northampton Dept. of Planning and Sustainability)*

one hundred tenements and was helping employees buy their own homes. In 1880, the company built a new mill in Leeds, "a handsome structure with a French roof, 122 feet in length by forty-two feet in width, five stories in height, every inch of which rests upon a solid rock foundation, formed by a ledge which makes into and forms the bed of the river."[8] The silk factory took over the village of Leeds from the late nineteenth century until its demise in 1931. It even took over the factory of the Northampton Emery Wheel Company after the latter ceased doing business in 1913.[9] Sometime prior to 1895 Northampton Silk took over the defunct Cooks Dam at the lower end of the village, where it constructed a small hydroelectric facility to run all its factories and the town's electric trolley. By 1900 Nonotuck Silk had occupied the old cotton mill in Haydenville and had even opened a factory in Quebec. They also had salesrooms in New York, Boston, Chicago, St. Louis, Cincinnati, St. Paul, and Gloversville, New York.[10]

Nonotuck's main manufacturing plant remained in Florence, where it employed 582 workers in 1920, producing a wide variety of silk products from hosiery and silk thread to silk for gloves (in Gloversville), lampshade silk, and dental floss. But financial conditions became difficult in the 1920s, and in 1922 the local owners sold the company to Brainerd, Armstrong and Co. of New London, Connecticut, who changed the company's name from Nonotuck to Corticelli in honor of its famous thread. The next year Corticelli workers unionized, and the next, 1924, saw them out on strike. The latter failed after a few months and the workers found their wages and benefits cut.[11]

Fig. 5.8 Late 19th-century Florence Manufacturing Company advertisement for "The Florence Brush," before the company changed its name to Pro-Phy-Lac-Tic. (Courtesy Historic Northampton)

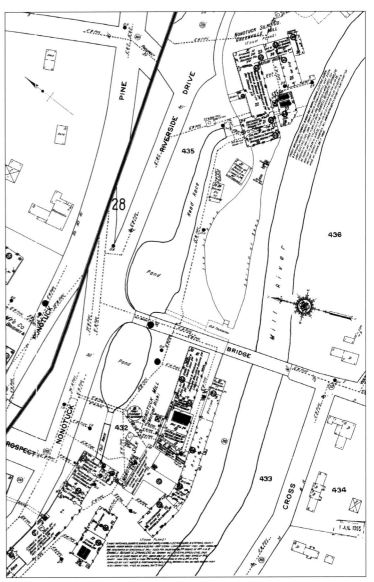

Fig. 5.9 1915 Sanborn map of the Nonotuck Silk Company's two factory buildings in Florence. While details on this map are illegible at this scale, it gives a sense of the complicated nature of the silk industry with its many components crowded together. Most notable is the use of waterpower throughout the factory with steam used as a reserve source. There are head and tail races in and out of both buildings and two small ponds. The dye houses border the river where they must have voided waste water that turned the Mill River various colors. (Courtesy Northampton Department of Planning and Sustainability)

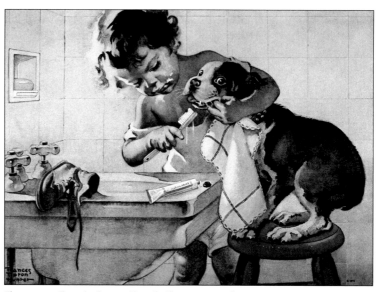

Fig. 5.11 *Prophylactic Brush Company advertisement ca. 1945* (*Courtesy Historic Northampton*)

Fig. 5.10 *Advertisement ca. 1942 for Pro Brush toothbrushes that used DuPont's new synthetic material to replace hog bristles, the original material for toothbrushes.* (*Courtesy Historic Northampton*)

"Behind the glamorous façade," writes Smith College professor Marjorie Senechal, "American silk manufacturers— all but the hosiery makers—grew increasingly nervous as the 1920s wore on."[12] Demand for silk slackened as fashions changed and readymade clothing became more easily available. The Crash of 1929 spelled the end of Northampton's silk industry: Corticelli closed up shop in 1931. The Pro Brush Company took over the Corticelli Silk building in the 1930s. It remains known today as the Nonotuck Silk Mill, the home of several small enterprises and nonprofits.

The Florence Manufacturing Company, which changed its name to the Pro-Phy-Lac-Tic Company in 1924 was by far the most successful factory along the Mill River. Throughout its one-hundred-fifty-year history from 1866–2007, the company continually adapted to new markets while adopting advanced molding and brush-making techniques. Locally known as Pro Brush, the firm maintained an enviable loyalty among its more than one thousand employees, providing them with vacation and benefits, and balancing out inevitable economic cycles by providing make-work in down times and avoiding layoffs by cutting hours rather than firing workers, many of whom were the grandchildren of those who made the first hairbrush in 1866 or the first toothbrush in 1884.[13] The company

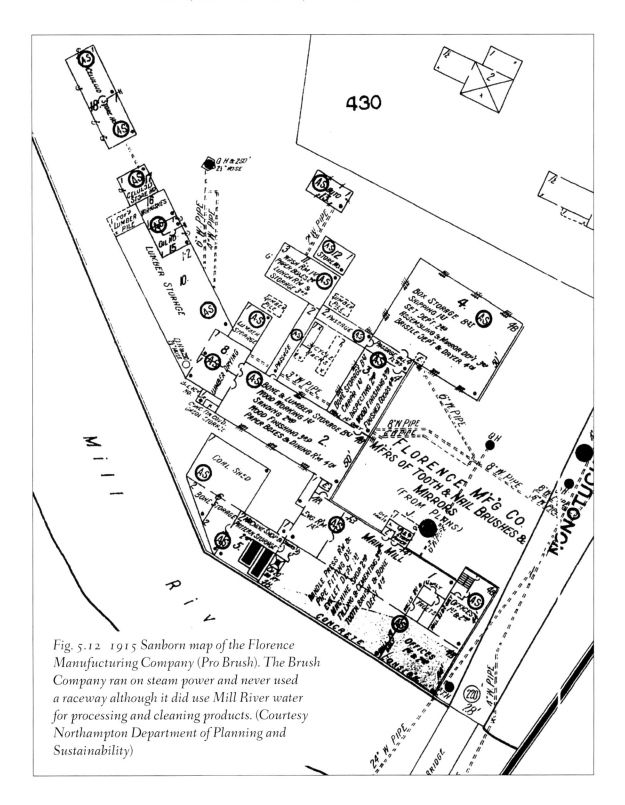

Fig. 5.12 *1915 Sanborn map of the Florence Manufacturing Company (Pro Brush). The Brush Company ran on steam power and never used a raceway although it did use Mill River water for processing and cleaning products. (Courtesy Northampton Department of Planning and Sustainability)*

never experienced a labor strike, although there were several attempts to unionize workers in the mid-twentieth century.[14]

At the beginning of the Great Depression, in his search for a toothbrush maker, Gerard Lambert, founder of Lambert Pharmaceuticals (of Listerine mouthwash fame), discovered Pro Brush. In 1930, Lambert bought out the local owners for five million dollars. He brought in a stable management team that continued prior labor practices, and an MIT engineer who ensured that the company would have cutting-edge technology. The result was that no workers were sent home during the Depression. Instead, the six-day week was reduced to five days and eventually to four until wartime increased demand and output.

Throughout the twentieth century, Pro Brush continued to use large amounts of water from the Mill River—not for power, but for cooling. The anonymous author of the Pro Brush Company's history wrote in praise of the river:

> Our Mill Stream still flows and serves us well in supplying water to cooling jackets on our many injection press machines. These cooling reservoirs demand amazing quantities of coolant. Except for the very warmest months of the year, a ram [for a pump] at the bottom of Mill Pond supplies cold water piped directly to the molding press floor. And happily, thanks to a series of straining devices, PRO voids this same water out of our jackets once more down-stream back to Mill River cleaner than when it was first diverted. Not one bit of stream pollution here! How jealous so many U.S. cities would be of our very low cost water service, Los Angeles, Phoenix, El Paso, Dallas, Tucson, Albuquerque, to name a few.[15]

Williamsburg Joins the Larger World

In the hilly upper section of the Mill River, twentieth-century life changed little between 1880 and 1940.[16] Transportation between Northampton and Williamsburg had already become much easier when, in 1868, the New Haven & Northampton railroad opened a branch line to Haydenville. A year later the line was extended to Williamsburg. Then, in 1894, electric trolleys began carrying travelers and commuters to work, a system that lasted until a bus service replaced it in 1927.

1903 was Williamsburg's year of modernization: the town established its first water supply with the Unquomonk Reservoir at the same time that the first telephone lines were strung. That same year, the Williamsburg Electric Company built a coal-fired generator where the Skinner mansion had stood. Williamsburg was quickly linked up to the larger world.

In Haydenville, Nonotuck Silk took over Hayden & Sanders' 1847 cotton mill at the downstream end of the village, and ran it until 1930 as an outpost of its main plant in Florence.[17] The Brass Works that Joel Hayden, Jr. had rebuilt after the flood continued through several changes of ownership until taken over in 1899 by the three Hills brothers, who ran it successfully until the middle of the twentieth century.[18]

The small flood plain where Skinnerville had once been located became known as the Village Green, which boasted the railroad depot, an electric company, and an ice and fuel distributor. Williamsburg Center became the town's residential and commercial district. In 1900, it hosted the Town Hall, two churches, the high school, two hotels, two livery stables, a carriage shop, two blacksmithies, three sawmills, and five shops, most of them located along Main Street. The manufacturing concerns had a harder time of it since few buildings remained standing after 1874. Henry James' cotton mill at the former 1813 Unquomonk Woolen Mill site changed hands in 1891 and again in 1903, burned down in 1913, became a sawmill, and ended life as a wood-turning factory in the 1950s.[19]

On the devastated East Branch, Onslow Spelman, the Williamsburg Reservoir overseer, rebuilt his stone dam and button factory, which he quickly sold (it was retooled as a sawmill). Hiram Hill rebuilt his gristmill, which the Hill family ran until 1926. It now houses the Williamsburg Historical Society's farm museum.[20]

The West Branch continued to house a series of different enterprises at several sites over the six decades from 1880 to 1940. Near the current town center stood a lead pencil shop, a wood products factory, and a shell-button business, which found success in Haydenville near the turn of the century. The most successful plant was the long-running Thayer Manufacturing Company, which produced hardware and tools and which now houses the Williamsburg Blacksmith.[21] Upstream at Searsville, three water-powered mills were still active in 1880 but led brief lives. Sears sold his woolen mill in 1862 to Thomas Nash, who re-sold it shortly thereafter, but it slipped into decay and on the night of July 3, 1890, thrill-seekers torched it to light up the night sky.[22] Gilbert

Bradford owned two sawmills, one of which went up in flames in 1913.[23] Bradford's son rebuilt it and ran it until 1926, when it fell silent after 163 years of continuous operation as a sawmill, blacksmith shop, gristmill and barrel shop. One lone sawmill remained in business into the 1930s, no longer running on water power. In 1950, an ice jam or other natural factors breached the Searsville Reservoir, leaving a final reminder on a woodland trail that Searsville had once been a major factory village.[24]

The Transformation of the Lower Mill Watershed from an Industrial to an Institutional and Recreational Landscape

Northampton's industrial and economic strength, unfortunately, proved more apparent than real by 1920. Unlike Springfield, Northampton found that its diverse industrial base had become a hindrance. Looking back on the first fifty years of the twentieth century, Gilbert Cestre, a visiting professor at Smith College from France,[25] surveyed the decline of Northampton's industrial base during the first half of the twentieth century. Cestre observed that not only were Northampton manufacturers small but highly specialized as well. With a population of less than 20,000 people in 1900, the city had a startling array of industrial concerns that included plastic moldings and brushes, silk thread and stockings, cutlery, the manufacture of millstones, brass objects, buttons, sewing machines, coffins, and several other kinds of firms, many of them with national reputations. However, only large industrial cities could support such diversity, and while Northampton's good fortune in 1900 appeared assured, the city was not equipped for the future.[26]

The first signs of trouble could be seen in the purchase of several local cutlery and silk hosiery factories by outside interests, and in the unsustainable economic expansion during the First World War. Northampton's small-scale industrial methods were poorly adapted to large-scale, fast-paced industrial change, and the result was a complete inability to adjust, which led to postwar unemployment. The Great Depression only exacerbated the decline of Mill River's industries.[27]

Those industries did not die outright, but continued throughout most of the twentieth century at a diminished level. Labor relations remained relatively calm, but once outside groups took ownership of the factories, several strikes occurred, beginning with the cutleries in the first decade of the twentieth century and in the silk industry in the 1920s. Prior to these strikes, industrialists had continued their extensive nineteenth-century welfare programs. They made sure their workers were housed well and the women properly protected from harm. Ira Dimock, president of Nonotuck Silk at the turn of the twentieth century, had fifty-seven workers' houses available for low rent, and a boarding house capable of accommodating sixty.

> We put the house up at a good deal of expense... We say to parents and brothers who live at a distance, 'You can safely let your sister or your daughter come down to the Nonotuck Mills. She is looked after, and is required to be in at suitable hours. We have an interest in her.'[28]

Had outmoded industry constituted the only employment available, Northampton's financial future after World War I might have been disastrous. Fortunately, an alternative already existed which, if not as exciting, was far more stable. The cutlery, silk, and brush and plastics molding industries provided

jobs for more than two thousand workers until the 1930s, but hospitals and the service industry provided thousands more new employment opportunities. The year 1924 saw the founding of the Veterans Affairs hospital in Leeds and the simultaneous expansion of the Northampton State Hospital and such educational institutions as Smith College and the Smith business and vocational schools. These changes, along with the growth of tourism, were remaking Northampton as a stable community of institutions rather than industries.[29]

The Mill River, as it always had, provided recreation as well, when families in summertime trooped down to the banks of the river and youngsters jumped off twenty-foot dams into the splash pools below. But in the late nineteenth century, the river's nearby residents for the first time looked on the Mill as an aesthetic asset.

Fig. 5.13 Young people at the Nonotuck Dam ca. 1940. (Courtesy Forbes Library)

The city of Northampton had always taken pride in its municipal buildings and churches, many of which still stand on Main Street, but the city had never cared for the riverside, which it had left to nature and industrial concerns. However, the shift away from waterpower occurred simultaneously with the demise of the weeklong, ten- to twelve-hour workday. Workers suddenly had leisure time, which created a demand for recreation, such as swimming, picnicking, and fishing on the Mill River. The Mill and its banks were falling into disrepair.

Fig. 5.14 *Paradise Pond from the Smith College President's House looking east with the Maynard Hoe Factory in the background ca. 1900. (Courtesy Sophia Smith Archives)*

In the 1890s, Smith College, then only about fifteen years old, hired the firm of Frederick Law Olmsted to design its campus. In the process, the Olmsted group beautified the banks of Paradise Pond, where the Maynard Hoe Factory sat at the head of the dam. A photograph at the turn of the century provides a glimpse of the romantic pond that Smith College alumnae hold nostalgically dear. The Hoe Factory in the background does not appear to detract from the aesthetics of the pond.

The City Beautiful Movement advocated the beautification of urban gardens and buildings to inspire citizenship and high morals among residents, as well as mitigating the blight of tenements and unsightly streets.[30] Northampton, having privileged commerce and industry in its growth, came late to the nineteenth-century idea of creating urban parks.

Finally, in 1934, a year and a half after the death of Calvin Coolidge, Gerald Stanley Lee, Congregational clergyman, author, and commentator on all things American, wrote a lengthy letter in the *Hampshire Gazette*, advocating a riverside park along the Mill in downtown Northampton as a memorial to Coolidge.[31] Foremost, Lee wanted the memorial to "Northampton's own president" to be characteristic of the man himself, certainly not some statue, whom "we have had all dolled up in bronze... If such a statue were going to get down off his pedestal and shake hands with us, one would feel different. But he won't. [He will] just keep on looking dolled up." Lee also rejected a museum that would put the thirtieth president in a glass case, making "some kind of glorified goldfish of him."

No, Lee wanted an expensive, original memorial, a striking feat in engineering that could become "a living, growing thing" that could be daily used by all citizens, so that should Calvin return, "he would be proud and glad of what he was daily doing, years and years after he was dead, to make Northampton happy!" That memorial would be called the Calvin Coolidge Riverpath Park.

> Mill river instead of being—very much of it from Pleasant street up, one great long disreputable ashamed back-yard—Northampton's tin-can, orange peel and ashes backyard—a kind of sl[e]azy sewer stringing itself shamelessly through the very heart of our fair city, would have become—thanks to Calvin Coolidge... a memorial that day after day, night after night down the years, will keep on remembering him the way he would like to be remembered.[32]

Lee detailed the run of his Riverpath Park from the Mill River Bridge at Pleasant Street, upstream past the old Mill River Footbridge at Old South Street, then along South Street at Fort Hill and down the steep slope of Hebert Street back to the river. Much of the path followed places where children played, swam, or fished. Lee chose locations where the city could create playgrounds and establish benches, spots the city could take by eminent domain. He specified ten entrances to the river path. "We would have," he wrote, "a memorial that stands out not only in Northampton but in the nation." It turned out that nature would have the last say, and did not favor the vision of Mr. Lee.

The Decades of Ceaseless Floods

Eight major floods in forty years, an average of two per decade: such was the result of a century of deforestation. Several of the floods would have had little human impact in the nineteenth century, but by the early twentieth Northampton residents had built out onto the Manhan Meadows and Venturer's Field in the southeastern part of town. The Fruit and Maple (Conz) Street section of town had been partially protected by the mid-nineteenth-century dike and a new sewer in the late 1880s that "very naturally [made] all residents living on Fruit street rejoice...transforming this belt of everlasting swamp into dry land and will essentially diminish the tendency to take on malarial diseases and economize the use of quinine."[33] Sadly, the eastern addition of building lots into Venturer's Field, namely Valley and Williams streets, became known as "Little Venice" for its frequent inundation.

Regardless of human folly, however, nothing would have prevented the havoc raised by the enormous flood of 1936, or the hurricane that followed in 1938. These were surely among the greatest storms since Northampton's settlement by English colonists. The storms came in the midst of the Great Depression when there was political will and plenty of labor available to dig a ditch and move the offending Mill River out of downtown. These actions both saved Northampton from flooding and wiped the collective memory clean of a town with a river running through it.

1890 *November Nor'easter*

"The High Water—Nearly up to the Biggest Flood of 1862" screamed the *Daily Hampshire Gazette* headline. Although the Connecticut River was three feet lower than during the Lincoln Flood, it still caused great damage. This November nor'easter dumped an enormous amount of rain over a twelve-hour period that caused the Mill River to rise fifteen inches at the Old South Street Bridge. Many houses on Williams and Valley streets had water up to their first floors, and fifty houses were entirely surrounded by water.

The old custom of merriment prevailed once again. The wedding festivities of a certain Louis N. Baker and his bride were celebrated "with as much joy and delight as though they were not shut off from all communication with the rest of the world except by boat. At the close of the feast, a boat containing a jolly party upset, giving the occupants a good ducking in several feet of water."

Meanwhile, a resident named Peter Marier put his cow on a raft to tow it to safety with his boat. "But the cow jumped off the raft and began to swim for the open meadows. Peter leaped out of the boat into the water up to his shoulders and fastening a rope to the cow's horns was pulled back into the boat by his father and the procession then started for the landing, the cow swimming on behind." He would have done better to have followed Joe Lapint's example. Lapint had kept his cow on the deck of his house until the water rose too high. He then stored the cow in the kitchen.[34]

1896 Spring Freshet

This was a typical early March freshet, during which the temperature warmed to fifty degrees and it started raining on top of a foot of snow. The resulting flash flood rose up to the floor of the Old South Street Bridge and fell several feet back within a few hours. Large chunks of melting ice on the Mill caused major jams that led to the flooding of the electric lighting company above the Lower Mills and the inundation of the lower floor of Maynard's Hoe Shop. Farther upriver, the bridge in Florence on Nonotuck Street at the Pro Brush shop was threatened, while Florence Fields were completely flooded and the road at the Ross Farm washed out. Ice blocks at Leeds and Haydenville accounted for the local damage of roads, dams, and bridges.

The main attraction of the flood came at noontime on March 1st on the Connecticut River where

> the force of the water broke the hold of the ice on the trees of the shores, and with a crunching and grating which could be heard a long distance off, the ice began to move down stream. Then came a grand sight. Trees six and eight inches through were broken off where they were frozen in, and even larger trees were bent and peeled of their bark by the irresistible force of moving ice. When the bank ran out against the direction of the flow the ice was forced up their sides, as high as 20 feet, and heaped up by the thousand tons... The river offered an attractive ice carnival all day, and was visited by hundreds of people, who went to the Hadley bridge for the purpose.[35]

One gets the sense that local folks had clearly become accustomed, indeed, happily anticipated, annual freshets. Entertainment had replaced fear—at least for the moment.

1902 Spring Freshet

April of 1900 brought some flooding of the east end of Northampton, but was otherwise a normal spring freshet.

> Williams and Valley streets in this city were all afloat, and while the water brought distress to the parents, it yielded increasing delight to their small children, who went about the neighborhood on rafts, poled with their mothers' clothes line props, and shouted and made merry from one end of their modern Venice to the other.[36]

The March freshet of 1902, however, was another story because such thick ice had built up in the Connecticut River that its quick breakup threatened major bridges.

Several of the large stones in the upper part of the pier [of the Hadley-Northampton Bridge] were knocked out by the great cakes of ice, nearly two feet thick, that almost constantly battered against it with tremendous force. The gorge [i.e., ice jam] was one of the largest ever seen in the river and presented a magnificent sight to the many who visited the scene during the afternoon and evening. Solid ice twenty feet high at the bridge covered an area of many acres. When the gorge was at its worst the surface of the ice was only about five feet below the tracks on the bridge. The strain became so great that workmen were sent by the railroad officials to destroy the ice jam by blowing it up with dynamite.[37]

Fig. 5.15 Little Venice (near Venturer's Field, Northampton) "presents a picturesque sight...people can get about only by using boats" in the 1913 Flood. (Courtesy Forbes Library)

Fig. 5.16 Children and boats in the Flood of 1913 in Little Venice (Courtesy Forbes Library)

As usual, Little Venice was underwater, in what had become so common a phenomenon that residents had finally begun complaining. "Councilman Mariz," noted the *Daily Hampshire Gazette*, "will be able to wax more eloquent than ever over the question of building a dike at the next meeting of the city council." The lower Mill River also became so congested with ice that the run of the river below the wire-mill dam at the Lower Mills was almost level with the water coming over the dam.[38]

1913 *Spring freshet*

Heavy rains in late March caused the flooding of the Northampton Meadows and Little Venice, which

presents a picturesque sight. The lower stories of the houses are partially submerged and the people can get about only by using boats. Thursday night families began moving household goods to upper stories of the houses, and pigs and hens were taken to places beyond the reach of the flood. Letter carriers, grocerymen and others who desire communication with the people of the flooded district paddle back and forth in boats and the children of the families find great enjoyment in sailing about in boats. There has been today a constant stream of people coming and going in visits to the lower part of Pleasant and Williams streets. The most interesting place visited is lower Williams street for there one gets a full view of the flooded section and the movement of the people.[39]

The joyous spirit of the season mirrored the upbeat temper of the times during the new century's Progressive Era leading up to the First World War. Fourteen years hence, a far more dramatic storm would dampen the spirits of the Mill River citizens.

1927 Nor'easter

The year 1927 marked the first of four devastating floods that hit the Mill River during the next decade. On November 5, the *Daily Hampshire Gazette* lead said it all: "Northampton awoke today to find itself in the grasp of the worst fall flood which ever struck the city. It surpassed the spring freshet of 1913, the highest water in recent years, and it is said to have equaled the great spring freshet which occurred in 1862."

Workers Build Dikes to Halt Waters in Flood Area.
Northampton. Mass., Nov. 1927

Fig. 5.17 Workers building dikes in Little Venice in 1927. (Courtesy Forbes Library)

Tremendous rains in early November followed on the heels of two dry months. The Meadows quickly flooded, and boats were sent out to rescue people and animals swimming in almost eight feet of water.

It was a Saturday, and "college girls arrived at the [train] station this morning, intent upon going to Springfield and points south, and were surprised that the flood had reached such proportions that train service had to be abandoned." The Hadley Bridge was closed and the only remaining transportation was by boat. Smith College boats at Paradise Pond were commandeered to rescue pigs and people caught in flood waters. Little Venice went underwater, of course, and the Fruit and Maple Street dike sprang a leak, forcing residents in that section to once again seek higher ground while men piled many thousands of bags of sand along the dike to prevent a break.

The 1927 flood was the first in which health authorities prominently warned against an outbreak of disease. The city's Board of Health announced that "Parents will be allowed to return to their homes to clean premises, but the children will not be permitted to return until an inspection is made…all food products touched by flood waters and not subject to cooking shall be destroyed."[40]

1936 Spring Freshet

This flood event changed everything, forcing the people of the watershed to face the choice of retaining the river in town or banishing it. The first of three great storms hit the Connecticut Valley, which had endured a bitter, snowy winter without a thaw during which two feet of ice had built up on the big river. On March 11, a warm front stalled over New Hampshire and Maine, dumping up to five inches of rain over three days before a second storm displaced it from March 16–19. A smaller storm followed the first two, adding to the misery. The Connecticut River rose thirty-eight feet in Hartford, and its waters receded only after almost two weeks of soaking rain that dumped up to thirty inches of water in parts of New England.[41]

Two days of warm rain had raised the anxiety levels of the citizens of the Mill River Valley on March 13. Stories began to appear in the *Daily Hampshire Gazette* about menacing conditions on both the Connecticut and Mill Rivers, where ice jams threatened bridges and dams. Residents of low-lying areas had to abandon their houses and "twelve pigs belonging to Mrs. Anthony Vaderlick, were lost on Meadow street, when a raft on which they were being carried tipped over." At Paradise Pond, ice had shoved the flashboards off the dam, and there was discussion of dynamiting the remaining ice to move it downriver to relieve the besieged Maple Street area.

By March 14, most of the families in Little Venice had to be evacuated and housed at the U.S. army drill hall on King Street while the city looked to generous local citizens to house more than two hundred flood victims. Northampton's mayor urged the department of public safety to blow up an ice jam in Easthampton to ease the danger of flooding in Northampton, but the first storm began to subside on the sixteenth, and most people expected that the town would escape further harm.

The second storm began on the eighteenth, cutting off the northern and western highway routes to Northampton and raising premonitions that the Flood of 1936 would dole out further punishment. The Mill River began to rise one foot per hour. The Pro Brush Company closed down when its engine rooms flooded. Residents feared that worse was to come as a dismal mist hovered over parts of the river. Farther upstream, flood waters took out several dams and bridges, washing out local roads and stranding many rural families.

The next day's *Gazette* headlines shouted out: "2000 Residents Here Flee Raging Waters; '27 Record Shattered: Mill River Runs On Rampage Into Maple Street Area." The Maple Street Dike failed, inundating the area and creating hundreds of refugee families. Pleasant and Hawley Streets went underwater along with part of King Street. The Turners Falls Power Company managed to keep some electric lines open, but the gas company was down to its last gas storage facility. The sewer system failed. "The water is so far above the sewerage system level that there is nothing the sewer department can do... to alleviate it."

Fig. 5.18 1936 Flooding on Pleasant Street looking toward Main Street, Northampton (Courtesy Forbes Library)

Fig. 5.19 *The sad remnant of a bar on the Meadows after the Flood of 1936. The 18th Amendment prohibiting consumption of alcoholic beverages had been abrogated barely two years before the flood.* (Courtesy Forbes Library)

In town on the nineteenth, a local reporter described what had become "a not uncommon sight— the picture of families stranded on the roofs of houses, waiting to be rescued by patrolling scouts and officers." Water began to flow over the main floor of the Hadley Bridge while huge blocks of ice on a fast current made transportation and rescue on the Big River almost impossible.

A large crowd gathered at Hadley bridge and vicinity yesterday afternoon to view the high water and ice jam against the bridge. Huge cakes were making a thundering noise as they struck the bridge and were forced underneath, where engineers reported that tie rods underneath the bridge flooring were being broken. The flood is so much higher and so much more disastrous than 1927 that there is no comparison, and the 1927 flood was far beyond any previous high water. It is by far the greatest disaster that has struck the Connecticut Valley."[42] Northampton's mayor Dunn estimated the number of refugees at over two thousand, or about 10 percent of the town's population, calling the flood "the worst disaster in Northampton's history."[43]

The flood peaked on March 20, six feet higher than the one in 1927. The waters took several days to recede, leaving behind weeks' worth of cleanup. Men from the Civilian Conservation Corps did banner work, and were finally called to dynamite the Maple Street Dike on March 25 to speed up floodwater drainage that had backed sewers up into basements, presenting residents with severe health hazards. Some even began to think of abandoning their homes in the Conz Street area, the section of the Meadows onto which residents had unwisely built.

During the Great Flood of 1936, the Mill River had simply been doing its proper job of moving water and materials from upstream to downstream, but people and their buildings and belongings were now in the way. Finally the possibility of diverting the Mill River out of town arose in earnest.

1938 Hurricane

Prior to the 1936 Flood, Northampton's engineers had already been reimagining the course of the river, and were prepared to propose safety measures. However, before any action was taken, another huge storm hit a year and a half later—the memorable Hurricane of 1938, a nasty reminder of the damaging potential of the little stream that had always run through the middle of town. Some sober scientists at the US Geological Survey described it in uncharacteristically emotional prose:

> During the brief interval of 6 hours on September 21, 1938, a West Indian hurricane passed over Long Island and New England. The hurricane as it struck New England was the climax of a 4-day period of rainfall which in itself was of outstanding amount and character and which produced river stages that inundated and damaged nearly everything on the river flood plains. When measured by the appalling loss of life [more than 650 dead] and property [more than $4.7 billion in 2017 dollars] by the combined forces of the hurricane winds and the associated ocean storm waves and river floods, these events constituted the greatest catastrophe in New England since its settlement by the white man.[44]

The eye of the hurricane passed just west of the Connecticut River Valley, and as punishing as was the rain, the wind was even more so. In fact, the flood event was less catastrophic than that of 1936, although both broke records. Normal high floodwaters on the Connecticut River at Northampton, ones that can be expected during an uncommonly strong spring freshet, would measure a flow of 50,000 cubic feet of water per second (cfs) as it passes Northampton. In 1936, the volume of water near Northampton was gaged at about 240,000 cfs, whereas the flood of 1938 reached about 200,000 cfs.[45] Both are four to five times the volume of a high freshet. The impacts are even now almost unimaginable, although global climate change, which may well usher in a series of severe storms, would normalize such numbers.

By the time the hurricane arrived, heavy rains had already flooded the meadows and had overtopped the island in Paradise Pond on the Mill River.[46] Planes at the Northampton airport were evacuated as were livestock on the Meadows and Elwell Island near the Hadley Bridge. The Connecticut River had already risen to fourteen feet above flood stage, half the height of the 1936 Flood. As the Mill River rose higher on September 22, factory basements began to flood upriver from Northampton, and the Lower Dam at Goshen gave way, sending a wall of water downstream. The wind gusts rose to ninety mph, blowing roofs off houses and Smith College dormitories and plunging the city into darkness. Some three thousand of Northampton's trees were downed within twenty-four hours. Smith College lost most of its great elms that F. L. Olmsted's firm had planted in the 1890s. Still, the Mill River watershed was spared from even worse conditions just across the river, where Hadley and Amherst experienced enormous destruction. "Literally hundreds of tobacco barns went down, carrying with them a summer's growth of valuable tobacco... In Amherst, nearly every fraternity house on the Amherst campus was damaged, and trees were torn up by their roots all over town."

The Mill River watershed escaped the worst of the hurricane, and, having gone through a disaster just a year and a half before, the city assessed the damage with some relief. The Maple Street dike held when hundreds of workers piled sand bags on top of it, stretching from Old South Street to the end of Maple Street. The upper watershed experienced little damage from the 1938 Hurricane. On September 23, the only mention of any news whatsoever in Haydenville concerned the occurrence of a wedding shower for Miss Margaret Devlin, but there were no reports of storm damage.

Unlike Nor'easters, which simply roll up the coast and pound everything in their paths, hurricanes destroy some places and spare others. It really depends on exactly where the eye of the hurricane is located, and a few miles one way or another can determine where damage occurs. The Mill River watershed was largely spared. Eugene Davis, a local engineer, surveyed all the dams on the Mill River and pronounced them safe: "Yesterday afternoon, I went to nearly all the dams on the Mill river watershed and found them in their usual condition," except for the Goshen dam that had given way earlier.[47] In summary, the Mill River watershed, especially the upper sections, fared better than many other areas of New England. Northampton's estimated loss was only $81,500 or about $320,000 in 2017 dollars.

Environmental Transformation V:

Alien Invasion and Native Resilience

Since the arrival of English colonists in the mid-seventeenth century, ecological and human impacts had deeply transformed the Mill River and its watershed. Early on, the Meadows had been outfitted with new grasses and forbs[48] suitable for European livestock, and the lower Mill River had been diverted and dammed, severely limiting the movement of migratory and local fish. By the end of the eighteenth century, the rush for potash as a cash crop encouraged the first major land clearings that began to erode the hillsides and silt up stretches of the river. Bare, eroded hillsides cropped up throughout the watershed as feeder streams ran lower and more turgid. The demand for wood slackened in the second half of the nineteenth century, allowing the woodlands to return, but they were no longer the diverse forest communities that existed earlier. Pines and hemlocks stood in dense stands, along with extensive patches of sugar maples. During the second half of the nineteenth century, factories from Williamsburg through Northampton poured a heavy load of pollutants into the river while a dynamically growing population dumped in household sewage. Although Northampton quickly developed clean drinking water and a sewer system after the Civil War, these measures were insufficient to keep up with the amount of effluent, especially during times of flood.

One last great ecological surprise awaited the Mill River as the nineteenth century ended. A new wave of exotic plants, insects, and diseases invaded on the heels of a population boom. Houses began to appear on the Mill River's flood plain, and machines shifted vast amounts of soil from one place to another through ditching, diking, building, and filling. Gardeners imported ever more ornamentals for their gardens, transplanting trees, shrubs and exotic herbaceous plants from distant origins to the banks of the Mill and its adjacent hillsides. New fish species appeared as well, dumped into the streams and reservoirs during the transplant craze of sport fisheries, around which grew a new sportsmen's bureaucracy.

The study of invasive species has become a fascinating, sprawling field, far too broad for us to do more than apply a few of its findings to our own Mill River watershed.[49] Most twenty-first-century Americans regard the arrival of exotic species and displacement of natives as inimical to a healthy ecosystem, but those who introduced these species insisted they were making the world a better place. The year 1900 was, after all, the beginning of the Progressive Era, a time of limitless optimism, when most thought that human action could only produce happy results, despite such naysayers as G. P. Marsh and John Muir. Americans could see no conflict in supporting both wilderness preservation and the introduction of exotic species. They had been importing and acclimating plants and animals since the seventeenth century to little apparent ill effect. At the turn of the twentieth century, forests appeared generally healthy, and the wetlands, floodplains, and grazing lands seemed to be intact, even if some pastures had begun to resemble shrublands unsuitable for livestock. The first great adoption of European food and fodder plants had been so successful that two centuries later, Americans simply accepted their fields and meadows as natural parts of their native communities even though there was scarcely a native plant remaining, save corn and cattails, and corn was a Central American import from about 1200 BP. The earliest exotics have now been with us almost four hundred years, and we have come to embrace most of them, from earthworms and honeybees to wheat and white clover. Some are problematic, such as dandelions and pigeons; others, like starlings and crabgrass, are simply reviled.

The late nineteenth century, however, saw an enormous expansion of exotic introductions, including insects and diseases that accompanied plants and animals. The early colonists had brought with them, intentionally or not, several score of European species. It has been estimated that another 140 exotic plant species became naturalized in America during the nineteenth century, and several hundred more came in the twentieth. As for insects, there were only some thirty exotic species in 1800, to which seventy more were added by 1860. Between 1860 and 1919, however, 475 new exotic insects were recorded.[50]

Nonnative insects have accumulated in the forests of the United States at a rate of about two-and-a-half per year over the last one hundred fifty years, arriving chiefly through live plants, pallets, and packing materials. The problem is particularly severe in the Northeast, which has the longest history of European settlement and contains tree species most closely related to those in Europe. Invasive insects and diseases are the only disturbance agents that have eliminated entire tree species and genera in our forests, changing the composition of our flora and altering the ecosystem, including wildlife habitat. The result has been economic damage that is likely in the billions of dollars.[51]

Exotic species find a host of ways to hitch rides. Settlers brought with them many fellow travelers including all the pets, farm animals, and fodder crops of the countryside, while other exotics were uninvited stowaways, such as rats and house mice. Hundreds more species were unceremoniously dumped as part of sailing ships' ballast in port cities (crabgrass) or came clinging to the hides of cattle and horses (cockleburs). Of the many thousands of plant and animal species introduced to America, only a small number thrived.

Native plants in the Mill River wetlands managed to maintain themselves throughout most of the twentieth century. In a 1970 comprehensive survey of the Mill's wetland vegetation, only about five out of seventy-five plant species were exotic.[52] The exotic plants that now overwhelm long stretches of the river never invaded extensively until the end of the twentieth century, most of them requiring a long lag time (often more than a hundred years) to adapt and expand.[53]

Many of the sixteen exotic plant species that have become the river's most noxious alien invasives have eighteenth- and nineteenth-century origins. The most recognizable, Japanese knotweed, was introduced as an ornamental in the 1870s but did not become pervasive until late in the twentieth century. Their dense stands along the banks of the Mill River obscure any view of the river itself along a number of reaches, especially between Williamsburg and Leeds. Other plants with lengthy lag times are multiflora rose (ca. 1800), exotic honeysuckles (early 1800s), Japanese barberry (1875), and Norway maple (late 1700s). These and other exotics, introduced years ago, have so overwhelmed native vegetation over the past fifty years that many of these landscapes would be almost unrecognizable to someone born in the first half of the twentieth century.[54]

In the forests, however, alien species had a devastating impact with little lag time at all. The American chestnut and American elm have all but disappeared, and eastern hemlock, American beech, and native ash are under attack.[55] Often it is not plants themselves that present a threat but their accompanying insects and diseases. Chestnut blight is a fungal canker, introduced on Asian chestnuts that were planted around 1900, and it proved so disastrous that as much as a quarter of forest biomass was destroyed throughout its range.[56] By 1920, almost all the chestnuts in New England were dead, leaving only the vigorous rootstocks that still refuse to die throughout the woodlands of the Eastern U.S. J. L. Harper, the most outstanding plant ecologist of the late twentieth century, describes this phenomenon as "probably the largest single change in any natural plant population that has ever been recorded by man."[57] Dutch elm disease was just as destructive as chestnut blight. Less important economically than chestnut, but just as important esthetically, elm had become perhaps the signature specimen tree of cities and towns. This beetle-born fungal disease probably originated in Asia, but is named after the European elms that it killed in Holland in the early 1900s. It came to America as an elm veneer imported into Ohio in about 1930, and most American elms were dead by 1960.[58]

The situation was quite different in the aquatic community, where the release of exotic fish into the waters of the Mill River did not significantly change the suite of fishes in the watershed. In the late nineteenth century, fly and bait fishing fanatics joined with the new state fisheries personnel to build fish hatcheries in which millions of exotic trout and bass were raised. The rage for bait and fly fishing led to the bassing and trouting of Massachusetts. First to be released were large- and smallmouth bass from the St. Lawrence watersheds in the 1860s, followed twenty years later by rainbow trout from California and brown trout from Germany and England. Bass quickly became a dominant predatory fish in the Connecticut River and lower reaches of the tributaries. Rainbow and brown trout fast became the favored stocked cold-water game fish because they grew large more quickly than brook trout, also known locally as "natives." Nonetheless, the exotics never managed to sustain their populations in the Mill, except for bass near its mouth in the waters of Hulbert's Pond. Rainbow and brown trout probably did not spawn in the Mill, and bass are not found upstream of Paradise Pond.

Fig. 5.20 Adult sea lamprey.

Some twenty species of native fish maintained a steady presence in the Mill River throughout the twentieth century, about half of them minnows and the rest white suckers and brook trout, along with a small number of yellow perch, pumpkinseed sunfish, and chain pickerel.[59] The natives held on despite a habitat deprived of migratory fish and polluted by industry and town sewage.[60] By 1900, at least two hundred years had passed since any significant number of salmon, shad, lamprey, blueback herring, or eel had run up the unhealthy and dammed-up waters of the Mill River.

Pollution in the Connecticut River, meanwhile, had blocked the major highway of almost all migratory fish. New England forests, the Mill River watershed included, suffered a devastating loss of nutrients when this enormous marine biomass was blocked from the Connecticut River. The millions of salmon, herring, and eels added fertility to the rivers and adjacent woodlands from their eggs, fry, and the dead that were left behind. But the sea lamprey, that ugliest champion of long-distance aquatic hitchhikers, contributed the most because they spawned and died in all the small brooks. Not a single individual returned to the sea, leaving their decaying bodies to fertilize the streams and forests.[61] Fisheries biologists Keith Nislow and Boyd Kynard described why the lamprey's contributions were so important: lampreys use the right spawning habitats (small, nutrient poor streams) at the right time (late spring during high nutrient demand), and do the right thing (die after spawning).[62]

We have plentiful accounts of fishing for salmon and shad on the Connecticut River but none on the Mill. Perhaps the fish runs were never large, but surely in the seventeenth century there would have been at least a modest number of fish, even if the first dam at the Upper Mills in 1666 hindered their travels. The 1710 diversion may have further reduced migration, but all we can do is surmise. We do know, however, that pollution played a major role in the decreased abundance and diversity of fish in the Mill during the late nineteenth and much of the twentieth centuries.

In the first quarter of the twentieth century, an official of the Massachusetts Division of Fisheries and Wildlife described the waters of the Mill above Leeds as unpolluted. The state annually released hundreds, sometimes thousands, of small brook trout during this period, and an occasional bunch of brown trout.[63] The lower watershed was a different story, and Northampton health officials were very much aware that water quality was dreadful

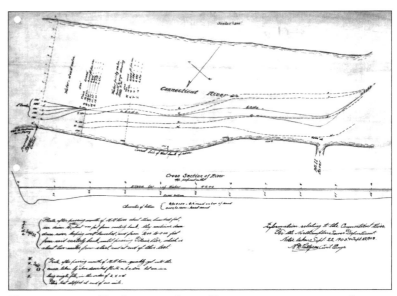

Fig. 5.21 1903 Northampton Sewer Department engineering plan to construct a sewer outfall a mile downriver from the mouth of the Mill River in a stretch of "dead calm" water 460 feet above the Hockanum Ferry. The writing in the lower left describes the use of floats to determine the flow of effluent down the Connecticut River, perhaps to determine the placement of the outfall. (Courtesy Doug MacDonald and Northampton Deptartment of Public Works)

in the city proper. They drafted a plan in 1903 to build an outfall pipe from their sewage collection system directly into the Connecticut River well downstream from the town.

Clearly the city had not alleviated the problem in a timely manner because, as Deputy Commissioner of Fisheries, P. F. McCarthy reported in 1914: "The river below Florence is of no value as far as fishing is concerned. The Northampton Gas Co. pollutes the stream with water gas char, and the river also receives the sewage from the city of Northampton." Three years later, however, on New Year's Day of 1917, Deputy Commissioner McCarthy wrote that the situation had dramatically improved:

> I have talked with the city engineer [of Northampton], the agent of the Board of Health and one of the sewer commissioners, and all three of them said that the only pollution now entering Mill River, above what is known as the 'Grist Mill' [Lower Mill], is some house sewerage, all acids and dye stuff having entered the city sewer. The city put in a special sewer for the Nonotuck Silk Co. for the purpose of taking off their dye stuff and was finished last year. I would consider Mill River above the 'Grist Mill' dam all right for food fish. The main sewer of the city empties into Mill River about one mile from its entrance into the Connecticut River. It is my belief that this sewer is very injurious to the fish at the lower end or its entrance into the Connecticut River.[64]

Northampton had improved its own water quality to the detriment of the Connecticut River. Katharine Hepburn, in a 1965 documentary entitled "The Long Tidal River," described the Connecticut River as "the world's most beautifully landscaped cesspool."[65] The Mill River continued to transport materials from upstream down and, in doing so, simply contributed its share of pollution to the 11,000 square miles of Connecticut River watershed that emptied into the dead zone at mouth of the Great Tidal River in Long Island Sound. The City of Northampton had gamed the natural system by storing pollutants in its collection system, which maintained a comparatively healthy Mill River, while dumping its waste into the Connecticut. Such is the ancient practice of letting people downstream bear the cost of upstream pollution.

In 1939, the citizens of Northampton had one more dramatic transformation in store for the Mill River—its diversion out of downtown Northampton. The river's health at mid-century was reasonably good even though some household sewage and the industrial waste from the cutleries were leaking into it.

While not up to twenty-first-century health standards, much of the river was fit for swimming and fishing, and the newspapers reported no accounts of water-borne disease in the news. Few exotic plants had invaded the banks and flood-plains, which still retained most of their native vegetation although the forests had been deprived of chestnut and elm. The most damaging exotic plants were chiefly sleepers, whose lag time limits would end with the end of the twentieth century. The waters of the Mill had been impoverished by the loss of marine nutrients from migratory fish, and nine dams had blocked the free passage of fish and blocked the normal transport of sediments and nutrients, which re-mained behind the dams. Yet native fish far outnumbered exotic transplants.

The one natural function of the Mill that its human residents could no longer tolerate was the river's insistence on occupying its flood plain in times of high water. Northampton had allowed too many people to move onto the Mill's secondary riverbed, and the cost of floods became far greater than their recreational benefits. The Mill River had to go.

The 1940 Diversion: From Greenway to Ghost Stream

Right after the 1938 Hurricane, engineer Eugene Davis gave a series of public talks to the citizens and officials of Northampton about the plan he had devised in 1936 to protect the town from future floods of record. "Flood protection for Northampton," announced the *Daily Hampshire Gazette* in 1936, "can best be obtained by diversion of the Mill river and the building of a higher dike for [the] Maple street section and a dike for the Williams street section in the city."[66]

What became known as the "Davis Plan" diverted the Mill River not far downstream from Paradise Pond, then near the north face of Fort Hill and "draining into the South street meadows to the Old Bed..." The mouth of the Mill once again emptied into the ancient oxbow leading to the mouth of the Manhan River (currently Massachusetts Audubon's Arcadia Sanctuary) just as it had prior to 1710. Unlike the pre-eighteenth-century riverbed, however, the new riprapped bed ran along the north rather than the south face of Fort Hill. The material from the old Maple Street dike was used as fill for the original riverbed.

In 1939, the U.S. Army Corps of Engineers began digging a ditch to divert the Mill according to the Davis Plan.

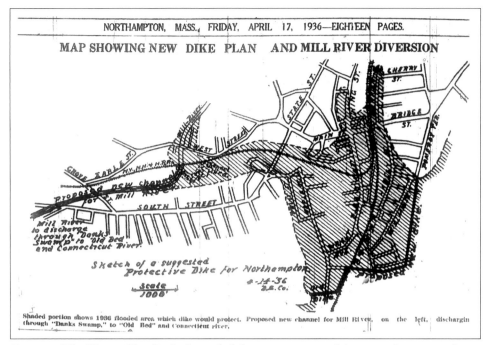

Fig. 5.22 *The "Davis Plan," which guided the construction of the 1940 diversion of the Mill River. The newspaper caption reads: "Shaded portion shows 1936 flooded area which dike would protect. Proposed new channel for Mill River, on the left, will discharge through "Danks Swamp" to "Old Bed" and Connecticut River. Daily Hampshire Gazette 4/17/1936.*

Fig. 5.23 *Photo of the ditch in 1939 that diverted the Mill River out of downtown Northampton into Hulbert's Pond near the Oxbow. (Courtesy Forbes Library)*

Thus, in six years, did the vision of the Mill River shift from Gerald Lee's public greenway to Eugene Davis' abandoned streambed. The river, which for centuries had been a major presence in the Nonotuck village and the colonial town, was gone from the city's collective consciousness. It was as though Paradise Pond, the defining landscape feature at Smith College, emptied into a void. The Mill had simply disappeared from downtown Northampton, leaving a palimpsest for the observant passerby.

After the Diversion: 1940–2018

The Mill River's disappearance barely raised a ripple in newspaper coverage during the 1940s. Everyone, after all, had more immediate concerns, namely the Second World War and the end of the Depression. When soldiers returned from the war, the U.S. economy, with some coughs and wheezes, took off. But New England's factories, textiles in particular, continued their long decline, as production moved to the South with its cheap labor and lack of unions. Larger cities like Springfield and Hartford, along with many factory villages, became hollowed out in the 1970s. Springfield, whose population grew from 150,000 in 1940 to its historic apogee of 175,000 in 1960, fell by 15 percent in 1980 to 152,000, where it has remained ever since.

The people of the Mill River fared somewhat better than many other New Englanders. Local populations remained remarkably stable: Williamsburg, with a population of 2200 in 1960, had 2400 in 2010. Northampton's population has remained between 28,000 and 30,000 from 1950 to the present.[67] We have seen how institutions, such as the colleges, the VA Hospital, and the State Hospital picked up the slack in industrial employment, and residents of the hilltowns became beneficiaries of employment opportunities as well.

Economic decline did indeed strike Northampton in the last third of the twentieth century, because institutional employment simply did not drive the economy as powerfully as industrial jobs had. Northampton in the 1960s was a rather sad town, as those of us who lived here at that time can tell you. Cultural activities tended to stay within the confines of campuses. There were few good restaurants, save some decent pizza places. Of the many bars, Rahar's on Old South (Lickingwater) Street was the most famous, especially among the underage college crowd. The upper watershed and Williamsburg settled into a somewhat drowsy period, with little local employment but enough regional jobs to provide the community with a decent quality of life. Northampton and Williamsburg remained as connected as ever to the wider world, but one could no longer sense the confidence or pride of place that marked life in the lower watershed.

Nonetheless, there remained several enterprising men and women with faith in Northampton's future, most notably a local group who bought a nineteenth-century Main Street department store to create "Thorne's Marketplace," filled with small shops from ice cream to clothing, pottery, and bookstores, along with quasi-public spaces. Thorne's served as an anchor to the development of downtown Northampton in the 1980s, ushering in a cultural renaissance that has turned the lower watershed into a regional destination for music, cultural events, and good eating and dancing. The size of Northampton's population remained the same, but the city gained a new sense of confidence and optimism.

The Mill River had, unfortunately, disappeared from downtown Northampton, leading residents and visitors alike to assume the river had always run elsewhere, but who knew where? On a happier note, the report card on the environmental health of the river and its creatures contains mostly good marks over the past seventy-five years. The best news is that the river's water is generally of high quality, except after heavy rains when fecal coliform from household sewage runs into it.[68] Environmental legislation in the 1960s and 1970s helped a great deal, but perhaps the greatest contributor to clean water was the loss of industry along the Mill. Factories no longer dump effluent from their processing plants. One of the only brownfield sites on the river is located at the Cutlery in Bay State, where heavy metals remain in the soil, preventing greenway advocates from building a path from Bay State to Florence.

The core problem in caring for the Mill has been the river's loss of integrity—it is divided into sections by nine dams and a diversion, so that its aquatic biota cannot move freely up- and downstream. Sand and mud build up behind the dams, destroying fish and invertebrate habitat. Many of its banks have been overwhelmed by exotics that appeared only near the turn of the twenty-first century. Japanese knotweed blocks the river from view along many stretches, and Asiatic bittersweet continues to destroy parts of the woodlands. Exotic shrubs have made for miserable walking on or near the stream banks. The river's dams hinder efforts to develop a sustainable, flexible, and resilient biotic system.

Some wonderful aquatic creatures and wildlife have returned to the river, in particular a rich array of river mussels that play vital roles in the aquatic ecosystem, filtering wastes from water and serving as food for birds, fish and animals. The Mill River has a total of nine species of freshwater mussels, several of which are endangered or of special concern, living in habitats from shallow ponds to deep pools and cascades to slackwater. It is among the richest in mussel diversity of all Connecticut River tributaries.[69]

Large and small mammals now inhabit riverbanks and hillsides, unconcerned with dams blocking their movements. Bears have become such a nuisance, often digging winter dens in the banks of the Mill, that the City of Northampton has had to enact regulations about when and where to hang bird feeders. Whitetail deer drive homeowners and gardeners as crazy as do bears. Bobcats lurk on the edge of the forest waiting to grab someone's house cat, and both gray and red fox have become common sights. Other fur bearers have returned for the first time in three hundred years—fishers are seen from time to time cleaning out gray squirrel nests. Minks patrol the banks, on the lookout for anything that moves, while muskrats remain common along all the banks. River otters lope easily from the Big River as far up as Williamsburg, and beaver leave their felled trees and chewed stumps all along the river.

We will take optimistic leave of our readers, knowing that the people of the Mill River have begun to steward its banks and waters as never before. In the first decade of the twenty-first century, a citizens group called the Mill River Greenway Initiative sprang up to give voice to the Mill River, tend its resources, and create a greenway along its banks. The group envisions a series of historic river walks that alternate with riversides and buffers for ecological research, multi-purpose paths, and even a major link between Haydenville and Williamsburg Center.

In 2017, the public enjoys long reaches of the river that run through the hills of Goshen and Williamsburg, where scores of people hike every year on pilgrimages to the site of the 1874 Dam Disaster. Williamsburg Center proudly designed a riverside pocket park where a summer farmers' market takes place, and Haydenville's Brass Works remains a river icon. The citizens of Leeds have created a self-guided river walk of the town and are trying to resuscitate an 1880 iron bridge. Downstream in Florence, the river is a signature feature of Look Park, which attracts crowds of regional residents for recreation, music, and picnics. One can often find anglers on the river looking for stocked trout to take home, and sometimes native brookies as well. Joggers, walkers, and dogs enjoy some three miles of trails on both banks of the Mill between Bay State and Paradise Pond. The latter attracts hordes of Smith alumnae, student boaters and local walkers. At the lower end of the Mill, the Arcadia Sanctuary offers seasonal paddles upriver.

Perhaps in time the river will yet become the quintessential feature of Northampton that Gerald Stanley Lee envisioned in 1934:

> Mill River [can] become one of the decorations and charms of our city, visited by people from all over the world as an original and beautiful thing just for itself—visited as a kind of redeemer of all small streams flowing through cities, throughout the nation, an example of possibilities, a living, flowing memorial... I can imagine hundreds of cities sending people on to Northampton to see what a little humble stream—a country boy's stream flowing through a city—through the very heart of a city, can do to make a city blessed![70]

Stanley's vision certainly seems like a far piece, but as the Book of Proverbs reminds us, "Where there is no vision, the people perish." Bringing the Mill River back into the lives of the people, enriching their experience of the river from top to bottom, would be a gift for seven generations.

AFTERWORD

Why the River Matters

> *El tiempo es un río que me arrebata,*
> *Pero yo soy el río.*
>
> — Jorge Luis Borges

Rivers have been my lifelong pursuit. How best to tell their stories, and explain why they matter? Were I an early Native American, I might grant rivers agency, cognition, and spiritual qualities. I could describe the Mill River as one of the earthshapers and placemakers that weave in and out of the origin stories of First People. I might then have a lively story to tell about the Mill and its creatures creating the landscape, and the evil moods of the river in flood. But I am descended from white immigrants, with barely a trace of prehistoric understanding, not even at the level of, say, Germans, who are still in touch with the living qualities of their founding river, the Rhine.[1]

I am a prisoner of my own time and place, who can only tell Mill River stories as a twenty-first-century American in New England. I can tell you that any river is, as Borges suggests, deeply personal. It can seize you in its flow and carry you back to your childhood passion for moving water. I can tell you that everyone I take to the river is grateful to be there. Like music, rivers require no intermediaries to explain their grip on you.

The Mill River carries American stories in its waters, both from Native Americans and from those the world over. Its history is proof that the Abenaki concept of the common pot, the *wlôgan*, cannot be obliterated, but can only be added to or subtracted from. The contents of the common pot change over the centuries and millennia, sometimes in balance and sometimes not. The landscapes and people of the Mill River bear a deeply American character: no other modern nation was born with so many Native people still living in a place where Europeans arrived so close to the birth of the Industrial Revolution or so well prepared for industrial life. We must give thanks to the Mill for doing what rivers can do so well—memorialize our past and float us toward the future. We must allow ourselves to reflect on the lessons its stories tell.

More concretely, the Mill River shaped this landscape and gave it character, carving its way between hills, creating the valley and dividing one part of the land from another. It also united the landscape, providing the pathway for aquatic life to move up and down the valley. One can follow the river from Paradise Pond up to its headwaters in Goshen using trails, both official and unofficial, as well as roadways. One can do some of it by bicycle and all of it on foot, although parts of the route are unpleasant, even dangerous because of traffic. But the river clearly defines your direction—its presence is real and a welcome friend to the hiker or cyclist.

From Paradise Pond downstream, however, the river has disappeared, resulting in a geographic and cognitive dysfunction. The New South Street Bridge has hidden any evidence of Lickingwater, the old fording place that once separated Meetinghouse Hill from Fort Hill. Even longtime residents who take the riverwalk from Paradise Pond to downtown Northampton become completely disoriented because they no longer carry mental maps of the river that defined the town. Visual clues are almost nonexistent: there is barely a hint of the river at Lickingwater near the base of Pulaski Park, or of water running along Pleasant Street and out into the Meadows, or of a river across the street from the old Hawley Street School below New South Street. When you lose the river, you lose your sense of direction and cannot understand why Northampton's street pattern is so peculiar.

Remember how important floods were to the lives of people in the lower watershed for almost three hundred years? Floods had presented regular opportunities to confront natural events, to wonder at the power of the river. The postwar era would hold few such occasions. The Davis Plan redirected the river out of town, and the Corps of Engineers installed a deep, riprapped ditch downstream of Paradise Pond, all the way to the south end of Northampton. The Corps included a wooden and iron barrier that could be erected across West Street in case of high water. That barrier has been raised twice since 1940, once during the hurricanes of 1955 and once during tropical storm Irene in 2011. In each instance, citizens came out in droves to witness the Mill River trying to regain access to its flood plain. The Davis Plan has worked: Northampton has not been flooded out so far. But its citizens, no longer accustomed to facing natural disaster, are unprepared for a future that could well include greater storm events. There is no Plan B, and there exists no communal memory.

The Mill River matters because it is part of the essence of this place. It is the reason why so many have gathered in the upper watershed to create a ten-mile greenway that will allow passage from the headwaters in Goshen to Florence in Northampton. It matters because it is lost as an essential element in much of the lower watershed. The recovery of the Mill River would mean the rediscovery of a landscape that lures its residents to its banks and allows them to see the river instead of a curtain of knotweed. Its recovery will offer children a playground and its residents a pathway through its villages. The Mill River's recovery will encourage sustainable populations of insects, crayfish, mussels, and fish. It will enrich the lives of the next seven generations who come after us.

Janine Norton photograph

ACKNOWLEDGMENTS

My deep appreciation goes to colleagues who have helped correct my ignorance on numerous points, and led me on both fruitful and wild goose chases. I hope I have done right by their remarks. Thank you, Marge Bruchac, for introducing me to the idea of Earthshapers and Placemakers; and to Lisa Brooks for introducing me to this land as seen from Native American perspectives. I hope I have not trod on or misused these concepts. Thank you, Neal Salisbury, whose knowledge of Native American history has given me a new pair of eyes. John Brady and Bob Newton have schooled me on geology, and Laurie Sanders and Fred Morrison's intimate knowledge of this watershed's natural history has accompanied me throughout this work. Jason Johnson provided invaluable insight into fisheries, and Boyd Kynard has extraordinarily deep knowledge of the lives of migratory fish and the whole of the Connecticut River watershed. Elizabeth Sharpe and Eric Weber have been the wise sources of all things 1874. Thanks, Steve Strimer, font of all mid-nineteenth-century people and places, and deep gratitude for shepherding the manuscript through the publication process. Thanks to Wendy Sinton for her passion and deep understanding of the world of Sojourner Truth, about whom she has been my guide.

Thanks, as well, to John Clapp, for introducing us all to the lost Roberts Meadow Village. Thanks to Stan Sherer, great photographer and gatherer of historic images. Speaking of historic photographs, Eric Weber has shown me great kindness in sharing his unparalleled collection of Williamsburg photographs and maps. I never thought that I would descend into the depths of the sewers, but Doug McDonald of Northampton's Public Works Department showed me the way. Without Andy Kuether, there would be no historic maps in this book. His work set the pattern for much of the history. To my co-moderators of the Mill River Greenway Initiative, Gaby Immerman and Neal Bastek: your constancy and love have given me the backbone to keep going. For keeping me grounded, I am indebted to my neighbors Patrick and Ellen McGrath.

I remain grateful for the support of my academic colleagues, above all to Reid Bertone-Johnson of Smith's Center for Environment Ecological Design & Sustainability (CEEDS). Reid, keeper of our geographic information system, is an irreplaceable asset and the most generous of colleagues. Thanks, Jack Ahern of UMass Landscape Architecture and Regional Planning, who warmly welcomed me back to the Valley in 2000 and gave me courage to pursue my work. Jon Caris of Smith's Spatial Analysis Lab has given freely of his time, expertise and students to complete tasks I thought impossible. Thanks to Drew Guswa, the most civil of engineers, who makes all our lives richer; and to David Glassberg, UMass public historian: your support has warmed our hearts. All of us are indebted to Gary Hartwell, Keeper of Paradise Pond.

Thank you, people of the Mill River watershed and all members of the Mill River Greenway Initiative. Thanks to Wayne Feiden for his original initiative to create a greenway, and especially to my dear friend Maggie Leonard. Peter Flinker, you were always there in the background working for our success. I would be remiss if I didn't thank the amazing people in Leeds and Burgy—John, Eileen, Paul, Gwen, Bill, Heidi, Sue, and Penny. You have all given me the support to remain optimistic about our river's future.

Of all those who have helped me along this path, my deepest gratitude goes to seven people: Elise Bernier-Feeley of Forbes Library and Marie Panik of Historic Northampton are two of the most wonderfully wise women of the Valley, who have shared their extraordinary knowledge of source materials. My hours of poring over Sylvester Judd's diary with Elise will remain seared into my memory. My colleagues Bruce Laurie and the late Elizabeth Farnsworth, who first challenged me to write this book, have literally saved me from dumping the project when I was convinced I'd lost my way forever. They are the most generous readers one could have, and much as I would wish otherwise, are not responsible for the inevitable gaffes that have crept into this work. Rob Stewart, the great graphic designer at Transit Authority Figures, made the maps and edited the images in this book so that readers could make sense of my scratchings. Much gratitude goes to my editor Robert Redick, without whose intervention this book would have become a recitation of facts and images. Robert's generosity of spirit is matched by his keen intellect; he has made a book out of a manuscript. Finally, deep thanks to my friend, the late, generous, and wise Ralmon Jon Black, a full twenty-two hours younger than me, but that much more knowledgeable about the world. He was the only person who could piece together the history of Williamsburg, and his passing leaves a great emptiness in our hearts.

APPENDIX

Notes On the 1874 Williamsburg Dam Disaster

Eric Weber, 2018

Eric Weber, President of Williamsburg's Historical Society, has analyzed the various heights of the flood wave at different points in the valley as it descended downstream from Williamsburg to Florence. Mr. Weber's notes were sent to the author in February and March, 2018.

Height of the Williamsburg Flood Disaster

The height of the flood varied widely. My estimates of it are based on the photographs taken later. Some reporters undoubtedly embellished it, but I have no doubt that the leading wave was at least twenty feet high where it entered the village of Williamsburg at Spelman's button shop. It knocked all the walls out from under the factory's heavily built, rigidly triangulated roof, then floated the intact roof three hundred feet downstream. Just below the confluence of the East and West Branches, where the valley widened to more than four hundred feet, the flood spread out and obviously grew shallower, but it was still deep enough to carry two dozen houses and other buildings entirely away before it reached where the pharmacy is today. A large pine tree at the confluence of the two branches had all its bark battered off to a height of about twenty feet. The flood appears to have gathered itself to about twenty feet again as the valley narrowed just above the Brass Works, where a house floating down from upstream stove in the second story (but not the first) at the upstream end of the mill complex. My guess is that the flats of Skinnerville were covered to not much more than seven feet at most of the houses, and less at some. Houses were swept away wholesale there, too, but I believe they were mostly quite small and lightly built. A few larger ones remained, and some of the tall first-floor windows on the upstream side of the Skinner mansion appear to be intact in photos taken afterward. I think their sills were at least six feet off the ground, and though some did let in water (the first floor had a foot of mud in it afterward), the fact that any windows survived suggests that even with the massive house acting as a dam across the flow of the current, the water level didn't rise above eight feet at the highest there.

So much of the initial wave was tumbling, thrashing debris that even eye-witnesses gave widely differing accounts of its depth. Some may have been making allowances for the part of it that wasn't water, while others may not. I think it would be safe to say that in the populated areas where it claimed many lives and carried away whole buildings before friction attenuated it, its depth ranged from twenty-five feet down to six to eight feet; it was certainly nowhere near uniform. Along the edges and after the bulk of it had passed, many places were flooded only to a depth of three feet or less. It was deepest in the first minutes in the ravine just below the dam, and at a sharp bend beside Ashfield Road, and possibly again at one or two points between Haydenville and Leeds. It must have been at least eight feet deep along the main street in Leeds to have done the damage it did there, and much deeper than that where it leveled the big brick boardinghouse beside the Mulberry Street bridge. But everywhere it went, it was pushed this way and that, piled against one obstacle and diverted away from others, by the underlying topography, by structures that resisted, and by temporary dams of flood-borne debris that changed from moment to moment. Many of those, and some of the topographic features, had disappeared by the time shocked residents came out to look for survivors, so it wasn't always easy to tell why the waters had been high in one place and lower in another.

Changes in the Mill River's Bed Caused by the Disaster.

1. For almost [the whole of its length], with a small handful of specific exceptions, the river valley is too narrow, its sides too steep, and the topography too closely underlain by bedrock for the river's course to have changed much as a result of the flood.

2. The available maps that show the river before the flood (notably the 1873 Beers maps) so closely match the river's present course that even if those maps could be trusted to be precise, mapping the small differences between them and recent maps would have to be done at quite a large scale. On any man-ageably-sized map that showed the river all the way from the reservoir to Florence, the differences would be barely perceptible.

3. Current and recent maps also show changes not attributable to the disaster — notably in Leeds, where almost incredibly, a freshet in the years after the flood caused a far more dramatic change in the river's course than the flood had — and in Haydenville, where I've just learned that part of the Brass Works mill pond was deliberately filled in sometime in the 1960s. What other changes have occurred since the flood that I don't know about?

4. There is no doubt that on the southeast end of Williamsburg village, on the level meadow across Route 9 from the end of Depot Road, along the lower end of Joe Wright Brook, on the flat in Skinnerville, on the floodplain above the Brass Works, on what are now the Northampton Country Club and Look Park grounds, and perhaps farther toward Florence, the flood did some erosional and depositional reshaping of the surficial sands and gravels adjacent to the riverbed. A lot of sand and gravel were certainly deposited between Leeds and Florence. Some of these changes can be deduced from the contours on recent USGS maps. But after the event, the river seems to have returned to its pre-flood course by itself except in Williamsburg village, where it had to be laboriously channeled back into its bed in the succeeding months to restore waterpower to the James Woolen Mill.

What I *have* mapped, zooming in on individual villages, is the approximate maximum extent of flooding, based on recent USGS post-flood topography, hundreds of photographs of the destruction and debris in the aftermath, and published accounts. No sophisticated computer modeling of the flood was involved in my estimates of flood elevations. Nor could any such modeling have been done, because there is no pre-flood topography data available for the valley. And even the maximum horizontal extent of flooding appears very narrow when viewed on a map that covers the upper eight miles of the river (to Meadow St. in Florence). At no point between the reservoir and Cook's Dam in Leeds was the flood more than about five-hundred feet wide. Most of the way it was less than three-hundred. Those widths are spectacularly greater than the river's normal fifteen- to thirty-foot width, but they look insignificant when drawn to scale on a map of more than half the river's thirteen-mile overall length. Even a fine pen or pencil line is too thick to accurately represent the normal width of the river except at millponds, and the full extent of the flood is represented by a variable line only a little wider. Such a map only makes the flood look trivial, and that's certainly not a message we want to deliver.

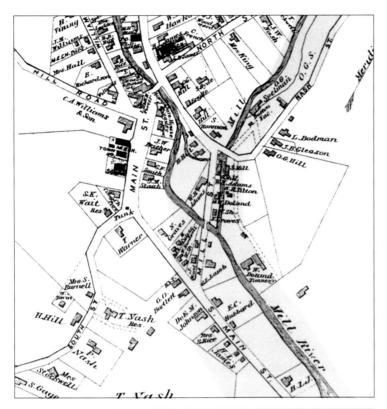

Williamsburg

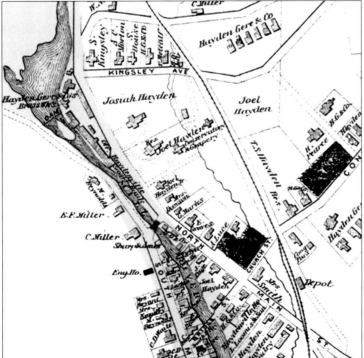

Haydenville

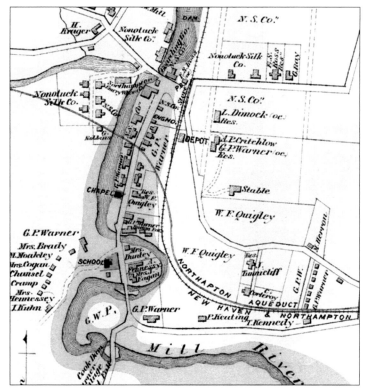

Leeds

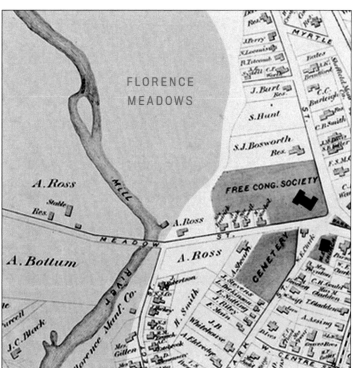

Florence

NOTES

Preface

1 Berger, J. & J.W. Sinton 1985. *Water, Earth and Fire: Land Use and Environmental Planning in the New Jersey Pine Barrens*. Baltimore: Johns Hopkins University Press.

2 Sinton, J.W. 1998. "La division des paysages partagés et le partage des paysages divisés aux Etats-Unis: l'exemple de l'estuaire du Delaware et de la région de Philadelphie, 1650-1990." (Sharing Partitioned Landscapes and Partitioning Shared Landscapes in America: The Case Study of the Delaware Estuary and Philadelphia Region, 1650–1990). *Géographie et Cultures*, #25 (Spring 1998):111–136.

3 Sinton, J.W. and W. Küpper. 2003. "The Heritage Value of Urban Rivers and Riverscapes: Cologne and Philadelphia," *Regards croisés sur le patrimoine dans le monde à l'aube du XXIe siècle* (A Global Cross Section of Views on Cultural Patrimony at the Dawn of the Twenty-first Century). Paris: Presses de l'Université de Paris: Sorbonne. Sinton, J.W. 2001. "200 Jahre Flächennutzungsstrukturen" (200 Years of Changing Land-Use Patterns). *Köln: Der historisch-topographische Atlas*, Wiktorin, Dorothea et al. eds. Köln: Emons.

4 Sinton, J.W., Elizabeth Farnsworth, Wendy Sinton. 2007. *The Connecticut River Boating Guide: Source to Sea*. Guilford, CT: Falcon Guide for the Connecticut River Watershed Council (now named the Connecticut River Conservancy). The river's first thirty miles are too narrow, shallow, or dangerous to paddle.

5 Some historians and scientists have succeeded in writing brilliant books on particular aspects of great rivers. Richard White, for example, wrote a fine history of the Columbia River as a source and symbol of power and energy from Native times through the twentieth century and the shifting relationship between the river and its people. (White, R. 1996. *The Organic Machine: The Remaking of the Columbia River*. NY: Hill and Wang.) The renowned French geographers Jacques Bethemon and Jean-Paul Bravard have spent their lifetimes studying human impacts on rivers from the Mekong to the Nile, and have written an exemplary study of their home river, the Rhône. Theirs is an extraordinary achievement, combining the natural and human sciences. Bethemont, J and J-P Bravard. *Pour Saluer le Rhône (In Homage to the Rhone)*. 2016. Lyon: Libel. No river history, however, is more fun than Mark Twain's magisterial memoir, *Life on the Mississippi*, but it retains the very randomness for which rivers are known—hard to pin down, flowing through one's hands.

6 The right bank/left bank convention always assumes one is looking downriver, as in the terms "river right" and "river left."

7 Laurie, Bruce. 2015. *Rebels in Paradise: Sketches of Northampton Abolitionists*. Amherst, MA: University of Massachusetts Press.

8 Brooks, Lisa. 2008. *The Common Pot: The Recovery of Native Space in the Northeast*. Minneapolis: University of Minnesota Presss, xxii

Chapter One

1 Extended quote from Denk, Jeremy. 2012. "Flight of the Concord," *The New Yorker*, p. 25. "My [Charles] Ives addiction started one summer at music camp, at Mount Holyoke College. I was twenty and learning his Piano Trio. There's an astounding moment in the Trio where the pianist goes off into a blur of sweet and sour notes around a B-flat-major chord. I knew the moment was important, but I wondered, was my sound too vague or too clear?... One afternoon, the violinist of the group and I were driving off campus and happened to cross the Connecticut River. Looking out of the window, he said, 'You should play it like that.' From the bridge the river seemed impossibly wide, and instead of a single current there seemed to be a million intersecting currents— urgent and lazy rivers within the river, magical pockets of no motion at all. The late-afternoon light colored the water pink and orange and gold. It was the most beautiful, patient, meandering multiplicity. Instantly I knew how to play the passage. Even better, Ives's music made me see rivers differently; centuries of classical music had prettified them, ignoring their reality in order to turn them into musical objects. ...Ives is different [from Schubert or Wagner]. He gives you crosscurrents, dirt, haze—the disorder of a zillion particles crawling downstream. His rivers aren't constrained by human desires and stories; they sing the beauty of their own randomness and drift."

2 Hurd, B. 2013. *Stepping Into the Same River Twice*. Frostburg, MD: Savage River Watershed Association.

3 Note from Robert Newton, Professor of Geology, Smith College. The increase in velocity downstream is caused by a significant decrease in friction in the downstream channel where the channel walls and bottom are much smoother than in upstream sections. (Personal communication, August 2015)

4 Photo by the late Joe Hartshorn, Professor of Geology at the University of Massachusetts, Amherst. It is actually a photo of a lake in Iceland, a re-imagining of the creation of Lake Hitchcock. Photo courtesy of Julie Brigham-Grette, Professor of Quaternary/Glacial Geology, University of Massachusetts, Amherst. It was published as the cover of the 63rd Reunion of the North Eastern Friends of the Pleistocene Field Conference, June 2000. University of Massachusetts, Amherst Department of Geosciences Contribution No. 73, http://www.geo.umass.edu. This visualization does not include such post-glacial features as Baker's Hill and Florence, which would have appeared as islands above the 300 foot level.

5 Robert Newton, personal communication, August 2015. Further geological explanation comes from John Brady, Professor of Geology, Smith College. Personal communication, September 2014: "This is what you will see in cross section if you drill down through the sediments at Smith College: on the surface are sandy soils that the post-glacial Mill River deposited in the center of Northampton. Below the sands are clays from the bottom of Lakes Hitchcock and Hadley, and below the clays are beds of glacial till from glacial periods prior to 20,000 years ago. Underneath the till is red sandstone, called arkose, part of the New Haven formation, more than 200 million years

old, which stretches south into Connecticut. Finally, below the sandstone is ancient bedrock, a metamorphic rock called schist that developed when 400-million-year-old sediment was heated under the immense pressure of high mountains."

6 Sanders, Laurie. 2014. "A Natural History of the Florence Meadows Conservation Area." Report to the Northampton Department of Planning and Sustainability. Northampton: Department of Planning and Sustainability.

7 Robert Newton, personal communication, August 2015. These soils are the source of New England "rock jokes," such as the one in which Cousin Ephraim asks Cousin Silas where the rocks in the field came from. Silas says that glaciers brought 'em. Ephraim asks where the glaciers have gone, and Silas replies, "Back to get more rocks, I guess."

8 Robert Newton, personal communication, August 2015.

9 We do not know precisely the origin of Fort Hill and would need to excavate a trench about ten to twenty feet deep or perhaps take a core. Robert Newton, personal communication, August 2015. Laurie Sanders and Fred Morrison have identified these two features as outwash deltas.

10 Goebel, T. 2008. "The Late Pleistocene Dispersal of Modern Humans in the Americas," *Science*, 319:1497–1502 (March 14).

11 What follows is taken from Elizabeth Farnsworth's path-breaking work on New England flora for the New England Wild Flower Society. Farnsworth, E. 2015. *State of the Plants: Challenges and Opportunities for Conserving New England's Native Flora.* Framingham, MA: New England Wild Flower Society, 5–6.

12 Anthropologists have developed a scheme of time periods for Natives based on changes in material culture, namely tools, weapons, and basketry. Pre-paleolithic: 17,000–15,000; Paleolithic 15,000–8,000; Archaic 8000–3000; Woodland 3000–Contact in the early to mid-seventeenth century.

13 Farnsworth relies on a large number of palynological (pollen profile) and lake varve (lake-bottom sediment) studies for her conclusions, 5. The climate periods for the Holocene are: cold, dry (14,600–12,900 YBP; very cold dry (12,900–11,600 YBP), cool, dry (11,600-8,200 YBP), warm, wet (8,200–5,400 YBP), warm, dry (5,400–3000 YBP), cool, wet (3000–present).

14 Evidence for this comes from the Public Archaeological Laboratory's recent study of three small areas near the Connecticut River in Northampton and suggests that we are unlikely to find intact, pre-contact Indian cultural deposits. Waller, J.N. and S.G. Cherau. 2009. *Cultural Resources Overview Study*, Silvio O. Conte National Fish and Wildlife Refuge. Vol. 1. Hadley, MA: Public Archaeology Laboratory for US Fish and Wildlife Service, Region 5.

15 An excellent primer on Native American understanding of chronology and geography can be found in Bruchac, Margaret. 2004. "Earthshapers and Placemakers: Algonkian Indian Stories and the Landscape," in Smith, Claire and H. M. Wobst, eds.

2004. *Indigenous Archaeologies: Decolonising Theory and Practice*. London: Routledge, 52–74.

16 Bruchac, "Earthshapers," 63.

17 Brooks, L., *Common Pot*, 2.

18 Bruchac, "Earthshapers," 64.

19 Bruchac, "Earthshapers,"73.

20 The most comprehensive archaeological study of this region is now more than thirty years old: Massachusetts Historical Commission. 1984. *Historic & Archaeological Resources of the Connecticut River Valley*. Boston, MA. A more recent study by the Public Arcaeology Laboratory is limited to the section of the Mill River along the Connecticut, part of the Silvio Conte USFWS Refuge: Waller and Cherau, 186.

21 Over the past thirty years, a picture has been emerging of Native American life and forest ecology prior to the arrival of the Europeans. The best summary for Massachusetts can be found in Hall, Brian; Glenn Motzkin; David R. Foster; Mindy Syfert, and John Burk. 2002. "Three Hundred Years of Forest and Land-Use Change in Massachusetts," *Journal of Biogeography*, Vol. 29, No. 10/11. Two important early sources are Crosby, A. 1973 (2003 rev. ed). *The Columbian Exchange: Biological and Cultural Consequences of 1492*. Westport, CT: Praeger and Cronon, W. 1983. *Changes in the Land*. NY: Hill & Wang. Charles C. Mann has published a popular summary of recent research: *1491: New Revelations of the Americas Before Columbus*. 2006. NY: Vintage.

22 There is now a sizeable bibliography on fire history, the most vocal proponent for which is Stephen Pyne, starting with his 1982 (1997 rev. ed.) landmark study, *Fire in America: A Cultural History of Wildland and Rural Fire*, Seattle, University of Washington. See also his *Vestal Fire. An Environmental History, Told Through Fire, of Europe and Europe's Encounter with the World*. 1997. Seattle: University of Washington Press, 2000. See also: Foster, D.R.S., Clayden, D.A. Orwig, et al. 2002. "Oak, chestnut and fire: climatic and cultural controls of long-term forest dynamics in New England, USA," *Journal of Biogeography* 29: 1359–1379; Parshall, T. and D.R. Foster. 2002. "Fire on the New England landscape: Regional and temporal variation, cultural and environmental controls," *Journal of Biogeography* 29:1305–1317; Abrams, M. D. and G. J. Nowacki. 2008. "Native Americans as active and passive promoters of mast and fruit trees in the eastern USA," The Holocene 18: 1123–1137; Patterson, W.A. III & Sassaman, K.E. 1988. "Indian fires in the prehistory of New England," *Holocene Human Ecology in Northeastern North America*, ed. G.P. Nicholas. NY: Plenum, 107–135.

23 Mann, 315. Wood bison (Bison bison athabasca), as distinguished from "woodland buffalo," are a subspecies inhabiting the northwestern quarter of North America.

24 Cronon, W. *Changes*, 51–52 See also http://en.wikipedia.org/wiki/Wood_bison.

25 Judd, Sylvester. 1863 (1905 edition reprinted 1976). *The History of Hadley, Massachusetts*. Somersworth, NH: New Hampshire Publishing Co., 96ff.

26 Farnsworth, *State of the Plants*, 7.

27 Much of this section is derived from notes and sources provided by Elizabeth Farnsworth, personal communication, August 2015.

28 Unlike a very few areas in America, such as the Pacific Coast, where redwoods reach multi-millenial ages, east coast forests are subject to more frequent disturbances, namely fire, hurricanes, disease, and high winds.

29 A witness tree is a large tree that serves as a boundary marker. Surveyors use witness trees to locate corners of original grants or surveys. A mark would be cut into the trunk and location of the witness tree noted in the surveyor's field report.

30 Cogbill, C.V., J. Burk, and G. Motzkin. 2002. "The forests of pre-settlement New England, USA: spatial and compositional patterns based on town proprietor surveys." *Journal of Biogeography*, 29, 1279 – 1304. See also Hall, Motzkin, et al. 2002, 1328.

31 Josselyn, J. 1665. *An Account of Two Voyages to New England, Made During the Years 1638, 1663*. William Veazie, Boston, MA.

32 For a summary of New England Indian diets, see Salisbury, Neal. 1982. *Manitou and Providence: Indians, Europeans, and the Making of New England, 1500-1643*. NY: Oxford University Press, 30 ff. See also Thomas, Peter A. 1979. "In the Maelstrom of Change: The Indian Trade and Cultural Process in the Middle Connecticut River Valley: 1635 – 1665." Ph.D dissertation in anthropology. University of Massachusetts, Amherst, 102-106.

33 In Manitou, 44, Neal Salisbury estimates the population between 126,000 and 144,000, but in 2016 suggested that 125,000 was, perhaps, a better estimate for the minimum number (personal communication). See also Thomas, P., 28. See also Snow, D.R. and K.M. Lamphear. 1988. "European Contact and Indian Depopulation in the Northeast: The Timing of the First Epidemics," *Ethnohistory*, 35:15 – 33 and Calloway, C.G. 1990. *The Western Abenakis of Vermont, 1600-1800: War, Migration, and the Survival of an Indian People*. Norman, OK: University of Oklahoma.

34 Brooks, L. *Common Pot*, 4.

35 Brooks, L. *Common Pot*, 17.

36 Brooks, L. *Common Pot*, 19-20.

37 Bruchac, "Earthshapers," 70.

38 Bruchac, Margaret. 2004. "Native Presence in Nonotuck and Northampton," in Buckley, K, ed. *A Place Called Paradise: Culture & Community in Northampton, Masssachusetts, 1654-2001*. Amherst, MA: University of Massachusetts, 18 –38.

39 Presentation by Doug Harris, the Narragansett tribal preservationist for ceremonial landscape, at a National Register conference: www.ncptt.nps.gov/blog/ceremonial-stone-landscapes.

40 Thomas, 33 ff.

41 Bruchac, personal communication August 2015.

42 In an unpublished research note of February 2018, Marge Bruchac first considers the confusion in the pronunciation of the place name "Nonotuck" (alternates include Norwottuck and Nolwatog). "The Nonotuck were surrounded by other Native communities: Nipmuc and Wampanoag to the east; Woronoco and Mohican to the west; Agawam to the south; and Pocumtuck and Sokoki to the north. Identifications of the area are thus inextricably entangled with the question of interpreting each of the places, peoples, and intentions encoded in colonial documents that refer to it." In response to the question "What was the Native language spoken by the Nonotuck people?" Professor Bruchac responded: "The simple answer is this: 'Nonotuck,' appears to have been an n-dialect version of the Massachusetts Algonquian language, similar to Agawam and Pocumtuck, and preserved in today's Western Abenaki."

43 Bruchac, "Native Presence," 24. A Massachusetts Historical Commission (MHC) report in 1982 listed, without description, three Indian sites: one contact site on Shepherd's Island near Old Rainbow and two Woodland Period sites on the Manhan Meadows. 1982. Massachusetts Historical Commission, "Reconnaissance Survey Town Report—Northampton." 4.

44 "Corn did not require permanent residence near the corn fields." Bruchac, "Native Presence," 24.

45 Delabarre, Edmund and Harris H. Wilder. 1920. "Indian Corn-Hills in Massachusetts," *American Anthropologist*, 22, #3 (July-Sept), 203-225.

http://anthrosource.onlinelibrary.wiley.com/hub/issue/10.1111/aman.1920.22.issue-3/ Delabarre, E. and H. Wilder. 1920. "That there should be any traces left at the present day of the gardens cultivated by the Indians two hundred and fifty years ago and earlier, may at first sight seem incredible. But there are many fields in New England, probably some in every town, that have always been used by white men as pastures, and have never been touched by the plough. Any of these which may have been used by the Indians as corn fields would stand an excellent chance of having the hills indefinitely preserved, because of the way in which the Indians did their planting." 204. What little may have remained of the fields from the 1920 photo was obliterated when the Corps of Engineers diverted the Mill River through this location. Judd noted that farmers and householders continued to plant corn in hills until the nineteenth century. Judd, S. *Hadley*, 356.

46 Delabarre and Harris. 1920. 220.

47 The Smith College fields are shown as agricultural fields on one of Cestre's maps, but not in the text. Cestre, G.R.J. 1963. *Northampton, Massachusetts; évolution urbaine*. Paris: Société d'édition d'enseignement supérieur.

48 Salisbury, *Manitou*, 105.

49 Calloway, 22.

50 Mann, 55. There are many excellent sources in which to find the impact of disease on Indians, including Mann and Calloway, who depend upon Denevan, W. 1976, ed. *The Native Population of the Americas in 1492*. Madison, WI: University of Wisconsin; Dobyns, H. 1983. *Their Number Become Thinned: Native American Population Dynamics in Eastern North America*. Knoxville, TN: University of Tennessee; Jennings, F. 1975. *The Invasion of America: Indians, Colonialism and the Cant of Conquest*. Chapel Hill, NC: Univ of North Carolina.

51 Mann, 314.

52 Jennings, Francis. 1975. *The Invasion of America: Indians, Colonialism, and the Cant of Conquest*. Chapel Hill: University of North Carolina.

53 Mann, 314 – 315.

54 Salisbury, *Manitou*, 50.

55 Salisbury, *Manitou*, 82. Salisbury has excellent analyses and descriptions of the impact on Indian groups of the combination of disease, trade, and English aggression. "The once-powerful Pawtucket, Massachusett, and Pokanoket were reduced to terror and humiliation before the numerically tiny Micmac as well as the formidable Narragansett... Even more critically, the epidemic [of the plague in 1618 – 19] enabled the hitherto inept English to establish a foothold for settlement." 109.

56 Salisbury, *Manitou*, 82.

57 William Bradford as reported in Salisbury, *Manitou*, 191.

58 Calloway, *Manitou*, 22.

59 Salisbury, *Manitou*, 166.

60 Salisbury, *Manitou*, 169.

61 Salisbury's description of the kind of Puritanism that installed itself in New England can be found in *Manitou*, 170 ff.

62 Trumbull, vol. 1, 5 ff.

63 Trumbull, vol. 1, 9.

64 Bruchac, "Native Presence," 23.

65 Bruchac, "Native Presence," 24.

66 In 1695 the Massachusetts courts granted the third division of Hatfield all the land west to Goshen, including the East Branch of the Mill.

67 Capawonk immediately reverted to Northampton, the proprietors of which sold it to Hadley in 1659 as part of "West Hadley," after which the residents successfully petitioned to incorporate Hadley's west bank into their own town of Hatfield in 1670. Judd, S. *History of Hadley*, 114. From the notes of Ralmon J. Black.

68 Thomas, 30.

69 Bruchac, "Native Presence," 26.

70 Bruchac, "Native Presence," 25. See also Peter Thomas' and Neal Salisbury's "Comments" in Ifkovic, J. and M. Kaufman, eds. 1984. *Early Settlement in the Connecticut Valley. Deerfield, MA*. Historic Deerfield & Westfield State University

71 Innes, Stephen. 1984. "The Pynchons and the People of Early Springfield," in Ifkovic and Kaufman, 34-45.

72 William got himself in terrible trouble with a book he wrote in 1650, entitled *The Meritorious Price of Our Redemption*, a critique of the brand of Congregationalism practiced in Boston. His was America's first banned book. It was burned on Boston Common, and Pynchon returned to England in 1652, remaining there until his death in 1662, having transferred all his Massachusetts property to his son John and his sons-in-law, who had absorbed William's lessons in running commercial and real estate enterprises. His daughter Mary, for example, married the wealthy Elizur Holyoke, after whom the city of Holyoke is named.

73 Salisbury, "Comments" in Ifkovic and Kaufman, 63.

74 Brooks, L., *Common Pot*, 21 –23.

75 Two of the best narratives of King Philip's War are: Lepore, J. 1999. *The Name of War: King Philip's War and the Origins of American Identity*. NY: Vintage; Schultz, E. and M. Tougias. 2017. *King Philip's War: The History and Legacy of America's Forgotten Conflict*. NY: Countryman Press.

76 Brooks, L. 2017. *Our Beloved Kin: A New History of King Philips War*. New Haven: Yale University, 8.

77 Bruchac, "Native Presence," 26 –27.

78 Haefeli, E. and K. Sweeney. 2002. *Captors and Captives: The 1704 French and Indian Raid on Deerfield*. Amherst, MA: University of Mass., 74.

79 Bruchac, "Native Presence," 21.

80 Trumbull, vol. 1, 485. "On one occasion Mary Sheldon received a visit from two squaws. Leaving their papooses in the bushes on Pancake plain, they came into the street, and found the house where Mrs. Clapp lived, by means of the step stones which had been described to them."

81 Salisbury, N. 1987. "Toward the Covenant Chain: Iroquois and Southern New England Algonquians, 1637-1684," in *Beyond the Covenant Chain: The Iroquois and their Neighbors in Indian North America, 1600-1800*. Richter, D. and J.H. Merrell. Syracuse: Syracuse University, 73.

82 Haefli and Sweeney counted more than 140 Indian raids in New England, large and small, just between the years 1703 –12, although few of them took place in the Connecticut Valley, 286 –89.

83 Bruchac, "Native Presence," 27. "Titus King from Northampton, for example, was adopted into Connecticut Valley Indian society in 1755 when they were living among the Abenaki in Canada. He escaped and returned to Northampton in 1758."

84 Haefeli and Sweeney, 266.

85 Bruchac, M., "Earthshapers," 65.

86 Thomas, 118.

87 The Massachusetts Court ordered, in 1650, that "wampumpeag should pass for debts to the value of 40 shillings, the white at 8 and the black at four for a penny, except for country rates." This law was repealed in 1661, and wampum had no legal value, but continued in use until 1675. Felt, Joseph B. 1839. "An Historical Account of Massachusetts Currency," Boston: Perkins & Marvin for the Massachusetts Historical Society.

88 Judd, S. *Hadley*, 97.

89 Judd, S. *Hadley*, 98.

90 Judd, S. *Hadley*, 99.

91 Judd, S. *Hadley*, 100.

92 A fine description of seventeenth-century livestock can be found on the Plymouth Colony's website at http://plymoutharch.tripod.com/id133.html Chartier, Craig, n.d. "Livestock in Plymouth Colony," the Plymouth Archaeological Rediscovery Project (PARP).

93 Judd, S. *Hadley*, 103. "Young cattle and horses often remained in the woods until winter, and some became wild and unruly, especially horses... Many days were spent in the winter in looking up horses and cattle in the woods. This mode of pasturing...was the best that the new settlers... could adopt."

94 Hall et al. 2002, 1329. "The most dramatic change has involved maple (primarily red maple), which increased from 7 to 27 percent in Massachusetts from the colonial to modern periods, presumably because of its rapid colonizing and sprouting abilities, high seed production, and tolerance of a wide range of moisture and light conditions."

95 The list of dams include: Upper and Lower Highland Lakes in Goshen, Haydenville (breached) in Williamsburg, the Upper, Middle, and Lower Dams and Cook's Dam in Leeds, the Nonotuck Dam in Florence, the Bay State Dam, Paradise Pond at Smith, and a cement barrier under the bridge at South Street near the end of Earle Street.

96 *Daily Hampshire Gazette,* June 3, 1904 "First Settlement" From the 250th celebration section of Northampton's founding.

97 Judd, Richard. 2014. *Second Nature: An Environmental History of New England.* Amherst, MA: University of Massachusetts, 75. Donahue, Brian. 2007. *The Great Meadow: Farmers and the Land in Colonial Concord.* New Haven: Yale University, 107.

98 Sheffield, Charles A., *History of Florence Massachusetts.* Florence, MA, 1894. 21.

99 Patricia Wright has a good explanatory essay of Northampton's original layout as described by J.R. Trumbull. Publication date 2004: "On the Ground: The Origins of Northampton's Peculiar Plan," in *Paradise Built: Shaping Northampton's Townscape,*

1654–2004. Florence, MA: Northampton Historical Commission.

100 Field, Barry. 1985. "The Evolution of Individual Property Rights in Massachusetts Agriculture, Seventeenth–Nineteenth Centuries," *Northeastern Journal of Agricultural and Resource Economics* 14 (October 1985): 97–109.

101 I am indebted to Laurie Sanders for her explanation of the relationship between land use and geology in Northampton.

102 Trumbull, Vol. 1, 461.

103 http://archive.northamptonma.gov/weblink/DocView.aspx?dbid=0&id=253804 &page=1&cr=1 The citation is to a web page on the City of Northampton's website on the history of a large tract of land called the Rust Block. "Theodore Rust was born in 1795 in the last house but one on Lickingwater Street (at today's 303 South Street). Like the rest of Seth Rust's children, he was educated in the nearby old schoolhouse (235 South Street)."

104 Trumbull, Vol. 1, 130.

105 Trumbull, Vol. 1, 452.

106 A wonderful short book about different paces of change can be found in Lynch, Kevin. 1976. *What Time is This Place*. Cambridge, MA: MIT Press. I remember chatting with one of the National Park rangers some years ago at the Little Big Horn battle site about various programs to help interpret the place. The most problematic attempt, he said, was to keep the battleground in the same condition as it was during the battle, a hugely expensive and ultimately useless effort because of the cost of labor in attempting to force some vegetation to grow while suppressing other plants. "What's the use?" he said, "the damn place is gonna do what it's gonna do!"

107 The poem's first stanza, the Invocation:

> My soul is wrought to sing of forms transformed to bodies new and
> strange! Immortal Gods inspire my heart, for ye have changed
> yourselves and all things you have changed! Oh lead my song in smooth
> and measured strains, from olden days when earth began to this completed time!

> In nova fert animus mutates dicere formas
> Corpora; di,coeptis (nom vos mutatstis et illas)
> adspiratemeis primaque ab origine mundi
> ad mea perpetuum deducite tempora carmen!

Ian Johnston of Vancouver Island, BC has created a list of more than 175 metamorphoses on the website: http://johnstoniatexts.x10host.com/ovid/transformationshtml.html

108 Indeed, prior to the seventeenth century, progress simply meant advancing forward whether walking or riding.

109 The settlers' objective "was to use the natural grasses as hay, to be mowed and stored for wintering livestock." Field, Barry and Martha Kimball, 1984 "Managing Common-Property Resources: Agricultural Land in Colonial New England,"

unpublished paper for a workshop in political theory and policy analysis given at Indiana University 11/14/84, 5. See also Chartier's webpage for The Plymouth Archaeological Rediscovery Project: http://plymoutharch.tripod.com/id133.html.

110 *Climate Change Adaptation Manual: Evidence to support nature conservation in a changing climate.* Published by *Natural England. 2014.* London: gov.uk.

http://publications.naturalengland.org.uk/publication/5629923804839936

111 Darby, H.C., ed. 1976. See Darby's article "The Age of the Improver: 1600−1800," in *A New Historical Geography of England after 1600.* Cambridge: University of Cambridge.

112 Thirsk, Joan, ed. 1985. *The Agrarian History of England and Wales: 1500-1640.* 1967. Cambridge, UK: Cambridge University, 49.

113 Hog's Bladder is locally known for an "Indian Massacre," namely, a small skirmish that took place between colonists and Indians, called the Massacre at Pascommuck. It occurred in May 1704, three months after the famous incident at Deerfield.

114 Elizabeth Robinton and John Burk developed a good baseline study of marsh vegetation on the river from 1973, which we will cite in a later chapter, but Robinton and Burk's study was not intended to address historical changes. Robinton, E. and J. Burk. 1973. "The Mill River and Its Floodplain, Northampton and Williamsburg, Massachusetts: A Study of the Vascular Plant Flora, Vegetation, etc." Amherst, MA: University of Massachusetts Water Resources Research Center.

115 Judd, S. *Hadley*, 302. Lists of native plants can be found in any reliable local seed catalogue.

116 Bowling, G. A. 1942. "The Introduction of Cattle into Colonial North America," *Journal of Dairy Science* 25:2 (Feb. 1942), 129−154.

117 Bidwell, Percy and J. I. Falconer. 1941. *History of Agriculture in the Northern United States, 1620-1860.* Washington, DC: Carnegie Institution. pp. 18−20; Carrier, Lyman. 1923. *The Beginnings of Agriculture in America.* New York: McGraw Hill, 26.

118 Judd, S. *Hadley*, 362.

119 Ralmon Black, personal communication May, 2016.

120 Frelich, L.E. et al. 2006. "Earthworm invasion into previously earthworn-free temperate and boreal forests," *Biological Invasions*, 8:6 (1235−1245).

121 Beavers live throughout the whole of the Mill River watershed, including the main stem, but they only build dams in the upper river, currently above Williamsburg and in the hills of tributaries in Westhampton, Ashfield, Conway, and Whately. They inhabit river banks as well as lodges.

122 "Beavers, once numerous in this region, were almost all caught by the Indians before Philip's War in 1675." Judd, S. *Hadley*, 347.

123 McMaster, Robert T, and Nancy D. McMaster. 2001. "Wetland plants of beaver

impoundments: Vascular flora of beaver wetlands in Western Massachusetts," *Rhodora*, Vol. 102, No. 910 (Spring, 2000), pp. 175 –197. Interestingly, the McMasters found very few invasive wetland plants, such as common reed (*Phragmites*) and purple loosestrife (*Lythrum salicaria*) in beaver ponds.

124 White, Sam. 2017. *A Cold Welcome: The Little Ice Age and Europe's Encounter with North America*. Cambridge, MA: Harvard University, 22. This excellent history of early, unsuccessful European expeditions to North America provides a detailed understanding of the factors involved in the Little Ice Age (LIA in Emmanuel Leroy Ladurie's abbreviation). The LIA was more than one phenomenon with more than one cause, including slight changes in the earth's orbit around the sun, oscillations in atmospheric and oceanic circulation, and an unusual number of volcanic eruptions.

125 Judd, S. Misc. 9, 120 and 288. Judd's records are supported by Arthur Watson's archival research into floods at Hartford in 1915. Watson was a local historian in Northampton whose family donated Child's Park. Watson, Arthur. 1915. "Flood History," typescript housed in the Hampshire Room of Forbes Library, Northampton, MA.

126 Trumbull, Vol. 1, 452.

127 Judd, S. I, 455 and Misc. 9, 288.

128 The following description was taken from Trumbull, James R., "Topographical Changes" *Hampshire Gazette* 3/22/1881 and a reprise of the article in the *Daily Hampshire Gazette* 6/3/1904.

129 Trumbull, "Topographical Changes."

130 One hundred thirty years later, with the coming of the Connecticut River Railroad in 1845, the riverbed was shifted several hundred yards eastward, emptying at a point directly into the Connecticut where it remained for the next 95 years.

131 *Hampshire Gazette* 9/20/1887.

132 There are five essential sources for mills on the Mill River: Ralmon J. Black's collection of primary sources, the Judd manuscripts, Charles Dean's manuscript, the (*Daily*) *Hampshire Gazette*, and Agnes Hannay's 1936 *A Chronicle of Industry on the Mill River*. Northampton, MA: Smith College Studies in History, vol. XXI, Nos. 1 –4. Since Charles Dean did not cite his sources and because his manuscript has at least one major error, his work on seventeenth and eighteenth century history may be problematic. Since he was the indexer for all the issues of the *Hampshire Gazette* from its founding in 1786 until the 1950s his information is generally accurate for that time period.

133 Every dam site has a head at the top and a discharge at the bottom. A given amount of water falling a given distance will produce a certain amount of energy. The greater the head, the greater the potential energy to drive waterwheels or turbines. More head and greater velocity mean more power.

134 Dean, "at a point just west of the site now occupied by the Northampton Gas Company's plant, and a little south of the lot now used by the Hawley Grammar School," 4 –6.

135 Judd, S. Vol. I, 455.

136 Dean, 8.

137 Judd, S. I, 455.

138 Dean, 9.

139 Dean, 10 –11; *Daily Hampshire Gazette* 6/3/1904 supplement.

140 Hadley had a sawmill in 1661, and it is difficult to imagine that Northampton did not have one as well. *Daily Hampshire Gazette* 6/3/1904; Dean, 11; Sheffeld, 24. The Hadley mill was actually in Hatfield or West Hadley. "Negotiations for its building were begun in April, 1661, and in December after he had 'expended considerable estate in building a mill the town of Hadley voted to have all the grain ground by Thomas Meekins "provided he make good meal.' Thomas Meekins was a millwright by trade. His mill was built on the Capawonk brook, which thereafter was called Mill river." Wells, Daniel W and Reuben F Wells. 1910. *History of Hatfield*, 46.

141 Dean, 11.

142 Judd, S. ms. Vol. 1, 449.

143 Judd, S. *Hadley*, 305.

144 Jason Johnson, fisheries biologist in Leeds, personal communication March 2015.

145 Moffitt, Christine. 1973. "Fish of the Mill River: a study of ecological and geographical aspects of black spot infestation." M.A. Thesis, Smith College. This is one of the few sources one can cite for native fish in the Mill. Of the seventeen fish species listed about a dozen would be considered native to the Mill River.

Chapter Two

1 Neuburg, N. O. 1955. "Land Use in Northampton: A Study in Various Ecological Aspects in a Specific Urban Community." Smith College honors thesis. Population statistics prior to the first national census in 1790 are notoriously inaccurate, and Neuberg puts the Northampton figure at 1200. The 1765 estimate is 1285 and that from 1790 is 1628. The original population in 1654 may have been about 100 people (24 families X 4 family members by my estimation). There are population data from 1765 and 1776, but these are suspect. For example, the Northampton population, according to this source grew by 400 people between 1765 and 1790, but the Springfield population decreased by 1,200! Greene, E. & V. Harrington. 1932. *American Population Before the Census of 1790*. NY: Columbia University.

2 While we are accustomed to imagining Springfield as the most important town in Western Massachusetts, Northampton, in fact, was Hampshire County's shire town, or county seat, with a larger population than Springfield's until the turn of the nineteenth century. Springfield only became a shire town when Hampden County was created in 1812, and, due chiefly to its location on major roads and rail lines between Boston, New Haven, and Albany, its population exploded during the industrialization of America.

3 Sweeney, Kevin M. 1986. "River Gods and Related Minor Deities: The Williams Family and the Connecticut River Valley, 1637–1790." Ph.D. dissertation. Yale University, History Deptartment. "A man's attire denoted his standing: the 1651 Massachusetts sumptuary law prevented the wearing of "excesse in apparel [by] men or weomen of meane condition." The following could wear the "garbe of gentlemen." 1. Wealth (an estate rated at more than 200 pounds). 2. So too did "any magistrate or publicke officer of the jurisdiction, their wives and children" regardless of wealth. 3. Military officers could attire themselves as gentlemen. 4. Former public officials or those who had once had considerable estate." 5 – 6.

4 Wars from 1670 –1783: King Phillip's (Metacom's) War 1675 – 78; King William's War 1689 – 1697; Queen Anne's War (War of the Spanish Succession) 1702 – 13; King George's War 1744 – 48; French & Indian War (Seven Years' War) 1754 – 63; American Revolution 1775 – 83.

5 Sweeney, 17. To exemplify the importance of military service, two Mill River watershed towns—Chesterfield and Ashfield—were organized as a result of grants to veterans of military expeditions, namely the Narragansett expedition of 1675 and the disastrous 1690 expedition to Canada during King William's War. They were among the sixteen "Canada Townships" that the Massachusetts General Court granted in the Connecticut Valley on the northern border of Massachusetts and southern border of New Hampshire and Vermont.

6 Edwards, Jonathan. 1957. *The Works of Jonathan Edwards*. Miller, Perry, ed. New Haven: Yale University, Vol. 8, 561 –62.

7 Edwards, Jonathan. 1758. "Personal Narrative," on the website http://www.cslewisinstitute.org/webfm_send/331, 3.

8 Jonathan Edwards has presented historians of colonial America with a wondrously complex puzzle: how could he be both deeply conservative and liberal minded at the same time? For a conservative view, stressing "sinners in the hands of an angry God," read Marsden, George M. 2003. *Jonathan Edwards: A Life*. New Haven: Yale University A more recent biography is Story, Ronald. 2012. *Jonathan Edwards and the Gospel of Love*. University of Massachusetts 2012. In his view, Edwards yearned for a loving community of compassionate, gentle people. My opinion is that, as twenty-first-century thinkers, we have trouble entering a seventeenth-century mind that saw no difficulty combining the concepts of predestination and hell with new scientific discoveries and the rational thought of the Enlightenment.

9 His death is chronicled in Marsden's book among many others.

10 Marsden, 143.

11 For an excellent discussion of this, see Nobles, Gregory. 1983. *Divisions Throughout the Whole: Politics and Society in Hampshire County, Massachusetts, 1740 –1775*. New York: Cambridge University Press. Another, deeper conflict began to appear in the eighteenth century as well. The people of Northampton, like others in New England, were facing great tensions in colonial life and thought. The historian James Henretta wrote that "on the one hand, [religious doctrine] directed them to immerse themselves in the things of this world without, on the other hand lavishing their affections on earthy pursuits. The contradiction was palpable. How many men and women could avoid the sin of covetousness, could pursue profits without succumbing to the temptations of profit?" For a thorough analysis of New England's early economic development, see Henrietta, James. 1991. *The Origins of American Capitalism*. Boston, MA: Northeastern University.

12 Tryon, Rolla M., Sr. 1966 (originally a 1916 dissertation for University of Chicago) *Household Manufactures in the United States, 1640 –1860*. NY: A. M Kelley, 5.

13 Sweeney, 718.

14 Laurie, Bruce. 2015. In writing the history of the "rebels," Laurie provides the conservative context against which they fought.

15 Dean, 12. Dean points out that there is an odd dearth of information from primary sources on mills and dams on the Mill River for the first forty years of the eighteenth century.

16 Dean, 12 –13.

17 Marsden, 143.

18 Sheffeld, Charles A. 1894. *History of Florence Massachusetts*. Originally self published, now available at Collective Copies in Florence and Amherst, 21 –22. Charles Sheffeld, grandson of the philanthropist and NAEI member Samuel Hill, was a careful researcher, using original town and NAEI records and the Judd manuscripts, as well as secondary sources, such as Trumbull.

19 Sheffeld, 20. His note reads: "This shows the three principal highways, the 'North,' 'South,' and middle roads, the latter called 'Isaac's Way.' The two vertical lines divided 'Inner Commons' from 'Long Division.' The lots in the Long Division were numbered in regular order from the Hatfield town line through to Easthampton. A space for a highway was left between lots Nos. 33 and 34, and for another road near the bridge between lots Nos. 40 and 41. By careful search one can find the three plains. Bear Hill, Broughton's Meadow, and Millstone Mountain, as well as other points of interest."

20 Sheffeld, 24.

21 Sheffeld, 25.

22 Dean, 27. "Hulburt's [sic] mill is believed to have been built about 1762."

23 Incorporation dates for districts in the Mill River watershed: Chesterfield in 1762 and Ashfield in 1765 were both granted to military veterans; Conway was separated from Deerfield in 1767; Whately and Williamsburg were partitioned from Hatfield in 1771 and Westhampton from Northampton in 1778; Goshen was split off from Chesterfield in 1781 and Easthampton from Northampton in 1785.

24 The surveying and laying out of eighteenth-century towns was a complicated, time-consuming task. In the case of Williamsburg, the Hatfield 3rd Division Lots were finally surveyed in 1735, whereas the Three-Mile-Addition Lots were first laid out in 1752.

25 The abutments of "The Great Bridge" that mark the former crossing of the East Branch of the Westfield River, can still be seen across the beautiful Chesterfield Gorge.

26 In fact Miller moved to Williamsburg from Northampton sometime after 1771. One must use Charles Dean's manuscript with care, especially when working with sparse seventeenth and eighteenth-century data. Dean's major contribution to Northampton researchers was his indexing of the *Hampshire Gazette* on which he may have relied too heavily or did not seek to check his sources when he wrote his "Mills of Mill River." Ralmon Black, Williamsburg historian, for example, found an error in Dean's reference to a John Miller, who, according to Dean, founded Williamsburg's first commercial establishment, an orchard. However, Black has found that this description was written by Benjamin Sydney Johnson, who published it as an article in the *Gazette* in July, 1860. Anecdotal as it was then, the errors have been replicated in many later histories. Black's research found that in 1735, John Miller's father died, leaving him land in the Northampton Meadows, along with other resources. He was twenty-three when he purchased the recently surveyed land in Hatfield's 3rd Division, built a shelter, and dug wolf pits when the bounty was equivalent to two weeks salary. He married in 1754, and his children were all born in Northampton. He was not settled in Williamsburg at least until after 1771. It is well documented that John Miller's great-grandson, Edwin F. Miller was the man who planted the 3,300 tree orchard towards the end of the next century.

27 *Hampshire Gazette and Northampton Courier*, April 2, 1867. In the late eighteenth century the Leeds area was called the Rail Hill District and referred to as Shepherd's Hollow for the first three decades of the nineteenth century.

28 Correspondence with Ralmon Black: in 1754, a County Road from Hatfield to Chesterfield was located over and through the Whately Reservoir and Adams Road. From Northampton there was a common path that Hampshire County ordered laid out in 1762 and is now North Farms Road and Mountain Street. Hampshire County Court Records, 1762, Book 7, 51.

29 This information comes from Ralmon Black's archival research, which includes a review of the 1771 Royal Charter. "It would be safe to say that all of those who settled Hatfield's Williamsburg District held title by deed of purchase, not by grant... The largest lot was 750 acres granted to Colonel Oliver Partridge, who never settled in Williamsburg." Personal communication in July 2017.

30 Josiah White's farm extended from what is now Old Goshen Road to Snow Farm three-quarters of a mile away to the west.

31 Although most of what is known as Haydenville today was specified as part of the District of Williamsburgh in the Royal Charter of 1771, the official border between Williamsburg and Hatfield was not established until 1845. Regardless of whether Haydenville was officially in Hatfield, inhabitants always considered themselves part of Williamsburg.

32 One finds such sentiments the world over. A Russian proverb states that "The Tsar has only two testicles, but every nobleman claims he is descended from one of them."

33 From Ralmon Black's research: Hampshire County Court Records, 1762, Book 7, 51 and the Bodman Papers in the Sophia Smith Collection, Smith College. Fairfield had a frame house that was mentioned in court records in 1762, and Downing Warner, who married in 1760, lived in a house on the County Road, now O'Neil Road, known to bicyclists as a swift down or brutal up.

34 *Hampshire Gazette and Northampton Courier,* "Historical Sketch of Williamsburg," March 5, 1861.

35 Specie money, backed by something with intrinsic value such as silver or gold, is contrasted with fiat money, with no intrinsic value. Fiat money can be backed, for example, by a government promise to pay. Potash, or potassium carbonate, is found all over the earth, including the oceans, but it is almost always chemically attached to other minerals. The water-soluble part of wood ash is mostly potassium carbonate and is purified by heating and recrystallization. In modern times it is derived from salt mines and from the electrolysis of seawater.

36 Black, Ralmon J. 2008. *Colonial Asheries.* Williamsburg, MA: Williamsburgh Historical Society.

37 Wood ash lye is potassium hydroxide.

38 An eighteenth-century hogshead cask had a capacity equal to 2 barrels or 64 gallons.

39 *Hampshire Gazette and Northampton Courier,* "Historical Sketch of Williamsburg," March 5, 1861.

40 From Ralmon Black's research: Boston Commercial Gazette, 3/18/1822.

"...The law requires Potash Casks to be made of perfectly seasoned Oak, 29 inches in length, measured from the outside of the heads, and 19 inches in the head, measured within the chimes [rims], and weigh as near as may be 14 percent, tare [allowing for the weight of the cask]... that casks be new. That they should be kept ... no longer than is necessary to fill them, but must be kept in a dry place to prevent stains... It is presumed that the Potash made in this State is inferior to none in the world, and a little attention in having Casks of a uniform size, and made in a workmanlike manner, will give to this important article of export such a character as will command for it the highest price."

41 Cronon, W. 1983. *Changes in the Land.* NY: Hill & Wang, 117–118.

42 Paynter, Henry M. 1990, revised 1998. "The First Patent," Invention & Technology Magazine, Fall 1990. Revised article: http://www.me.utexas.edu/~longoria/paynter/hmp/The_First_Patent.html. Samuel Hopkins' invention of the process to increase the quality and quantity of black salts from potash was the first patent ever given in the United States, by George Washington in 1790.

43 Judd, *Hadley*, 99.

44 Black, *Ahseries*, 14. An interesting argument has recently erupted about the ethics and economics of eighteenth- and nineteenth-century forest clearings, namely, it was right and proper to conserve resources and invest in long-term productivity or, as in the present case, to use resources in a laissez-faire manner since tomorrow's demands and technologies will change to meet resource scarcity and environmental damage? See especially Brian Donohue, 2007. "Another Look from Sanderson's Farm: A Perspective on New England Environmental History and Conservation," *Environmental History*, 12 (January 2007), 9−34.

45 Black, *Asheries*, ii.

46 Paynter, H.M. "The First Patent." https://www.me.utexas.edu/~longoria/paynter/hmp/The_First_Patent.html. The potash yield from 3 species of tree is as follows: 1 cord of hickory = 4 lbs of potash; 1 cord of birch = 4lbs potash; 1 cord of oak = 2 lbs potash. Blake, William P., ed. 1886. History of the Town of Hamden, Connecticut. New Haven: Price, Lee & Co., 78.

47 The question of ecological succession—one community of tree species that follows another over time—is complicated, but it should be noted that pine, birch, juniper, and cherry are the first species to occupy the landscape after cutting or fire, followed by oak, maple, and beech, which sprout in the shade of the "pioneer" pines and birch. The pioneer community requires open sunlight to establish itself while the second generally requires shade.

48 http://harvardforest.fas.harvard.edu/dioramas. An explanatory book accompanies the dioramas. Foster, David and John O'Keefe. 2000. *New England Forests Through Time: Insights from the Harvard Forest Dioramas*. Petersham, MA: Harvard Forest.

49 Cumbler, John. 2001. *Reasonable Use: The People, the Environment, and the State, New England 1790 −1930*. New York: Oxford University, 96.

50 This detail and the following materials are from Cumbler, 5-16 and 24-27.

51 Judd, *Hadley*, 309.

52 Judd, ms. 2/5/1856.

53 Judd, *Hadley*, 307.

54 Many descriptions of floods in the mid-eighteenth century come chiefly from Ebenezer Hunt's journal as copied by Sylvester Judd in his manuscripts I, p. 25 and Miscellaneous 9, 120 and 288. For other flood descriptions see the Judd manuscripts, vol. 1, 25 and 455; Misc. 4, 71 and 123; Misc. 9, 288 and 229. Misc. 10, 145 and 229;

Misc. 13, 229. Ebenezer Hunt was a wealthy man as described by James Henretta, *Origins of American Capitalism*, 231: "Ebenezer Hunt presided over a store and hatmaking enterprise that had 550 open accounts in 1773. In return for store goods and felt and worsted hats, local men and women provided Hunt with dressed deerskins and beaver pelts, meat, hoops, and barrels. They also spun and wove and lined hats for this small-scale merchant entrepreneur. The returns from domestic manufacturing thus bolstered local farm income and raised living standards."

55 Judd Misc. 9, 120 and 288.

56 The 1752 Judd Misc. 9, 288. This date was marked NS for new style, which means that England had finally adopted the Gregorian (modern) calendar almost 200 years after its adoption by the Pope and Italian states. It meant that 1752 lost 11 days, so that September 2 was followed immediately by Sept. 14.

57 Judd Misc. 9, 288.

58 Judd Misc. 9, 288.

Chapter Three

1 Following are the dates of the incorporation of the 72 towns in the four counties of Western Massachusetts: Between 1630 and 1700 = 6 towns; 1700–1760 = 4 towns; 1760s = 15 towns; 1770s = 25 towns; 1780s = 6 towns; 1790s = 5 towns; 1880–1980 = 11 towns.

2 Ashfield 1765, Williamsburg 1771, Goshen 1781, Westhampton 1778

3 After its founding in 1786, the *Hampshire Gazette* kept close track of international and national news, which mirrored the cultural and economic interests of Hampshire County communities.

4 If you are taking the Advanced Placement Test in American History, you would have to name at least eight parties from the following ten: Democratic, National Republican, Working-Men's, Anti-Masonic, Whig, Liberty, Know-Nothing, American, Free Soil, Constitutional Union, and Republican.

5 Darby, H.C., ed. 1976. See Darby's article "The Age of the Improver: 1600–1800," in *A New Historical Geography of England after 1600*. Cambridge: University of Cambridge, 53. The Industrial Revolution began in the last quarter of the eighteenth century. Darby points out that improvements in spinning and weaving, for example, which began with John Kay's 1733 flying shuttle, were not sufficiently refined until Edmund Cartwright's powered weaving loom in 1785 and not in general use until after 1800.

6 Muir, Diana. 2000. *Reflections in Bullough's Pond: Economy and Ecosystem in New England*. Hanover, NH: University Press of New England, 78.

7 Numbers come from the US Census.

8 Clark, Christopher. 1990. *The Roots of Rural Capitalism: Western Massachusetts, 1780-1860*. Ithaca: Cornell University, 28–31. A brief glance at the contents of the *Hampshire Gazette* reveals a society glued to news of the nation and the world. Save for the occasional event of local concern, such as Shays' Rebellion, the paper focused on foreign wars, national affairs, and items from Boston and Hartford.

9 Clark, *Roots*, 122.

10 Clark, *Roots*, 122.

11 Clark, *Roots*, 155. "The 1820s and 1830s marked a crucial period in the transition to rural capitalism. Not only did households shift their production and consumption strategies but, in doing so, they created unprecedented opportunities for local merchants to expand their role and influence in the countryside. The people most carefully calculating profits were not farmers but shopkeepers and traders, who began to handle more business. They expanded their role, inserted themselves into existing exchange patterns, and extended their influence beyond trade itself into the control of household labor. It was this, in particular, that signaled the beginnings of a new rural social structure and the curbing of the autonomous household system."

12 Clark, *Roots*, 246. See also Hannay's chart of interconnected investors, 78–80.

13 Clark, *Roots*, 252. Critchlow, an Englishman, was one of the few immigrants.

14 One can find a wonderful collection of historical and engineering facts from Carl Walter's heroic undertaking, "Hampshire and Hampden Canal, 1829–1847." 2006. A map and notes published by Carl Weber. Currently out of print.

15 Clark, *Roots*, 196–97.

16 Laurie, *Rebels*, 17.

17 For present purposes, we use the term manufacturing to mean the use of machines to mass produce objects, in contrast to the simple milling of a natural resource (flour, felt, timber).

18 In 1849 the inhabitants of "Shepherd's Hollow" petitioned the United States Government for a Post Office, and that it be granted to "Leeds, Massachusetts" in honor of the large textile city in England. The request was granted and the Post Office was established May 27, 1850. Source: Sue Carbin, Leeds historian.

19 Dean, 18. It's difficult to imagine a factory at that site, which is several hundred yards away from the Upper Mills Dam unless that facility did not require water power. It may, instead, have been built closer to the dam itself, not far from the boat house.

20 Judd ms. as quoted in Goldscheider Tom. 2012. Independent study paper for Barry Levy, UMass, Amherst, 11.

21 Goldscheider, 12.

22 Dean, 21.

23 Dean, 14 – 15.

24 The following analysis comes from Richards, Leonard L., 2002. *Shays's Rebellion: The American Revolution's Final Battle*. Philadelphia: University of Pennsylvania.

25 In fact, as Bruce Laurie has pointed out, Massachusetts was one of the few states that refused to establish its state capitol near the middle of state population centers, and Boston remains the only capitol city that is both the largest in size and the largest seaport of any in the United States. Personal communication 2/16.

26 How ironic that the crop of sagebrush rebels in 2016 decry the "regulators" as government bureaucrats who regulate land use!

27 Richards, 58.

28 Goldscheider, 21.

29 William Butler, only twenty-two years old, arrived in Northampton in the summer of 1786 after a three-year apprenticeship at the print shop of Hudson & Goodwin in Hartford. He published the *Gazette* until 1815, when he sold it to William Clapp of Boston, who sold it in 1817 to the law firm of Bates & Judd, who hired Thomas Shepard (Levi Shepherd's son) as publisher. In 1822 Sylvester Judd, of Judd manuscripts fame, bought the paper and ran it until 1835. Source: Historic Northampton http://www.historic-northampton.org/members_only/gazette/gazhistory.html

30 On the state and national scene, there is no doubt that Shays' Rebellion put the fear of God into government officials. Samuel Adams, among other leading Bostonians, demanded harsh punishment for the rebels, insisting they be hung. Furthermore, the Constitutional Convention was then meeting in Philadelphia, and Shays' Rebellion provided a perfect rationale for the constitutional framers to create a republic that limited the direct representation of the general public, such as the election of senators by state legislatures.

31 Dean, 20-21. Paper at the time was made from rags and linen (flax), and later, cotton. Wood pulp for paper, invented in the 1840s, was not in general use until the late nineteenth century.

32 *Daily Hampshire Gazette*, 6/3/1904.

33 Dean, 91.

34 Judd ms, Vol. 2, 340.

35 Judd includes a strange note that this "was the place for the new Silk Factory." Vol. 2, 340.

36 Judd ms., Vol. 2, 340.

37 Sheffeld, p. 53 White advertised his new grist mill in the *Hampshire Gazette* in 1829 as "a new Grist-mill, with three runs of stones – one for grinding Provender, including ears of corn in the cob, another for Indian Corn, and a third for Flouring, with a superfine Bolt. And as he [White] is [l?]ocated [sic] it is not probable that he will have

a large run of business, so that customers may rationally calculate upon being served without going a second time." Dean, 30.

38 Sheffeld, 33 describes the process: White "took the flaxseed and expressed the linseed oil, the seeds being first bruised or crushed, then ground and afterwards subjected to great pressure. Henry Shepher, Esq., remembers the huge hydraulic press, and especially the massive lever connected with it..."

39 Josiah White apparently cut quite a figure in the village: a self-made man, whose "scholarly turn of mind gave him the name of 'Old Cicero.'" He died at the age of 74 in 1832, just 15 years before Broughton's Meadow was renamed Florence, by which time the village had taken on a startlingly new character. Sheffeld, 36.

40 Sheffeld, 53-54.

41 Sheffeld, 38.

42 Flip was a staple of New England taverns. Concocted from eggs, sugar, rum, brandy, and ale, the mixture was heated with a red hot flip-iron to cause it to froth or "flip."

43 Sheffeld, 46.

44 Kilborne, Sarah Skinner. 2012. *American Phoenix: The Remarkable Story of William Skinner, a Man Who Turned Disaster into Destiny.* NY: Free Press, 88.

45 Kilborne, 88.

46 Sheffeld, 61.

47 Clark, Christopher. 1995. *The Communitarian Moment: The Radical Challenge of the Northampton Association.* Ithaca, NY: Cornell University, 33.

48 Sheffeld, 63.

49 Dean, 29.

50 We have no word on the subsequent fate of Burnell, Cotton, or Brewster.

51 Dean, 32; Massachusetts Historical Commission 1982. Reconnaissance Survey of Northampton, 11.

52 Laurie, Bruce, personal communication 2/16.

53 Broadcloth, a densely woven, lightly napped weave of any number of textiles, was made at least as far back as the fifteenth century in Belgium. Leeds' reputation as the "first" American broadcloth may really be the first produced by powered looms. MHC, 1982, 11.

54 Dean, 33; Massachusetts, Historical Commission Reconnaissance Survey, Northampton. 1982, 11.

55 Stephen Brewer, a Mainer, managed the company through the 1830s when Northampton Woolen won first prize for its broadcloth at the Baltimore International Fair in 1835 against foreign competition. A popular figure in the Valley, Brewer sadly died, drowned in a sailboat accident on the Connecticut River in 1842. Dean, 45.

56 The historic dam was demolished in 2018. The great granite foundation blocks are to be transported down to Pulaski Park in downtown Northampton as a memorial to the site. The advocates to save the dam created a website: https://sites.google.com/site/savethechesterfieldroaddam/home.

57 John Clapp describes Robert Lyman as something of a seventeenth-century reprobate, who had discovered the region's lead deposit, which was in use into the nineteenth century. In his later life, he apparently descended into "a state of distemperature," lost custody of his children, and ended up as a lonely hunter. Clapp, John I. 2016. *Lost Village of Roberts Meadow: Northampton's Forgotten Settlement.* Amherst, MA: Off The Common Books, 1–3.

58 This idea originated in a discussion the author had with Ralmon Black. Its source is word-of-mouth, and we have no citation to rely on.

59 The original foundations are still discernable below the little bridge by his house at Snow Farm on Hyde Hill Road.

60 Josiah Hannum was a nephew of Downing Warner.

61 The site was at Dwight's sawmill above the Searsville Bridge on the West Branch.

62 Axes were made by folding a bar of iron over a handle pattern, then welding a bit of hardened high-carbon steel at the bezel. In forging scythe blades, a bar of steel and iron was welded together and, under glowing heat, it was passed under the trip-hammer, shaping the blade in just two or three heatings at the forge. Shanks were then welded and adjusted on the blades.

63 As it was a fickle little stream, a mile or more up on the south end of Walcott Hill, Guilford found he was able to divert the Town Lot Brook through a short canal to flow down the north side of Gere Hill, enhancing the volume of water at his shop. Successively, Steven Hyde and Levi Hitchcock used this location as a grinding shop. Guilford may have been working in concert with Hyde, finishing the ax heads and scythe blades at his grindstone and making hickory helves and bentwood ash snathes. Note from Ralmon Black.

64 Nathaniel Sears was schooled at Hawley and taught there awhile, but on reaching his majority, went to Cambridge, Massachusetts to learn the dyers trade.

65 Satinet was a strong cloth fabric made with cotton warp and wool filling, fulled and finished to resemble satin, used chiefly for trousers.

66 *Hampshire Gazette and Northampton Courier.* 4/2/1861.

67 Sears, Lorenzo. 1946. *A History of Williamsburg.* Williamsburg, 111. Lorenzo was the son of Nathaniel and his second wife, Cordelia Morton.

68 The 1829 road severely sliced across the riverbank, creating such a narrow dugway that it is, to this day, dangerous for any but motor vehicles to travel on. The new River Road also turned at the end of North Main Street in Williamsburg Center, over what is now the Buttonshop to ascend more gradually along the West Branch to Searsville,

which made travel easier. Taking advantage of the new highway in 1831, Levi Hitchcock left the grinding shop to build a dam above a new bridge where he established an ax factory and a dwelling. The factory was at 40 Goshen Road and the dwelling still stands at number 41. His millpond was still a favorite nighttime skating rink a century later, and his sons were in the business for many years. Levi Hitchcock's sons were Andrew and Hemen. After Rufus Hyde's death, his brother-in-law went out on his own and acquired the old Wild millsite, placing a bold sign on it, "B.K. Baker—Edgetool Maker." Baker's nephew Levi Bradford owned both millsites after Baker's death. Ralmon Black, personal communication.

69 Joel Hayden's rise to prominence was not foreshadowed by his grandfather, Josiah Hayden, Sr., one of Searsville's first settlers. Josiah was a husbandman, who had fallen into debt, having borrowed six pounds from the wealthy Levi Shepherd. In 1785 Shepherd went to court to recover various debts that local people owed him, and Josiah was among the debtors. The court had him jailed for his 42 shillings 8 pence debt, a sum that amounted to 28 days of unskilled labor. It was the kind of event that fed anger against the government and led the Shays' Regulators to rebel in 1786. Goldscheider, 11.

70 Laurie, B. *Rebels*, 114.

71 Laurie, Bruce. 2016. "'Chaotic Freedom' in Civil War Louisiana: The Origins of an Iconic Image," *The Massachusetts Review*, Working Titles series, Vol. 2, No. 1 (November).

72 Agnes Hannay, for all her fine work on mills in Northampton, is an untrustworthy source for Williamsburg, so her description of the early development of industry should be read with care. For example, A.H. Bodman never became a pillar of the town (was first a hog reeve, then a fence viewer and a highway surveyor). There is more to the story than her description that Williamsburg "seems to have been the center for clothiers." Note from Ralmon Black re. A.H. Bodman.

73 "to accommodate the Public and the greater part of the Inhabitants of Chesterfield and at all Seasons of the Year, if Two Bridges be built and maintained across the man branch and the Westernmost branch of Northampton Mill River—that over the Main branch a Little South of the Road now laid out, And the other in the said road—Thereupon Ordered by this court." Hampshire County Court Records, 1762, Book 7, 51.

74 The house is located at #2 South Street and the tanning yard at 12–14 Main St. He also owned more than a hundred acres along the river, from Fenton's Bridge to the Great Bridge near the current pharmacy. Note from Ralmon Black.

75 There can be no mistake from the description of this property that it is the same one still visible along the hillside from the bridge on Goshen Road to the Blacksmith Shop (24 Williams Street) that Wild dug and where he was operating the "upper gristmill" in 1788. This is documented in town records. Bodman Papers, Wm Bodman file, Sophia Smith Collection, Smith College. Research by Ralmon Black.

76 The fence viewer was a magistrate charged to review the boundary line between

neighbors, to decide whose share of the boundary belongs to whom, and to see that legal fences were built and maintained. He might also mediate disputes over fences and boundaries. New England towns had a large number of elected and appointed officers to ensure the efficient administration of town affairs. The author, for example, was once elected field driver to the town of Leverett in evident preparation for higher office. The field driver is on call to drive stray livestock back home.

77 "...for $475.50 paid by Gross Williams and Aaron Warner...I hereby sell...one half of the building erected for the Carding Machines together with the priviledge of... water for use of the Machines, Also the half of the Machines...the above described Buildings & Machines now Standing on Mr. Saml Bodmans land [25 –29 Main Street] in Williamsburgh." Hampshire County Registry of Deeds, Book 25, 454. Research by Ralmon Black.

78 Abner Williams died in 1807, and his sons, Prince and Phineas, sold the Williams' house to Uncle Gross Williams. They all three began the cotton factory at the upper gristmill that Wilde had operated two decades earlier. The cotton mill near the center of town was operated by Erastus Hubbard and Edmund Taylor. Note from Ralmon Black.

79 *Hampshire Gazette and Northampton Courier*, 4/9/1861.

80 In 1797 the Bodman brothers were too young to have been on their own. Samuel Bodman had sold Edmund Taylor, a millwright, the place in 1781 (Hampshire Co. Registry of Deeds, Book 32, 174.) The Bodman sons' father William or another family member probably started the business. Note from Ralmon Black.

81 Lewis sold the property to Simeon P. Graves and Charles Hayden in 1842. Ralmon Black and Eric Weber have taken the trouble to trace the paths of many properties in the county sometimes with success, sometimes not.

82 Gilmore, William J. 1989. *Reading Becomes a Necessity of Life: Material and Cultural Life in Rural New England, 1780–1835*. Knoxville, TN: University of Tennessee.

83 Daniel Hayden's brother David contributed financial support to purchase the property from John Miller, Jr. and Samuel Fairfield, Jr, sons of two of Williamsburg's first settlers. Note from Ralmon Black.

84 The only other industrial enterprise of note in Haydenville during the first half of the nineteenth century is an iron foundry that is shown on the 1831 map and had been in operation since 1824. David Hyde, George W. Holmes, William Lewis, Lyman Litchfield, Josiah Hayden, and John A Root were, at different times, the proprietors. Note from Ralmon Black.

85 Barrus, Hiram. 1881. *History of the Town of Goshen from its First Settlement in 1761 to 1881*. Boston: H. Barrus, 21.

86 Barrus, 111.

87 Barrus, 89.

88 In the 1940s, when Lou Cranson owned the land, Ralmon Black's father, then Scout Master, convinced Cranson to make a gift of that beautiful stretch of the river, which he deeded in 1945 to the Trustees of Williamsburg Boy Scout Properties, with the hope the Scouts would keep the Devils Den Reservation open to the public as a park in a natural condition.

89 You will notice that descriptions of floods become more detailed and dramatic as the nineteenth century progresses. This is likely due to two causes: the source materials and an increase in flood intensity. Flood descriptions come from two sources—the Judd notebooks and manuscripts and the *Hampshire Gazette*. We are fortunate to have Sylvester Judd's descriptions of floods in the mid-nineteenth century for Judd was a great diarist and stickler for detail. It's simply a quirk of history that he left us such a wealth of material. The *Hampshire Gazette* also saw its purpose as providing real "news" to the public, news that subscribers could not otherwise get, which meant articles about the nation and the world, not local material. In 1790 there were about 1,600 people in Northampton and by 1860 there were almost 7000. Most people knew each other in 1800, and local news traveled by word of mouth, so floods and other local events passed from person to person. Thus, local weather events were seen less as "news" than as immediate experience.

90 Arthur Watson, local Northampton historian, noted these two floods in his typescript with no further details. Watson, Arthur. 1915. "Flood History," typescript lodged in the Hampshire Room of Forbes Library.

91 *Hampshire Gazette* 4/8/1801.

92 *Hampshire Gazette* 4/20/1836.

93 *Hampshire Gazette* 3/22/1859.

94 *Hampshire Gazette* 9/10/1828.

95 Connecticut River Watershed Council. 2005. "Currents & Eddies," (newsletter) vol. 55, No.1.

96 *Hampshire Gazette* 9/10/1828.

97 Judd edited the *Gazette* from 1822–35, so he may well have written the flood descriptions of 1821 and 1828. The news reports, especially in 1828, reflect the style of his manuscript writings in their detail and syntax.

98 Judd Notebooks: Jan. 27-31, 1939, 238–243.

99 *Hampshire Gazette* 2/26/1840.

100 Judd Notebooks, 2/25/2840, 292.

101 *Hampshire Gazette* 2/26/1840.

102 Judd, Hadley, 307. Judd's observation is supported by Louis Everts in his *History of the Connecticut Valley in Massachusetts*. 1870 Philadelphia: L.H. Everts, 88 "The

salmon remained in the river until some time after the construction of the dam at Montague [in 1796]." Many fish were found after the first year of the dam, but then there was a sharp decline "until about the last seen of them were a few stragglers at South Hadley Falls, about the year 1800."

103 Judd, *Hadley*, 310.

104 Barrus, p. 115 The deer was shot by John W. White, an ancestor of Williamsburg historian Ralmon Black.

105 The process by which one mix of species replaces another mix after a disturbance is called ecological succession.

106 Hall et al. 2002, 1329-30.

107 Donahue, Brian 2007. "Another Look from Sanderson's Farm: A Perspective on New England Environmental History and Conservation," *Environmental History*, vol. 12, No. 1 (January), 18.

108 Old Sturbridge Village documents. 1980."Early New England Farm Crops." http: /resources.osv.org/explore_learn/document_viewer.php?Action=View&DocID=732 The Commonwealth taxed different types of hay-producing land from salt marsh to fresh meadow to upland. "The relative merits of hay from each type of land were subjects of vigorous debate. English or upland hay was generally considered the best and became the standard against which the other two types were measured. Each farmer also had his own preferences among the individual varieties of these three general types of hay. Of the varieties of upland hay, for example, some preferred timothy or herds grass to orchard grass, while the makers of salt marsh hay were given to debating the relative merits of fox grass and sedge.

Chapter Four

1 1874 Williamsburg Dam Disaster—139 lives lost. 1889 Johnstown Disaster—2209 dead.

2 Steinberg, Theodore. 1991. *Nature Incorporated: Industrialization and the Waters of New England.* Amherst, MA: University of Massachusetts Press, 144.

3 Steinberg, 244.

4 Steinberg, T., 44 –45. Steinberg, a history and law professor at Case Western Reserve, describes the transformation of water law in Massachusetts from its origins in protecting the rights of landowners to "a vision of water and law that sanctioned the maximization of economic growth [by the mid-19th century]," 16.

5 See Chapter 3, Williamsburg Center subsection.

6 Hannay, 127.

7	1840	Northampton	3,750	Williamsburg	1,309	Goshen	500
	1860	Northampton	6,788	Williamsburg	2,094	Goshen	440
	1880	Northampton	12,172	Williamsburg	2,234	Goshen	327
	2013	Northampton	28,400	Williamsburg	2,400	Goshen	1,050
	1840	Holyoke (1850)	3,200	Springfield	10,985		
	1860	Holyoke	5000	Springfield	15,199		
	1880	Holyoke	22,000	Springfield	33,340		
	2013	Holyoke	40,000	Springfield	153,700		

8 Westhampton's population peaked in 1830, with 918 residents. By 1870 it had only 587. Ashfield's population peaked in 1840 with 1,579 people and lost about 500 by 1880 when it was down to 1,066 .

9 Laurie, *Rebels*, 6

10 Laurie, *Rebels*, 6.

11 Readers interested in the political history of mid-19th-century Northampton are urged to read Bruce Laurie's outstanding story in which he describes life through the lives of five prominent local men—Sylvester Judd, Jr (our 19th diarist), John P. Williston, David Ruggles, Henry S. Gere, and Erastus Hopkins. The political currents of the time are far more complex than our brief descriptions suggests. They include both political and apolitical approaches to abolitionism, the place of women and the suffrage, prohibition and temperance, and the treatment of workers.

12 Laurie, *Rebels*, 87.

13 Clark, *Roots*, 246.

14 "This must be the paradise of America," is the quote most often attributed to Jenny Lind in 1851.

15 Brian Turner, an instructor at Smith College, tracked down the origin of "Paradise City," and found no confirmation that the source was Jenny Lind. He did discover, however, that the Round Hill Water Cure advertised its hotel as located in "The Paradise of America" three years after Mme. Lind's stay in 1855. An advertisement to that effect appeared that year in the Charleston, South Carolina *Courier*. Personal communication with Meadow River Historians, a group of local historians supported by the non-profit Historic Northampton.

16 Hannay, 78 – 80 The backgrounds of the entrepreneurs and investors were diverse. "Of forty-two men active as proprietors or agents between 1845 and 1860 whose backgrounds could be traced, ten started out as skilled craftsmen and eight as farmers. Five other men, migrants to the Valley from other states or abroad, had previous careers in the factory system. But the largest single group, nineteen men, had mercantile origins." Clark, *Roots*, 1990, 247.

17 The original gas plant building called the Roundhouse remains below Pulaski Park and beside the ditch where the Mill River used to run.

18 Rudd, Kassia 2011. "Dams, Industry and Power in Northampton 1831–1895." Kassia Rudd (Smith College '11) wrote this work as a senior thesis. It can be found on the Mill River Greenway Initiative website on the following page: http://millrivergreenway.org/greenway-projects/mapping-the-historic-mill-river/dams-industry-and-power-in-northampton-1831-1895-by-kassia-rudd/

19 Lamb started his wire business across the Connecticut River in Hadley in 1852, making wire for brooms at a time when there were only four or five wire factories in the country. After his move to the Lower Mills and the rebuilding of the mill in the 1870s, his new machinery produced much more uniform wire of various sizes, from telegraph wire on down. Lamb was apparently "a 'square man' to do business with, and always does as he agrees. No one doubts his word, and his verbal promise is as good as his note." He died in 1896. *Hampshire Gazette*, 2/4/1879.

20 Strimer, Steve. 2013. "Historical Function of the Lamb Wire Mill and Its History to the Present," application to the Northampton Community Preservation Committee for renovation of the Wire Mill Building. Northampton Community Preservation Committee papers.

21 *Springfield Republican* 3/2/1869

22 *Hampshire Gazette*, 12/27/1881; DHG 4/28/1898

23 Dean, 65–66.

24 *Hampshire Gazette*, 10/30/1866

25 A short history of Northampton State Hospital can be found in Moore, J.M. 1993. "The Life and Death of Northampton State Hospital. Northampton: Historic Northampton." This website http://northamptonstatehospital.com/ offers a fine short description and good citations.

26 http://northamptonstatehospital.com Within a decade of its founding, the formidable Dr. Pliny Earle took the helm and "immediately began to cultivate a strong work therapy program by expanding the farm, and constructing a greenhouse as well as other service oriented buildings."

27 The last eleven patients left in 1993. Anna Schuleit's memorial installation of Bach's Magnificat was recorded in a video of the event in 2000: https://www.youtube.com/watch?v=zg4jOBR083I

28 Dean, 66, 68, 121, 151–52.

29 Dean, 91.

30 Hannay, 85; Massachusetts Historical Commission Reconnaissance Survey 1982, 15.

31 Maynard built his tool factory at the Upper Mills, and, when the Bay State

Company foundered in the post-war depression, Clement and Hawke sold to J.H. Lyman, who ran the Riverside Cutlery Company from 1870 to 1871, and, within a year, sold it to Judge Hinckley. "Background on Northampton Cutlery Company" from the Northampton Cutlery Company Records 1869-1987, University of Massachusetts, Amherst Libraries, Special Collections & University Archives. Call no: MS58.

32 *Hampshire Gazette,* 10/30/1866

33 Clark, Christopher, *The Communitarian Moment,* 2.

34 Christopher Clark goes into the details of various sorts of abolitionism from colonizers (return the slaves to Africa) to the Garrisonians' refusal to participate in politics, to radical political abolitionists and those who demanded temperance (abstinence), as well as religious convictions. It was a complicated scene. Clark, *Communitarian Moment,* 34ff. See also Bruce Laurie in *Rebels in Paradise.*

35 Letter from June 9, 1839 quoted in Strimer, Steve, n.d. "On the Trail of the Josiah White Cottage Where Lydia Maria & David Lee Child Lived Between May 1840 and May 1841 in Florence, Massachusetts." Northampton: David Ruggles Center, 3.

36 Lydia Maria moved to New York where she became editor of the *National Anti-Slavery Standard.* David remained several more years, but was never able to make a success of beet sugar or, later, peat mining. Strimer, Steve, "On the Trail of the Josiah White Cottage." See also Karcher, Carolyn L. 1998. *The First Woman in the Republic: A Cultural Biography of Lydia Maria Child.* Durham, NC: Duke University

37 Clark, *Communitarian Moment,* 2.

38 Clark, *Communitarian Moment,* 157.

39 Clark points out that even before the Community's dissolution, members were mapping out an alternative future that would bring about the vision of a "neighborhood community...a collection of individual family houses and properties whose proximity to one another would retain some of the community's spirit." *Communitarian Moment,* 187.

40 Painter, Nell I. 1996. *Sojourner Truth: A Life, A Symbol.* NY: Norton, 87.

41 For further information, check with Steve Strimer, who helped establish the David Ruggles Center in Florence. See: www.davidrugglescenter.org. See also Hodges, Graham R. 2010. *David Ruggles: A Radical Black Abolitionist and the Underground Railroad in New York City.* Chapel Hill, NC: University of North Carolina.

42 Strimer, Steve, n.d. "History of Nonotuck Street, 1835–1891." For further information on census data see the 2007 registration form to nominate the Ross Farm for national historic site status, 9.

43 George Benson had teamed up with Samuel and John Williston to turn the silk mill into a cotton factory in 1846. The enterprise was called the Bensonville Manufacturing Company, which appears on a contemporary map, but, after Benson joined the

Anti-Sabbatarians, the Willistons kicked him out and took over in 1848, changing the name of the enterprise to the Greenville Manufacturing Company. Benson moved away in 1850 and Samuel Hill was left to clean up his debts.

44 When traveling in England in 1843, Joel Hayden met in Nottingham "a young man in whom he became much interested. There was something about the fellow that appealed to the American manufacturer," so Hayden brought him to the Mill River Valley to help start a horn button factory in 1844. Critchlow was soon in business for himself and developed a line of buttons made from mountain laurel and others of paper mâché. Dean, 68.

45 The chief inventor, Lucius Dimock, was a local man, who would later move his factory and family to Leeds.

46 The authoritative story of Northampton's silk industry can be found in Senechal, Marjorie. 2004. *Northampton's Century of Silk*. Northampton, MA: Northampton Historical Commission.

47 *Hampshire Gazette*, 2/24/1852. The citizens also rejected the names Bensonville and Greenville.

48 The unknown author of the "50th-anniversary Brochure for Florence Manufacturing" wrote that the organizers of the company—George Burr, Isaac Parsons, and D.G. Littlefield—began by making buttons, jewel and revolver boxes, along with medallion and daguerreotype cases from Florence Compound. Recognizing that many of these items were going out of fashion, "they began to talk about what else they could make. Just as an experiment a small oval medallion frame was picked up, a fat piece of wood whittled out to fit it and this piece was punched full of holes. Then somebody bought some bristles and stuck them in these holes. This piece was then glued to the medallion back. And lo, there was a brush. It is true that nobody knew what kind of a brush it was. It was certainly not a hair brush, nor a clothes brush, nor a shoe brush. It was crude, but it was a BRUSH. Here was a new use for Florence [Compound]."

49 "Florence Manufacturing Company 1916. Fifty Years of Brush Making." Copy from Historic Northampton.

50 Florence Manufacturing Company, "Fifty Years of Brush Making."

51 National Register of Historic Places. 2007. Registration form for the Hill-Ross Farmstead, 123 Meadow St., Northampton (Florence) 01062

52 Dean, 47.

53 Sharpe, E. 2004. *In the Shadow of the Dam: The Aftermath of the Mill River Flood of 1874*. NY: Free Press. Sharpe has a colorful description of the process: "In the boiler house, roaring fires produced steam heat, which shrank the hard shell... In the brick mill...men wielded small circular saws to cut slices off the kernel's exterior... In the dye house, workers dunked the buttons in huge vats—some in white to brighten their natural color and others in darker colors..." 26.

54 In the 1870s, Critchlow retired and passed his ownership of the Button Shop on to his manager, George Warner, who became a village leader and one of the heroic figures saving lives during the 1874 Flood. Sharpe, 25.

55 Like William Skinner, J. L. Otis was a self-made man. He entered the workforce as an eight-year old child laborer in a cotton factory, toiling almost fourteen hours a day. He became an outstanding self-taught machinist and took a job as superintendent of the Otis Manufacturing Company in Manchester, Connecticut, then helped establish his own company while consulting for another silk and wool-knit goods simultaneously. After serving in the Connecticut 10th Volunteer Infantry Regiment during the Civil War from 1861-64, chiefly along the Mid-Atlantic Coast, and achieving the rank of Brevet Brigadier-General, Otis settled in Northampton where he became superintendent of the Florence Sewing Machine Company. Otis became a substantial presence in Northampton and held positions as a selectman, state legislator, and state senator. He was instrumental in writing the charter that changed Northampton's status from town to city in 1883. Research by Ralmon Black.

56 Joel Hayden was smart and inventive from an early age, and, after an apprenticeship as a machinist, locksmith and gunsmith in Pittsfield, set up shop with his partner in 1822 at the only mill site at that time in Haydenville. Besides his extraordinary expertise in millwork, machinery, and tool making, Joel was deeply devoted to the cause of changing society through religion and social movements. He became a founding member of the local anti-slavery society, and co-founded with J.P. Williston the first abolitionist newspaper, the *Hampshire Herald* that Henry S. Gere edited. The paper was known as the voice of the Liberty party. He was an ardent advocate for temperance and the banning of alcohol in social settings, and he helped found and support a variety of churches. Notes from Ralmon Black and Sharpe, 14.

57 Sharpe, 10.

58 Letter from Daniel Webster Tarnten (?) from Haydenville to his family, May 3rd, 1856 in the possession of Ralmon Black. The Warren, Dawson & Hyde Pen Shop was on the right bank above the Cotton Mill Dam.

59 Lt. Joshua Thayer was the first to buy a water privilege at that site where he built a gristmill after the Revolution, but soon lost it in a freshet. In 1832, J. J. Lewis and J. J. Goodell started a small blacksmith shop where they manufactured bits and bitstocks. Four or five others in succession occupied this water privilege, smithing spoons made of Britannia (a tin-based alloy), harness trimmings, faucets, hoes, and tacks. In the 1850s Samuel S. Wells enlarged the factory building and began making portmanteaux frames, but in two years time removed his business to Boston. Notes from Ralmon Black.

60 Sarah Skinner Kilborne paints a fascinating picture of her great-great grandfather, who beat the odds in a grim corner of England. He worked in the dyehouses of Spitalfields and was found always carrying around books, many of which he memorized. He sailed for America in 1845, became foreman of a Florence dyehouse, married Nancy Warner, the sister of his business partner, Joseph Warner, fell out with Joseph, established his

own dyeing business, and moved upriver to Sweetfern Plain. Kilborne, 74 ff.

61 One of the dyers, Lewis T. Black, was Ralmon Black's great grandfather. Lewis was born in 1840 and died in 1880, having survived the Civil War and the Great Flood. He learned the dyer's trade from his father Captain Milton Black, who worked at the Unquomonk Woolen Mill in Williamsburg Center. Notes from Ralmon Black.

62 Willison Thayer built the Searsville Reservoir Dam higher than six feet to provide a reservoir for more reliable flow at his works on Buttonshop Road in the Center. At Sears Woolen Mills, Sears retired in 1862, and Thomas Nash carried on for two decades or more. The edgetool factory fell into the hands of B. Franklin Sears. D. Warner Graves turned out button molds at the same water privilege. At that same site, S.K. Wait operated a gristmill in the 1860s followed by Levi Bradford. Just downstream Marcus Way & Sons turned wood button molds. Notes from Ralmon Black

63 *Hampshire Gazette*, 4/30/1872.

64 *Northampton Courier*, June 4, 1878. In 1890, the woolen mill at the bridge in Searsville succumbed. It had twice changed hands after Nathaniel Sears retired, and was left unoccupied and dilapidated for several years. On the Fourth of July, 1890, some local boys torched it. And finally, "the saw mill of Gilbert M. Bradford, at Searsville on the Goshen road, was burned in 1897. It was run by steam, which was substituted for water about a year ago. *Daily Hampshire Gazette*, February 23, 1897. It burned again in 1901.

65 *Hampshire Gazette*, 4/18/1843.

66 Judd, Northampton Vol 4, 4/23/1847.

67 Judd, Northampton Vol 5 4/28-5/3/1850. Judd was a fanatic measurer of flood heights, taking his measuring rod through town, asking residents about historic floods, and noting it all down. Here is an example from the 1850 notes: "Flood of 1843—2'1" above top of Conn. River/Hadley Bridge abutment as determined by the mark on the storehouse, since there was no abutment for the bridge in 1843.

> 1845 flood—4.5' lower than 1843
>
> 1847 flood—2'2" lower than 1843
>
> 1850 flood—2'7" lower than 1843

"It is certain that the flood of 1847 was from 5 to 6 inches above that of 1850 at the abutment. It is certain that the flood of 1845 was from 2'4" to 2'8" below that of 1850. It is certain that the flood of 1843 at the storehouse was 2' and 7" or 8" below that of 1850."

68 *Hampshire Gazette*, 5/2/1854.

69 Judd notebooks Vol. 7, 4/29/54.

70 *Hampshire Gazette*, 5/2/1854.

71 *Hampshire Gazette*, 3/22/1859.

72 *Hampshire Gazette,* 3/22/1859.

73 Since the Upper Mill site was first dammed in the 1660s, property owners had had a hard go of it. The mid-nineteenth century was no different. "These misfortunes, while they cause great inconvenience to the people of the town, are especially hard for the owners of the mills. Messrs. Damon & Son have at two other times suffered severely from damage by water, and they are richly entitled to the warm sympathy of our citizens. They are men of energy, and the wish is irrepressible, that they may speedily overcome this misfortune and again move along in a condition of prosperity." *Hampshire Gazette,* 3/22/1859.

74 *Hampshire Gazette,* 5/2/1854. From the *Gazette* report, it appears that Fruit and Maple Streets had no flood protection. "The water came up into the first floor of all the houses at the lower end of the two streets above named, and surrounded them all up to the south street road, which for the time, seemed to be at the head of ship navigation.

75 *Hampshire Gazette,* 4/22/1862.

76 *Hampshire Gazette,* 10/5/1869.

77 *Hampshire Gazette,* 10/5/1869.

78 *Hampshire Gazette,* 10/5/1869.

79 There were 139 lives lost in the Williamsburg Disaster, and 15 years later the 1889 Johnstown Dam Disaster killed 2,209.

80 *Hampshire Gazette,* 5/26/1874.

81 Sharpe, E. *In the Shadow of the Dam* and Kilborne, Sarah S. 2012. *American Phoenix: The Remarkable Story of William Skinner, a Man Who Turned Disaster into Destiny.* NY: Free Press

82 This whole process is described in detail in Sharpe, 39–45.

83 Sharpe, 46.

84 Sharpe, 49.

85 Under Massachusetts law, a coroner's inquest was the legal method for investigating the cause of death of persons who may have died as a result of a violent act. The lengthy inquest provides details of the flood from eyewitnesses as well as testimony from the owners of the reservoir company and engineering inspections. Sharpe, 152ff.

86 Sharpe, 56.

87 *Hampshire Gazette,* 5/26/1874.

88 Eric Weber's explanation of the flood wave's height can be found in Appendix 1.

89 Eric Weber's notes, Appendix 1.

90 Sharpe, Elizabeth. 2012. "Mill River Flood of 1874," on website of Pioneer Valley History Network, https://pvhn3.wordpress.com/1800s/mill-river-flood-of-1874/

91 Sharpe, 56.

92 Sharpe, 61.

93 Sharpe, 61.

94 Sharpe, 63.

95 Kilborne, 23.

96 Kilborne 27.

97 Sharpe, 67.

98 Sharpe, 68.

99 Kilborne, 55.

100 Sharpe, 72.

101 Sharpe, 74.

102 Sharpe, 76.

103 Sharpe, 77-85.

104 Sharpe, 82-83.

105 Kilborne, 209.

106 Sensing profit in tragedy, the city fathers in Holyoke, located between North-ampton and Springfield, had already been approaching the industrialists of the Upper Mill Valley to lure them to the new city that Boston capital had built in the 1850s. As America's first planned industrial city, Holyoke had enormous advantages, not the least of which were a steady supply of waterpower and land available for the large factories that flanked the canals fed by the Connecticut River.

107 Taken from William Cobet-Skinner's diary, which Ralmon Black transcribed from a copy in his possession.

108 As Skinner's great-great-granddaughter Sarah Skinner Kilborne tells this story: William Skinner became an American phoenix whose second chance allowed him to participate in America's Gilded Age. Skinner built his new Unquomonk Silk Mill in Holyoke six months after the Great Flood and re-hired half the men from his Skinnerville workforce, including all his dyers. He re-hired only about a quarter of the women and girls, but was using fewer women at the Holyoke mill than he had in total at Skinnerville. Many of the men decided in the end not to move to Holyoke. Kilborne, 325–26.

109 Kilborne, 364.

110 Kilborne, image caption, 26.

111 The cleanup operations are colorfully described in Elizabeth Sharpe, 90ff.

112 Sharpe, 140.

113　Sharpe, 143–44.

114　Sharpe, 218.

115　Sharpe, 152.

116　Sharpe, 197.

117　Spelman had a substantial interest in the Textile Manufacturing Company of Westfield where he served as president and general manager. Notes of Ralmon Black.

118　Kilborne, 357.

119　*Hampshire Gazette*, 12/17/1878.

120　*Hampshire Gazette*, 12/17/1878.

121　*Hampshire Gazette*, 12/17/1878.

122　*Hampshire Gazette*, 12/17/1878.

123　As of this writing, the village of Leeds is raising money to repair the Hotel Bridge so that it can be used by foot traffic. This is a rare iron bridge from the late nineteenth century that Leeds hopes to place on the National Historic Register.

124　*Hampshire Gazette*, 5/26/1874.

125　Barrus, H., Barrus, Hiram. 1881. *History of the Town of Goshen from its First Settlement in 1761 to 1881*. Boston: H. Barrus, 110

126　The work of Harvard Forest researchers show that forest clearing in Massachusetts peaked between 1830 and 1885, and their maps shows sparse forest cover in our watershed in 1830. The 1830 data were chiefly taken from the series of 1831 maps that the state required every town to complete at that date. Hall, B., G. Motzkin, et al. 2002. "Three Hundred Years of Forest and Land-Use Change in Massachusetts," *Journal of Biogeography*, Vol. 29, No. 10/11, 1327.

127　The American ambassador to Portugal, William Jarvis, smuggled more than 3000 merino sheep from Spain from 1809-1811 past the eyes of the Spanish authorities, who were preoccupied with the Napoleonic Wars.

128　Judd as quoted by Clark, *Roots*, 292.

129　Pitch/yellow/hard pine was used for tar, charcoal, and candlewood, which was burned as a source of light. Yellow pine was the most common material used for structural timbers in the Connecticut Valley until the early 19th century and the most common wood for floorboards, some of which were up to 15 inches wide. White pine was used less frequently for flooring, but were sawn up to 2 feet wide. Motzkin, G. et al. 1999. "A Historical Perspective on Pitch Pine-Scrub Oak Communities in the Connecticut Valley of Massachusetts," *Ecosystems* 2:255–273, 262.

130　Judd Notebooks Vol. 4, 1847 4/16. The author would also note that as construction timber became more and more scarce in the Connecticut River Valley, the great log drives on the Connecticut River, which began in the late 1860s, supplied the region with plenty of logs from the Great North Woods of New Hampshire and Vermont.

131 The competition was between two groups of an unknown number of hunters headed by Colonel J. Thayer and Major B. Cook from unnamed local towns. Heading the list of dead mammals were over 6000 red squirrels, followed by 2,300 grey squirrels, 1,400 "striped squirrels" (we assume these were chipmunks), 950 raccoons, 700 muskrats, 700 rabbits and a few flying squirrels and weasels. The numbers of feathered game were led by 2,600 blue jays, followed by 800 grouse (partridge), 700 woodpeckers, 320 owls, 300 pigeons (unknown whether passenger pigeons or mourning doves), 175 crows, 115 hawks, 20 ducks, and a handful of "larks" and woodcock. During this time, two turkey had been shot in the nearby town of Palmer. The total kill was 19,114. Judd manuscripts, Vol. 5, Oct. 28-Nov. 1, 1848. From the *Hampshire Herald*, Tuesday Nov. 9 1848.

132 Based on the amount of land assessed as woodland: Northampton had 5625 acres in 1841 and 2498 in 1860; Williamsburg assessed woodland went from 1925 in 1841 to 1395 in 1860. Clark, *Roots*, 291.

133 There is a considerable literature on the 19th-century rural economy of New England, particularly that of Western Massachusetts, because of work done at the Harvard Forest in Petersham http://harvardforest.fas.harvard.edu. I have cited Christopher Clark's work, and would also suggest a more recent work by the Brandeis historian Brian Donohue 2007. "Another Look from Sanderson's Farm: A Perspective on New England Environmental History and Conservation," *Environmental History*, vol. 12, 9–34. One of his provocative conclusions is that "continuous grazing encouraged the spread of pasture weeds such as hardhack, juniper, red cedar, and (notably) white pine—whatever the cows wouldn't eat. Controlling these native woody invaders...took hard labor with the brush whack, in the face of diminishing returns... In the end, they decided that the only sensible thing to do was to let most of their spent pastures go, and stop clearing new ones. Pastures were not filling up with pines because farms had been abandoned. Even on prosperous farms, pastures were abandoned because they were filling up with pines." 19–29.

134 Marsh, G.P. 1864. *Man and Nature; or, Physical Geography as Modified by Human Action*. 36. In his 80 years of life (1801-82) he packed in several lifetimes of achievement as a lawyer, newspaper editor, sheep farmer, mill owner, lecturer, politician, diplomat, scientist and America's foremost authority on Scandinavian languages. See David Lowenthal. 2000. George Perkins Marsh: Prophet of Conservation. Seattle: University of Washington Press.

135 Melosi M. 1999. *The Sanitary City: Urban Infrastructure in America from Colonial Times to the Present*. Baltimore: Johns Hopkins University (Abridged edition in 2008 published by University of Pittsburg Press). In Great Britain and Europe, households began linking their waste to the stormwater sewers after the invention of running water systems and water closets at mid-century. These systems, however, worked poorly because of bad designs, so sanitarians suggested separate systems with the added benefit

that human wastes could be recovered for fertilizer. Some European cities adopted expensive separate systems, but most stuck with the cheaper combined ones. 117.

136 Cumbler, *Reasonable Use,* 110.

137 The Board of Health was given authority to regulate pollution in waterways in 1878. Cumbler, *Reasonable Use,* 115.

138 Groundwater movement and the leaching of pollutants by soil organisms was poorly understood at the time. Pollution dilution by soil organisms works, and cesspools and leach fields are common everywhere in less densely populated areas. Their installation and maintenance are now regulated, but these systems can be overburdened by heavy use and are unsuitable for built-up areas with lots of impervious surfaces.

139 Cestre, *Northampton, Massachusetts,* 71. Prior to 1871, drinking water came from wells and from springs, chiefly near Round Hill. Northampton's current drinking water comes from a reservoir in West Whately, outside the Mill River Watershed. It was built in 1901.

140 The most encyclopedic history of environmental health in the US can be found in Melosi's *The Sanitary City.* A series of fundamental essays is collected in a work by Tarr, J. 1996. *The Search for the Ultimate Sink: Urban Pollution in Historical Perspective.* Akron, OH: University of Akron.

141 A vast literature on wilderness exists, and a good starting place would be Cronon, W., ed. 1995. *Uncommon Ground: Rethinking the Human Place* in Nature. NY: Norton.

142 1872 Congressional Act of Dedication.

143 Steinberg, T. 1991. *Nature Incorporated: Industrialization and the Waters of New England.* Amherst, MA: University of Massachusetts, 76.

144 Steinberg, T., *Nature Incorporated,* 205.

145 Cumbler, *Reasonable Use,* 55–61. Industrialists developed financial and legal tools to assert control over waterways, which included changes in water law that allowed factory owners to build dams and foul waters to a much greater extent than earlier in the 19th century. See Steinberg, 146 ff. for an explanation of the development of the "reasonable use" doctrine that allowed for inevitable damage from industrial use so long as that use was reasonable and in the communities' interests.

146 Hannay, 128 estimated the number of manufacturing establishments, as defined by the Massachusetts census, as 44 in 1845, 74 in 1855, and 64 in 1865. The Commonwealth had changed its definition of "establishment" between 1855 and 1865.

147 Sharpe, 197–98.

148 Although agricultural research and outreach have attenuated the contention inherent in the relationship between soil and water on the one hand, and agriculture on the other, arguments persist to this day. Think, for example, of the bumper sticker once common on cars in Washington state: "Are You an Environmentalist or Do You

Work for a Living?" Although modern Americans tend to link recreation and aesthetics with nature, the fact is that people have experienced nature through work from the very beginning. Historian Richard White probed deeply into this theme in his essay entitled "Are You an Environmentalist, Or Do You Work for a Living," in Cronon, W., ed. *Uncommon Ground*, 1995, pp. 172 ff.

149 Sinton, J.W. 1998. "La division des paysages partagés..."

Chapter Five

1 Krugman, *Paul*. 2016. "Review of Robert Gordon's The Rise and Fall of American Growth," *New York Times Book Review*, 1/31/16, p. 64.

2 Gordon, Robert J. 2016. *The Rise and Fall of American Growth: The US Standard of Living Since the Civil War*. Princeton, NJ: Princeton University p. 2 Gordon engagingly details the impacts of inventions from the obvious—extending the hours of light, networking houses and cities, preserving food, reducing epidemics—to the subtle—elevators enabled skyscrapers to be built, motor vehicles replaced horses, thus increasing by 25 percent the amount of agricultural land devoted to human instead of animal feed, even transforming the understanding of time: "Dramatic changes in working conditions over a long, contentious period changed the whole concept of time, including the introduction of blocs of time that were barely known a century earlier, such as the two-day weekend and retirement.", 6

3 Following is a chart estimating the number of workers in four industrial sectors. For unknown reasons, the workers in the Florence Manufacturing Company/Pro Brush concern are not included. Data from Hannay, 131

Date	Silk workers	Cutlery workers	Other Metals	Wood Products
1891	1245	403	509	130
1910	1509	398	591	94
1920	1927	369	375	213
1930	1815	435	200	79

4 Springfield became the first city in Western Massachusetts in 1852, followed by Holyoke in 1874, Northampton in 1883, and Pittsfield in 1891. All settled areas in New England were originally called towns, governed by all certified voting residents at "Town Meeting," which appointed town officers and established the town budget. Many towns with more than about 20,000 or so people in the nineteenth century found that the town form of government was inefficient, and switched to a mayor/council, or city form of governing. More than 90 percent of New England communities are still towns.

5 Massachusetts Historical Commission 1982 Reconnaissance Survey. From 1890–1915, 30 percent of the immigrant population of Springfield were Irish, 14 percent French Canadian, and 9 percent Italian. In the period following, Italian and Russian immigrants surpassed other groups.

6 The 1930 Sanborn map showed a large portion of the downsized factory as vacant.

7 Strimer, Steve. 2013. Application for Community Preservation Funds to the City of Northampton. 12/17 personal communication.

8 Senechal, 29.

9 New England Woven, Inc. bought the Emery Wheel building in 1938 and manufactured labels there until the 1960s.

10 Kilborne, 222.

11 Hannay, 116.

12 Senechal, 54.

13 The anonymous author of this 1974 pamphlet wrote that the company never had more than 1500 employees and noted, no doubt with some exaggeration, that Pro Brush paychecks supported some 25 percent of Northampton's families. Anon. 1974. "50 More Years of Brush-Making—1916–1974." Typescript in special collections at the Du Bois Library, University of Massachusetts, Amherst,1 and 9.

14 *Daily Hampshire Gazette*, 12/15/1960 Strike votes were held in ca. 1940, 1951, 1953, and 1960.

15 "50 More Years of Brush-Making," 3.

16 At the turn of the century, Fannie Clary at Clary Farm, now known as Snow Farm, entertained many notable thinkers of the time. Fannie herself was at ease among that company, an educator, suffragist and prohibitionist. In 1902, the Prohibition Party nominated her for State Representative from this district and she received 500 votes. Again in 1904, she was nominated on the Prohibition ticket for Secretary of State—the first woman in Massachusetts to receive a state-wide nomination for a state office. Of course, she was too far ahead of her time to be taken seriously, let alone elected. Ralmon Black, personal communication 3/17. By the mid-twentieth century, Williamsburg had become a classic New England town, content to care for itself while fully participating in the life of the larger world. As Phyllis Deming, a contemporary local historian, wrote: "Beautiful, energetic, largely residential with the exception of a few industries familiar to us, Williamsburg still reflects the trends and progress of a great nation." She further noted that while the town supported women's rights, it frowned upon strong drink, no doubt the legacy of Fannie Clary. Deming, Phyllis. 1946. *A History of Williamsburg in Massachusetts*. Northampton, MA: The Hampshire Bookshop, 403.

17 The silk company had about fifty operatives who produced silk twist thread for sewing machines in 1931 when the plant closed. Following that, a group called the College Weavers manufactured rayon for a short time, after which H. R. Sharpe and D. Outhouse made paper milk bottle caps, and during the Second World War, Noble Manufacturing Company manufactured weapons parts for the US government. Ralmon Black, personal communication.

18 Christian, Albert, and Reuben Hills were sons of Jacob Hills, a German metallurgist

whom Joel Hayden, Sr. hired in the 1850s. Ralmon Black, personal communication.

19 Henry James ran the woolen mill after the Flood until poor health forced him to sell it to George Cook from New York, who produced cotton blankets for a decade before he left town. Gilbert Bradford, who was operating two woodworking facilities in Searsville, bought the property and produced tobacco boxes and apple barrels, outfitting the factory with a steam engine. The mill burned down in 1913, after which two other men used the site as a sawmill. The factory finished its life in the 1950s as a wood turning plant for handles and dowels. Ralmon Black, personal communication.

20 Spelman sold the site to his partner, Frederick Crosby, in 1882, who then ran it with his new partner, Albert Morton, as a sawmill for at least three more decades. Ralmon Black, personal communication.

21 The button factory had a particularly interesting history that involved a constant adaptation to changing styles, purchasing a plant on the Mississippi River to cut blanks from clamshells, then shifting from buttons to studs, cuff links and jewelry. In 1963 the high price of shell spelled the end of the button shop, which is now a funeral home. Ralmon Black, personal communication.

22 Ralmon Black, personal communication.

23 *Daily Hampshire Gazette*, 11/17/1913. "Williamsburg had at 5 o'clock yesterday afternoon (November 16, 1913) the largest fire in its history when Gilbert M. Bradford's sawmill was burned to the ground…"

24 Nathaniel Sears' old woolen mill shut down in the 1880s. On the night of July 3, 1890, thrill-seekers torched it to light up the night sky. Ralmon Black, personal communication.

25 Cestre was a French social historian, who had spent a year researching the city of Northampton from his research position at Smith College in the 1960s.

26 Cestre, 92.

27 After the founding of Holyoke in 1850, not a single new textile firm came to the Mill River. In the late nineteenth century, Paterson, New Jersey cemented its hold bit by bit on the silk industry, condemning Corticelli Silk to failure during the Great Depression. Cheap electric energy, low tariffs, declining transportation costs, and superabundant skilled labor all contributed to lower prices for industrial goods and spelled the doom of many industries in the Mill River watershed. Cestre, 92.

28 Hannay, 101

29 Cestre, 91

30 F.L. Olmsted finished Central Park in 1857, Hartford's Bushnell Park along the Park River was done in 1861, and Forest Park in Springfield, another Olmsted design, was completed in 1884. Central Park and Forest Park, each about 775 acres, are among America's largest urban parks. The largest urban parks, both begun in the 1860s and 1870s are the 1000+ acre Golden Gate Park in San Francisco and Chicago's Lincoln Park at more than 1,200 acres.

31 Gerald Stanley Lee (1862–1944) was a major literary presence in early twentieth century Northampton, writing a dozen books, many essays, and much commentary in his magazine entitled *Mount Tom*. Lee's letter was headlined "Gerald Stanley Lee Suggests "Riverpath Park" Be Built Along Stream from Wright Ave. Bridge to South Street—Opposes "Taking Advantage of Name of Coolidge to Get a Good Bridge Bargain" *Daily Hampshire Gazette*, 6/2/1934.

32 *Daily Hampshire Gazette*, 6/2/1934

33 *Daily Hampshire Gazette*, 9/20/1887

34 *Daily Hampshire Gazette*, 11/1/1890

35 *Daily Hampshire Gazette*, 3/2/1896

36 *Daily Hampshire Gazette*, 4/21/1900

37 *Daily Hampshire Gazette*, 3/3/1902

38 *Daily Hampshire Gazette*, 3/3/1902

39 *Daily Hampshire Gazette*, 3/28/1913

40 *Daily Hampshire Gazette*, 11/5/1927

41 US Department of Interior, Geological Survey. 1937. *The Floods of March 1936: Part 1. New England Rivers*. Geological Survey Water-Supply Paper 798. Washington, DC: US Printing Off.

42 *Daily Hampshire Gazette*, 3/19/1936

43 *Daily Hampshire Gazette*, 3/19/1936

44 US Department of Interior, Geological Survey. 1940. *Hurricane Floods of September 1938* (Water-Supply Paper 867). US Government Printing Office, 1.

45 USGS paper 867, 149.

46 The following discussion is derived from reports in the *Daily Hampshire Gazette*.

47 *Daily Hampshire Gazette*, 9/23/1938.

48 A forb is an herbaceous flowering plant that is not a grass.

49 Some good sources to mine for an understanding of the last generation of research on invasives/exotics include: Baskin, Yvonne. 2002. *A Plague of Rats and Rubber Vines: The Growing Threat of Species Invasions*. Washington, D.C.: Island Press; Cox, George W. 1999. *Alien Species in North America and Hawaii: Impacts on Natural Ecosystems*. Washington, D.C.: Island Press; Davis, Mark. 2009. *Invasion Biology*. NY: Oxford University; Terrill, Ceiridwen. 2007. *Unnatural Landscapes: Tracking Invasive Species*. Tucson, AZ: University of Arizona; Heberling, J.M. and J.D. Fridley. 2013. "Resource-use strategies of native and invasive plants in Eastern North American forests," *New Phytologist*, vol. 200:2, 523-533; Lovett, Gary M. et al. 2016. "Nonnative forest insects and pathogens in the United States: Impacts and policy options." *Ecological Applications*, 0 (0), 1 –19.

http://www.caryinstitute.org/sites/default/files/public/downloads/project/lovett_etal_ecological_applications_2016.pdf

The origin and spread of many species and their diseases are known, while many others remain to be studied. There is no agreement on language, either, whether one should use value-free words (adventive, non-indigenous or neophyte), as contrasted with names related to war (invasive, eradicate), disease (infestation, epidemic), or human migration (alien, immigrant, exotic). See especially Baskin, 12.

50 Cox, 43.

51 Lovett, et al.,1.

52 Robinton and Burk, 72 –74. Robinton's and Burks's is the only known comprehensive study of vegetation of the Mill's wetlands, which surveyed wetlands in Haydenville, Leeds and two sites in Arcadia Refuge. The exotics were *Agrostis solonifera* creeping bentgrass, a possible invasive; *Bidens* sp. beggar-ticks mostly native with a possible invasive species mixed in; *Gnaphalium uliginosum* brown cudweed; and *Solanum dulcamara* climbing nightshade.

53 Lag time can be attributed to any or all of three factors: the time it takes for a very small number of individuals to multiply; the necessity for the species to adapt genetically to begin to flourish; and, perhaps most commonly, a change or disturbance in the environment that will enable previously limited species to explode. Baskin, 82, quoting the UC Santa Cruz biologist Michael Soulé.

54 Smith College. 2016. "Making Room for Native Plants and Wildlife: A Guide to Invasive Species in the Mill River Watershed." Framingham, MA: New England Wild Flower Society. This handbook, the brainchild of Smith College's horticulturist Gaby Immerman, has become the guide for invasive plant management in the Mill River and neighboring watershed. It can be found online at http://millrivergreenway.org/the-river-2/natural-history.

55 New England forests are notoriously resilient, returning time and again from fire, cutting and hurricanes, but after each disturbance, a different assemblage of tree species occupies that woodland landscape. Researchers from Harvard Forest, fifty miles east of the Mill River, have been studying forest transformation since the early twentieth century. See, for example Hall, B. et al., 1319–1335

56 Cox, 99.

57 Cox, 95, quoting from J.L Harper's *The Population Biology of Plants*, 1977. NY: Academic Press.

58 Cox, 99.

59 Moffitt, C. The suite of fish species in the Mill was never very large because of the impact of the Wisconsin glaciation. For some 50,000 years, vertebrate life ceased to exist in freshwater habitats, after which fish from refugia south of New England (and perhaps from islands to the east where Georges Bank is currently located). Hartel, K. E.,

D.B. Halliwell, and A.E. Launer. 2002. *Inland Fishes of Massachusetts*. Lincoln, MA.: Massachusetts Audubon Society, 34.

60 Moffitt, 18-19. Moffitt surveyed the Mill River in 1971 when the water quality was probably similar to that in 1940 upstream of Paradise Pond although the lower river would have been more healthy since it had been diverted away from the sewage treatment plant. Williamsburg continued dumping its untreated effluent into the river until the 1970s. Moffitt's survey found that the clean waters from Williamsburg upstream held the largest diversity of fish—eight species of minnows plus suckers, sculpin, and trout—whereas the most polluted lower section had four kinds of minows, suckers, perch, and sunfish. The only exotic species were some bluegills and a few smallmouth and largemouth bass at Hulbert's Pond.

61 Sea lamprey have a fascinating life history. Adults spend two years parasitizing large marine fish by feeding off their fluids, then migrate into freshwater, far upstream to gravelly spawning beds. By the time they spawn, they are blind and beginning to deteriorate. After spawning, they die, and their bodies are absorbed into the ecosystem, marine nutrients and all. The tens of thousands of eggs they deposit hatch in less than two weeks, after which the larvae drift downstream to quiet water and burrow into sandy and muddy sediment where they remain generally five years or more filter feeding on algae and plankton. The larvae then metamorphose into free swimming "transformers," traveling downstream for several months, often attached to fish although not yet necessarily parasitizing them. The cycle begins again when they assume their adult form in the ocean. Lamprey, which entered the Great Lakes from the St. Lawrence River, wreak havoc on trout and salmon in the lakes because this population is not anadromous, that is, they have no path back to the sea.

62 Nislow, Keith and Boyd Kynard. 2009. "The Role of Anadromous Sea Lamprey in Nutrient and Material Transport between Marine and Freshwater Environments," *American Fisheries Society Symposium*, 69: 485–494.

63 Massachusetts Division of Fisheries and Wildlife. There were exceptions to this, for example, a 1906 report that Charles Coville of Whately, owner of a sawmill in Haydenville had been charged with "letting all [his] sawdust into the brook," and asking Coville why he should not be served notice to desist. Coville responded that he would do the best he could, "but my honest opinion is there will not be one more fish in the brook by what sawdust I let into the stream... I am told by the old fishermen here that they do not think it will make any difference with the fish... I hope you will be as lenient towards me as possible. I expect to abide by the law, but I cannot help but think this is a damage to me, and no advantage to anyone else." After receiving a considerate letter back from the commissioner, the local state fisheries official visited the mill once more, "finding a pile of sawdust under blower. Stream very low, banks of stream and bed covered with sawdust. Followed stream and found pile of sawdust about 50 by 25 feet in size. Conditions bad." n.b.: The Massachusetts Division of Fisheries and Wildlife has kindly given the author permission to publish historical accounts that are held in their headquarters at Westborough, MA.

64 Massachusetts DFW. Letter of Deputy McCarthy dated Jan. 1, 1917..

65 The quotation is usually written as "the country's best landscaped sewer." Hepburn's brother-in-law, Ellsworth Grant, who had written a book on the Connecticut River, was the film's writer and producer. Mullens, Jo Beth & Robert S. Bristow. 2003. "Overcoming the Nation's Best Landscaped Sewer: Recreators' Perceptions of the Connecticut River. *Journal of the American Water Resources Association*, 39:1, 7–15.

66 *Daily Hampshire Gazette*, 5/26/1936

67	1940	1960	1980	2000	2010
Northampton	24,794	30,058	29,286	28,978	28,483
Williamsburg	1684	2186	2237	2427	2482
Springfield	149,554	174,463	152,319	152,082	153,060

68 The Connecticut River Conservancy (formerly Connecticut River Watershed Council) now monitors one water-quality station between Bay State and Paradise Pond, distributing the records online. That station consistently records water clean enough to swim in except after significant rainstorms.

69 Nedeau, E.J.. 2008. *Freshwater Mussels and the Connecticut River Watershed*. Greenfield, MA: Connecticut River Watershed Council. Freshwater mussels have a fascinating life cycle. They are dioecious (pronounced dye-ee-shus—stress on the second syllable), meaning separate male and female individuals exist. During breeding season, males release sperm, which females filtrate to fertilize their eggs. The eggs develop into very small glochidia that look almost like adult mussels, which the females release into the water, sometimes prompted by a curious fish inspecting it's shell. The glochidia attach themselves to the gills of fish where they filter feed for weeks or months, doing the fish no harm. They metamorphose into cysts, which drop off when the glochidium turns into a mussel and drop from the gill to the river's substrate. Some mussels are generalists, happy with any kind of fish, but others require specific fish on which to attach themselves. Some species can live several years and others to at least 100 years. Because mussels use fish to distribute their progeny, and dams prevent fish from moving upstream, this means that glochidia can't move upstream either, so mussel numbers are much lower than they should be above Paradise Pond.

70 *Daily Hampshire Gazette*, 6/2/1934.

Afterword

1 A sidenote: The Rhine is the only river in the German language that is of the male gender—der Rhein—all other rivers are feminine as in die Elbe or die Donau/Danube). Furthermore, Father Rhine carries in its flows the ghosts of Teutonic times with historic landmarks impressed on children's memories of boat journeys down that river.

INDEX

HE MILL RIVER

WESTERN MASSACHUSETTS

NORTH

MILES

.5   1   2

Mill River Watershed

Mill River Pre-1710

Mill River 1710-1940

Mill River Post-1940

Hulbert's Pond

Goshen

Upper Highland Lake

Lower Highland Lake

Rogers Brook

West Branch Mill River

Devil's Den

East Branch Mill River

West Branch Mill River

Searsville

Williamsburg

Skinnerville

Haydenville

Beaver Brook

Mountain Street Reservoir

Leeds

Roberts Meadow Brook

Mill River

Florence

Bay State

Lower Mills

Upper Mills

Lickingwater

Connecticut River

The Oxbow